M000167341

B-WESTERN
BOOT HILL

A FINAL TRIBUTE
TO THE COWBOYS AND COWGIRLS
WHO RODE
THE SATURDAY MATINEE MOVIE RANGE

by Bobby J. Copeland

Published by
Empire Publishing, Inc.
P. O. Box 717
Madison, NC 27025-0717
336-427-5850

Also by Bobby J. Copeland:
Trail Talk, published by Empire Publishing, Inc.
The Bob Baker Story, self-published
The Whip Wilson Story, self-published
Bill Elliott, The Peaceable Man, published by Empire Publishing, Inc.
Roy Barcroft, King of the Badmen, published by Empire Publishing, Inc.
Silent Hoofbeats, published by Empire Publishing, Inc.
Charlie King, We Called Him "Blackie," published by Empire Publishing

Empire Publishing, Inc.
PO Box 717
Madison, NC 27025-0717
phone: 336-427-5850
fax: 336-427-7372
email: movietv@vnet.net

B-Western Boot Hill © 1999 by Bobby J. Copeland

Library of Congress Catalog Number 99-73384
ISBN Number 0-944019-28-5

COVER LAYOUT: Debra DeLancey

Published and printed in the United States of America

First Printing: 1999
Second Printing: 2002
Third Printing: 2005
1 2 3 4 5 6 7 8

CONTENTS

ACKNOWLEDGMENTS AND SELECTED BIBLIOGRAPHY

(In no particular order)

Western Clippings, published by Boyd Magers
International Film Necrology by Stewart, McClure & Jones
Western and Frontier Film and Television Credits 1903-1995
    (Volume One) by Harris Lentz, III
Richard B. Smith, III
Bill McDowell
Luther Hathcock
Bill Sasser
Norman Foster
John Leonard
Boyd Magers
Joe Copeland
Lance Copeland
Ron Downey
Ed Wyatt
Scott D. Groll

WHAT IS A B-WESTERN?

by Bobby J. Copeland

If you were fortunate enough to have lived in the 1930s and 1940s—and if you were lucky enough to obtain a dime—you could visit your local movie house to view an exciting B-Western movie.

The B-Western is a true piece of Americana, and, it reflects on a time when we believed in God, country, Mom, apple pie, and Saturday matinee heroes. Many have asked, "Just what does the 'B' stand for in B-Western?" Well, it stands for budget—low budget. However, these films should not be thought of as inferior just because so little money was spent on making them. To a great segment of the population, these little gems are still considered very special. They made an impression on the youths of that era that is still etched in the hearts and minds of those individuals today. Fans of the B-Westerns now gather at Western film festivals to meet the performers whom they idolized as youths in an attempt to recapture memories from the past. Through the years, the fans have enjoyed meeting in person Roy Rogers, Lash LaRue, Sunset Carson, Buster Crabbe, Rex Allen, Don "Red" Barry, Eddie Dean, Bob Steele, Charles Starrett, Monte

Hale, Bob Livingston, Clayton Moore, and many others.

The B-Westerns had simplistic and repetitive plots, and there was never a mystery about the identity of the hero or the villain. Everyone knew that there would be a rip-roaring climax, where good would triumph over evil, and that the hero would ride off into the sunset ready to fight another day. The cowboy hero had the fastest horse, quickest draw, fanciest clothes, sang the sweetest song, and he possessed a heart of purest gold. Even on his worst day, he could beat the daylights out of the meanest bad guy and clean up the most wicked town in the West—without even getting dirty.

For decades, critics have maligned the B-Westerns and regarded them as nothing more than juvenile fare, or simply thought of them as a waste of film. Yet these grand old movies probably did more than any one thing to shape our ideas and ideals. The films gave us action, comedy, music, and good wholesome entertainment for the entire family. They taught us faith, hope, loyalty, honesty, and gave us heroes. We knew they were not real, but we loved them just the same. They made no attempt to show life as it is, but rather how life should be. The B-Westerns were not a substitute for church, but they certainly complemented the message presented by the church. After watching one of these movies, you felt a tingle of goodness spread throughout your body...like your soul had been cleansed.

Unfortunately, the advent of television sounded the death knell for the B-Western films, and they are gone, never to return. Gone now are Tom Mix, Buck Jones, Gene Autry, Roy Rogers, Wild Bill Elliott, Hopalong Cassidy, The Durango Kid, and all the other heroes of the celluloid range.

Yes, our beloved B-Westerns are gone forever, but wouldn't it be fun if we could turn back the clock and start them all over again?

INTRODUCTION
by Richard B. Smith III

December 1950 was an important month in my young life. Being 9 years of age, I attended a Saturday matinee at the small Pitts-Clarco Theatre in Berryville, Virginia, and cast my eyes on Chapter One of Republic's gun-blazing serial, *The James Brothers of Missouri* (1949).

A 7-year-old buddy and I focused our attention on the James brother possessing this beefy build and deep-throated voice.

Once Roy Rogers' *Bells of Coronado* (1950) in Trucolor came on the screen, we both saw the same individual again. My little friend, more mentally alert, said excitedly: "He was in the serial."

Years later, I'd learn the man's name was Robert Bice, a support movie actor of this period, who became my first real introduction to numerous B-Western players. Their lives, as happened to many of them, were never recorded with proper facts for access in an easy-to-locate obituary book.

Bobby J. Copeland corrects such massive information lapses with this handy reference guide which highlights over 1200 births and deaths of Western favorites as tribute to their longevity. His goal was to list every performer who appeared in at least three B-Westerns using available data.

Bobby did this 10-year research project not as a moneymaker, but out of his admiration for those old, beloved films. Sadly, this guide will be just about complete and current because most B-Western people are now gone.

The B-Western's fabulous era officially ended during 1998 when singing cowboy greats Gene Autry and Roy Rogers passed away. Their respective deaths were mourned and sadly felt by many personally devoted individuals.

Both entertainers had decades of continuous popularity after they ended 1950s oater production. Such an unbelievable outreach by these two film industry giants powerfully sustained fan interest for the Western genre that will never be matched again.

Bobby J. Copeland has produced a literary milestone which surely will rank at the top among those important Western film history books printed within the past 30 years.

BIRTH & DEATH DATES OF B-WESTERN PERFORMERS

Note: I have attempted to list the names of all performers, where data is available, who appeared in at least three sound B-Western pictures. I have also included actors who appeared in starring roles, although they made less than three films. Tex Fletcher and Gene Austin fit into this category. The names in parentheses indicate the performer's real name.

NAME	BIRTH DATE	PLACE	DEATH DATE
Acuff, Eddie	Jun 3, 1908	Caruthersville, MO	Dec 17, 1956
Acuff, Roy	Sep 15, 1903	Maynardville, TN	Nov 23, 1992
Adams, Ernie	Jun 18, 1885	San Francisco, CA	Nov 26, 1947
Adams, Ted	Mar 17, 1890	NY	Sep 24, 1973
Adrian, Iris (Iris Adrian Hosteller)	May 29, 1913	Los Angeles, CA	Sep 17, 1994
Alcaide, Chris	Oct 20, 1924	Youngstown, OH	Jun 30, 2004
Alderson, Erville	Sep 11, 1882	Kansas City, MO	Aug 4, 1957
Alexander, Dick (Richard)	Nov 19, 1902	Dallas, TX	Aug 9, 1989
Allen, Bob (Theodore Baehr)	Mar 28, 1906	Mt. Vernon, NY	Oct 9, 1998
Allen, Ethan	May 11, 1882	MO	Aug 21, 1940
Allen, Harry	Jul 10, 1883	Australia	Dec 4, 1951
Allen, Judith (Marie Elliott)	Jan 28, 1911	New York, NY	Oct 5, 1996
Allen, Maude Pierce	Nov 30, 1887	MA	Apr 24, 1960
Allen, Rex	Dec 31, 1920	Willcox, AZ	Dec 17, 1999
Alvarado, Don (Joseph Page)	Nov 4, 1904	Albuquerque, NM	Mar 31, 1967
Alyn, Kirk (John Feggo, Jr.)	Oct 8, 1910	Oxford, NJ	Mar 14, 1999

NAME	BIRTH DATE	PLACE	DEATH DATE
Andre, Lona (Laura Anderson)	Mar 2, 1915	Nashville, TN	Sep 18, 1992
Anderson, Charles (Cap)	Oct 27, 1882	Sweden	Mar 24, 1956
Anderson, Robert (Bob)			Jan 4, 1996
Andrews, Slim (Lloyd)	Dec 8, 1906	Gravette, AR	Apr 3, 1992
Andrews, Stanley (Stanley Andrzejewski)	Aug 28, 1891	Chicago, IL	Jun 23, 1969
Ankrum, Morris (Stephen Morris)	Aug 28, 1897	Danville, IL	Sep 2, 1964
Appel, Sam	Aug 8, 1871	Mexico	Jun 18, 1947
Armida (Vendrell)	Mar 29, 1911	Mexico	Oct 23, 1989
Arnt, Charles	Aug 20, 1908	Michigan City, IN	Aug 6, 1990
Ash, Sam	Aug 28, 1884	KY	Oct 20, 1951
Askam, Earl	May 10, 1898	Seattle, WA	Apr 1, 1940
Atchley, Hooper	Apr 30, 1887	Ebenezer, TN	Nov 16, 1943
Ates, Roscoe	Jan 20, 1895	Grange, MS	Mar 1, 1962
Aubrey, Jimmy	Oct 23, 1887	England	Sep 2, 1983
Austin, Gene	Jul 24, 1900	Gainesville, TX	Jan 24, 1972
Austin, Frank	Oct 9, 1877	Mound City, MO	May 13, 1954
Austin, Vivian	1919	Los Angeles, CA	Aug 1, 2004
Autry, Gene	Sep 29, 1907	Tioga, TX	Oct 2, 1998
Aylesworth, Arthur	Aug 12, 1883	Apponaugh, RI	Jun 26, 1944
Bacon, Irving	Aug 27, 1897	Danville, IL	Sep 2, 1964
Bailey, William Norton (George Reineck)	Sep 26, 1886	NE	Nov 8, 1962
Baker, Benny	May 5, 1907	St. Joseph, MO	Sep 20, 1994
Baker, Bob (Stanley Leland Weed)	Nov 8, 1910	Forest City, IA	Aug 29, 1975
Baker, Floyd (Silvertip)	1887		Mar 15, 1943
Bakewell, William	May 2, 1908	Los Angeles, CA	Apr 15, 1993
Baldra, "Chuck" (Charles)	Aug 18, 1889	Albany, OR	Apr 14, 1949
Baldwin, Walter	Jan 2, 1889	OH	Jan 27, 1977
Ball, Frank (Francis)	May 25, 1876		Mar 1968
Ballew, Smith	Jan 21, 1902	Palestine, TX	May 2, 1984
Bane, Holly (Mike Ragan)	Feb 18, 1918	Los Angeles, CA	Aug 25, 1997
Bannon, Jim	Apr 9, 1911	Kansas City, MO	Jul 28, 1984
Barclay, Don	Dec 26, 1892	Astoria, OR	Oct 16, 1975
Barclay, Joan (Elizabeth Geear)	1914	MN	Nov 22, 2002
Barclay, Stephen	Nov 20, 1918	Baltimore, MD	Feb 2, 1994
Barcroft, Roy (Howard Ravenscroft)	Sep 7, 1902	Crab Orchard, NE	Nov 28, 1969
Bardette, Trevor	Nov 19, 1902	Nashville, AR	Nov 28, 1977
Barlow, Reginald	Jun 17, 1866	Springfield, MA	Jul 6, 1943
Barnett, Griff	Nov 12, 1884	TX	Jan 12, 1958
Barnett, Vince	Jul 4, 1902	Pittsburgh, PA	Aug 10, 1977
Barrat, Robert	Jul 10, 1889	New York, NY	Jan 7, 1970
Barron, Robert	Mar 13, 1896	AL	Jun 21, 1971
Barry, Don "Red" (Don Barry d'Acosta)	Jan 11, 1911	Houston, TX	Jul 17, 1980

NAME	BIRTH DATE	PLACE	DEATH DATE
Barton, Buzz (William Lamoreaux)	Sep 3, 1913	Gallatin, MO	Nov 20, 1980
Barton, Greg (Hal Barker)	Jun 5, 1912	Long Island, NY	Nov 28, 2000
Basquette, Lina	Apr 19, 1907	San Mateo, CA	Sep 30, 1994
Baxter, Warner	Mar 29, 1889	Cleveland, OH	May 7, 1951
Beddoe, Don	Jul 1, 1889	Pittsburgh, PA	Jan 19, 1991
Beery, Noah, Jr.	Aug 10, 1915	New York, NY	Nov 1, 1994
Beery, Noah, Sr.	Feb 17, 1882	Smithville, MO	Apr 1, 1946
Bell, Hank (Henry)	Jan 21, 1892	Los Angeles, CA	Feb 4, 1950
Bell, James	Dec 1, 1891	Suffolk, VA	Oct 26, 1973
Bell, Rex (George Beldam)	Oct 16, 1903	Chicago, IL	Jul 4, 1962
Bellamy, Madge (Margaret Philpott)	Jun 30, 1900	Hillsboro, TX	Jan 29, 1990
Benedict, Billy	Apr 16, 1917	Haskell, OK	Nov 25, 1999
Bennett, Lee	1911	Chicago, IL	Oct 10, 1954
Bennett, Ray (Raphael)	Mar 21, 1895	Portland, OR	Dec 17, 1957
Bertram, William	Jan 19, 1880	Canada	May 1, 1933
Betz, Mathew	Sep 13, 1881	St. Louis, MO	Jan 26, 1938
Bevans, Clem	Oct 16, 1879	Cozaddake, OH	Aug 11, 1963
Bice, Robert	Mar 4, 1913	Dallas, TX	Jan 8, 1968
Big Tree, Chief John (Isaac Johnny John)	1865		Jul 5, 1967
Bill, Jr. Buffalo, *see Jay Wilsey*			
Bishop, Julie (Jacqueline Wells)	Aug 30, 1914	Denver, CO	Aug 30, 2001
Blackmer, Sidney	Jul 13, 1895	Salisbury, NC	Oct 5, 1973
Blaine, James			Mar 18, 1967
Blair, Reno, *see Reno Browne*			
Blane, Sally (Elizabeth Jung)	Jun 11, 1910	Salida, CO	Aug 27, 1997
Bletcher, Billy (William)	Sep 24, 1894	Lancaster, PA	Jan 5, 1979
Blue, Monte (Gerald Montgomery Blue)	Jan 11, 1887	Indianapolis, IN	Feb 18, 1963
Blystone, Stanley	Aug 6, 1894	Eau Claire, WI	July 16, 1956
Blythe, Betty	Sep 1, 1893	Los Angeles, CA	Apr 7, 1972
Bolan, Eddie	Dec 27, 1885	San Francisco, CA	Feb 3, 1935
Bond, Johnny (Cyrus Whitfield Bond)	Jun 1, 1915	Enville, OK	Jun 12, 1978
Bond, Lillian	Jan 18, 1908	England	Jan 25, 1991
Bond, Ward	Apr 9, 1903	Benkelman, NE	Nov 5, 1960
Borden, Eddie	May 1, 1888	Deer Lodge, TN	Jun 30, 1955
Borden, Renee (Edith Lavoy)	Jan 26, 1908	CA	Sep 8, 1992
Borg, Veda Ann	Jan 11, 1915	West Roxbury, MA	Aug 16, 1973
Boteler, Wade	Oct 3, 1888	Santa Ana, CA	May 7, 1943
Botiller, Dick	Oct 10, 1896	Bakersfield, CA	Mar 24, 1953
Boyd, Bill "Cowboy Rambler"	Sep 29, 1910	Ladonia, TX	Dec 7, 1977
Boyd, William "Hoppy"	Jun 5, 1895	Hendrysburg, OH	Sep 12, 1972
Bradford, Lane (Myrtland LaVarre, Jr.)	Aug 29, 1922	New York, NY	Jun 6, 1973
Bradley, Harry	Apr 15, 1869	San Francisco, CA	Oct 18, 1967

NAME	BIRTH DATE	PLACE	DEATH DATE
Brady, Edwin J.	Dec 6, 1889	New York, NY	Mar 31, 1942
Brady, Pat (Robert O'Brady)	Dec 31, 1914	Toledo, OH	Feb 27, 1972
Brandon, Henry	Jun 8, 1912	Germany	Feb 16, 1990
(Heinrich Kleinbach)			
Bray, Robert	Oct 23, 1917	Kalispell, MT	Mar 7, 1983
Brennan, Walter	Jul 25, 1894	Swampscott, MA	Sep 21, 1974
Brent, Evelyn	Oct 20, 1899	Tampa, FL	Jun 4, 1975
(Elizabeth Riggs)			
Brent, Lynton	Aug 2, 1903	Chicago, IL	Jul 12, 1981
Bridge, Alan	Feb 26, 1891	PA	Dec 27, 1957
Bridge, Loie	Oct 16, 1889	PA	Mar 9, 1974
Bridges, John	Oct 24, 1888	AL	Jul 11, 1973
Bridges, Lloyd	Jan 15, 1913	San Leandro, CA	Mar 10, 1998
Briggs, Harlan	Aug 17, 1879	Blissfield, MI	Jan 26, 1952
Brinkley, Charles	Nov 15, 1880	Yuma, AZ	Feb 17, 1946
Brodie, Steve (John Stevens)	Nov 25, 1919	Eldorado, KS	Jan 9, 1992
Bromley, Sheila	Oct 31, 1910	San Francisco, CA	Jul 23, 2003
Brower, Tom	Feb 20, 1878	Birmingham, AL	Jul 19, 1937
Britton, Barbara	Sep 26, 1920	Long Beach, CA	Jan 17, 1980
Brooks, Rand	Sep 21, 1918	Los Angles, CA	Sep 1, 2003
Brown, Johnny Mack	Sep 1, 1904	Dothan, AL	Nov 14, 1974
Brown, Raymond	Aug 16, 1874	Champaign, IL	Jul 30, 1939
Brown, Stanley (Brad Taylor)	Aug 18, 1914		Sep 29, 2001
Browne, Lucile	Mar 18, 1907	Memphis, TN	May 10, 1976
Browne, Reno	Aug 20, 1921	Reno, NV	May 15, 1991
(Josephine Ruth Clark)			
Brownlee, Frank	Oct 11, 1874	Dallas, TX	Feb 10, 1948
Buchanan, Edgar	Mar 30, 1903	Humansville, MO	Apr 4, 1979
Bucko, Buck (Ralph Boukou)	1892		Aug 6, 1962
Bucko, Roy (Roy Boukou)	Aug 22, 1893	CA	Aug 6, 1954
Burgess, Dorothy	Mar 4, 1905	Los Angeles, CA	Aug 20, 1961
Burke, James	Sep 24, 1886	New York, NY	May 23, 1968
Burnette, Smiley (Lester)	Mar 18, 1911	Summum, IL	Feb 16, 1967
Burns, Bob	Nov 2, 1888	Glendive, MT	Feb 2, 1956
Burns, Edmund	Sep 27, 1892	Philadephia, PA	Apr 4, 1980
Burns, Forrest	Sep 21, 1879	MT	Jul 24, 1954
Burns, Fred	Apr 24, 1878	Ft. Keough, MT	Jul 18, 1955
Burns, Marion	Aug 9, 1907	Los Angeles, CA	Dec 22, 1993
Burns, Paul	Jan 26, 1881	Philadelphia, PA	May 17, 1967
Burns, Robert E.	Nov 21, 1884	MT	Mar 14, 1957
Burson, Wayne	1920		May 6, 1997
Burtis, James	May 12, 1893	Emporia, KS	Jul 24, 1939
Burton, Frederick	Oct 20, 1871	Indianapolis, IN	Oct 23, 1957
Burton, George	Sep 17, 1898	MT	Dec 8, 1955
Bush, James	Oct 14, 1907	Greenfield, OH	Apr 9, 1987
Buster, Budd (John)	Jun 14, 1891	Colorado Springs, CO	Dec 22, 1965
Butler, Roy	May 4, 1893	Atlanta, GA	Jul 28, 1973
Buttram, Pat (Maxwell)	Jun 19, 1915	Addison, AL	Jan 8, 1994

NAME	BIRTH DATE	PLACE	DEATH DATE
Byron, Marion	Mar 16, 1912	Dayton, OH	Jul 5, 1985
Calvert, E. H.	Jun 27, 1863	Alexandria, VA	Oct 5, 1941
Cameron, Rod (Roderick Cox)	Dec 7, 1910	Canada	Dec 21, 1983
Campana, Nina	1897		Jun 21, 1950
Campeau, Frank	Dec 14, 1864	Detroit, MI	Nov 5, 1943
Camron, Rocky	Aug 4, 1902	CO	Jun 16, 1967
(aka Gene Alsace & Buck Coburn)			
Canutt, Yakima (Enos)	Nov 29, 1896	Colfax, WA	May 24, 1986
Cardwell, James (Albert C.)	Nov 21, 1921	Camden, NJ	Feb 1, 1954
Carey, Ed	1905		Oct 30, 1979
Carey, Harry, Sr.	Jan 16, 1878	New York, NY	Sep 21, 1947
Carle, Richard	Jul 7, 1871	Somerville, MA	Jun 28, 1941
Carleton, George	Oct 28, 1885	NY	Sep 23, 1950
(Charles Nicholas Carleton)			
Carlton, Claire	Sep 28, 1913	New York, NY	Dec 11, 1979
Carmen, Jean	Apr 7, 1913	Portland, OR	Aug 26, 1993
Carpenter, Horace	Jan 31, 1875	Grand Rapids, MI	May 21, 1945
Carpenter, Johnny	Jun 25, 1914	Debinsville, AR	Feb 27, 2003
Carr, Mary	Mar 14, 1874	Philadelphia, PA	Jun 24, 1973
Carr, Nat	Aug 12, 1886	Russia	July 6, 1944
Carradine, John	Feb 5, 1906	Greenwich Village, NY	Nov 17, 1988
Carre, Bartlett	Jul 10, 1897	Melrose, MA	Apr 26, 1971
Carrillo, Leo	Aug 6, 1881	Los Angeles, CA	Sep 10, 1961
Carson, Sunset	Nov 12, 1920	Gracemont, OK	May 1, 1990
(Winnifred Maurice Harrison)			
Carver, Lynne	Sep 30, 1909	Birmingham, AL	Aug 12, 1955
Cason, John	Jul 30, 1918	TX	Jul 7, 1961
Cassidy, Ed	Mar 21, 1893	IL	Jan 19, 1968
Cavan, Allan	Mar 25, 1889	Concord, CA	Jan 19, 1941
Cavanaugh, Hobart	Sep 22, 1886	Virginia City, NV	Apr 25, 1950
Cecil, Edward	Sep 13, 1878	San Francisco, CA	Dec 13, 1940
Chambers, Wheaton	Oct 13, 1887	Phildelphia, PA	Jan 31, 1958
Chandler, Eddie	Mar 12, 1894	Wilton Junction, IA	Mar 23, 1948
Chandler, George	Jun 30, 1898	Waukegan, IL	Jun 10, 1985
Chandler, Janet	Dec 31, 1915	Pine Bluff, AR	Mar 16, 1994
Chandler, Lane	Jun 4, 1899	Culbertson, ND	Sep 14, 1972
(Raymond Oakes)			
Chaney, Lon (Creighton)	Feb 10, 1906	Oklahoma City, OK	Jul 12, 1973
Chase, Colin (Colin Callings)	Apr 13, 1886	Lewiston, ID	Apr 24, 1937
Chase, Stephen	Apr 11, 1902	Huntington, NY	Apr 1, 1982
Chatterton, Tom	Feb 12, 1881	Geneva, NY	Aug 17, 1952
Chesebro, George	Jul 29, 1888	Minneapolis, MN	May 28, 1959
Cheshire, Harry "Pappy"	Aug 16, 1891	KS	Jun 16, 1968
Chester, Alma	Apr 30, 1870	IA	Oct 10, 1940
Church, Fred	Oct 17, 1889	IA	Jan 7, 1983
Churchill, Berton	Dec 9, 1876	Canada	Oct 10, 1940
Clancy, Ellen	Jan 23, 1919	Beatrice, NE	Oct 15, 2000
Clark, Cliff	Jun 10, 1893	NY	Feb 8, 1953

NAME	BIRTH DATE	PLACE	DEATH DATE
Clark, Davison	Jan 15, 1881	CA	Nov 4, 1972
Clark, Frank	Dec 22, 1857	Cincinnati, OH	Apr 10, 1945
Clark, Harvey	Oct 4, 1885	Chelsea, MA	Jul 19, 1938
Clark, Steve	Feb 26, 1891	IN	Jun 29, 1954
Clemente, Steve	Nov 22, 1885	Mexico	May 7, 1950
Cleveland, George	Sep 17, 1885	Nova Scotia	Jul 15, 1957
Clifford, Jack (Virgil James Montani)	1880	Italy	Nov 10, 1956
Clyde, Andy	Mar 25, 1892	Blairgowrie, Scotland	May 18, 1967
Coats, Tommy	1901		Jun 6, 1954
Cobb, Edmund	Jun 23, 1892	Albuquerque, NM	Aug 15, 1974
Coburn, Buck, *see Rocky Camron*			
Cody, Bill	Jan 5, 1891	St. Paul, MN	Jan 24, 1948
Cody, Bill, Jr.	Apr 18, 1925	Hollywood, CA	Aug 11, 1989
Cody, Iron Eyes (Oscar DeCorti)	Apr 3, 1904	Gueydan, LA	Jan 4, 1999
Coffin, Tristram	Aug 13, 1909	Mamouth, UT	Mar 26, 1990
Colcord, Mabel	Jul 30, 1873	San Francisco, CA	Jun 6, 1952
Coleman, Charles	Dec 22, 1885	Australia	Mar 8, 1951
Coleman, Don	Jan 15, 1898	Sheridan, WY	Dec 24, 1985
Collier, Lois (Madelyn Jones)	Mar 21, 1919	Salley, SC	Oct 27, 1999
Compson, Betty	Mar 19, 1897	Beaver, UT	Apr 18, 1974
Compton, Joyce (Eleanor Hunt)	Jan 27, 1907	Lexington, KY	Oct 13, 1997
Conklin, Chester	Jan 11, 1886	Osakaloosa, IA	Oct 11, 1971
Connors, Buck (George W. Connors)	Nov 22, 1880	San Sabag, TX	Feb 4, 1947
Conrad, Mikel	Jul 30, 1919	Columbus, OH	Sep 11, 1982
Cooley, Spade (Donnell)	Dec 17, 1910	Pack Saddle, OK	Nov 23, 1969
Cooper, Clancy	Jul 23, 1906	Boise, ID	Jun 14, 1975
Cooper, Dee	May 25, 1920	Muleshoe, TX	Dec 14, 1989
Cooper, George (George Cooper Healey)	Dec 12, 1892	Newark, NJ	Dec 9, 1943
Cooper, Tex (Judge)	Apr 21, 1876	TX	Mar 29, 1951
Copeland, Nick	Oct 14, 1894	Omaha, NE	Aug 17, 1940
Corbett, Ben	Feb 6, 1892	Fludson, IL	May 19, 1961
Cordell, Frank	Feb 3, 1898	OK	Oct 25, 1977
Cording, Harry	Apr 29, 1891	England	Sep 1, 1954
Corey, Jim (Arthur)	Mar 22, 1889	NY	Mar 26, 1950
Corrado, Gino	Feb 8, 1895	Italy	Dec 23, 1982
Corrigan, Lloyd	Oct 16, 1900	San Francisco, CA	Nov 5, 1969
Corrigan, Ray "Crash" (Ray Benard)	Feb 14, 1902	Milwaukee, WI	Aug 10, 1976
Costello, Don	Sep 5, 1901	New Orleans, LA	Oct 25, 1945
Cotton, Carolina (Helen Hagstrom)	Oct 20, 1925	Cash, AR	Jun 10, 1997
Cowan, Jerome	Oct 6, 1897	New York, NY	Jan 24, 1972
Cowles, Jules	Oct 7, 1877	Farmington, CT	May 22, 1943
Coxen, Ed	Aug 8, 1884	England	Nov 21, 1954

NAME	BIRTH DATE	PLACE	DEATH DATE
Crabbe, Buster (Clarence Linden)	Feb 17, 1908	Los Angeles, CA	Apr 23, 1983
Craig, James (James Meador)	Feb 4, 1912	Nashville, TN	Jun 28, 1985
Cramer, Dick (Richard)	Jul 3, 1890	Bryan, OH	Aug 9, 1960
Crane, Frank	Jan 1, 1887	San Francisco, CA	Aug 31, 1948
Crane, Richard	Jun 6, 1918	Newcastle, IN	Mar 9, 1969
Crehan, Joseph	Jul 12, 1884	Baltimore, MD	Apr 15, 1966
Cripps, Kernan	Jul 8, 1886	CT	Aug 12, 1953
Crockett, Luther	Sep 3, 1890	MO	Apr 6, 1952
Crosby, Wade	Aug 22, 1905	Cedar Rapids, IA	Oct 2, 1975
Curtis, Billy	Jun 27, 1909	Springfield, MA	Nov 9, 1988
Curtis, Dick (Richard Dye)	May 11, 1902	Newport, KY	Jan 3, 1952
Curtis, Don	Feb 17, 1915	Cheney, WA	May 23, 1997
Curtis, Ken (Curtis Gates)	Jul 2, 1916	Lamar, CO	Apr 27, 1991
Custer, Bob (Raymond Glenn)	Oct 18, 1898	Frankfort, KY	Dec 27, 1974
Daheim, John			1990
Dale, Virginia (Virginia Paxton)	Jul 1, 1917	Charlotte, NC	Oct 2, 1994
Daley, Jack	Aug 21, 1882	MA	Aug 30, 1967
Dalroy, Harry (Rube)	1879		Mar 8, 1954
Daniels, Harold	Jun 25, 1903	Buffalo, NY	Dec 27, 1971
D'Arcy, Roy	Feb 10, 1894	San Francisco, CA	Nov 15, 1969
Darcey, Sheila (Rebecca Heffener)	Aug 8, 1914	York, PA	Feb 27, 2004
Darien, Frank	Mar 18, 1876	New Orleans, LA	Oct 20, 1955
Darrell, Steve	Nov 19, 1904	Osage, IA	Aug 14, 1970
Darro, Frankie	Dec 22, 1918	Chicago, IL	Dec 25, 1976
Davidson, Max	May 23, 1875	Germany	Sep 4, 1950
Davis, Art (Audrey)	May 31, 1913	Paradise, TX	Jan 16, 1987
Davis, Gail (Betty Grayson)	Oct 5, 1925	Little Rock, AR	Mar 15, 1997
Davis, Jim	Aug 26, 1915	Dearborn, MI	Apr 26 1981
Davis, Jimmie	Sep 11, 1899	Quitman, LA	Nov 5, 2000
Davis, Robert O.	Dec 17, 1910	Germany	Sep 22, 1971
Davis, Rufe (Rufus Davidson)	Dec 2, 1908	Dinson, OK	Dec 13, 1974
Day, Marceline	Apr 24, 1908	Colorado Springs, CO	Feb 16, 2000
Dean, Eddie (Edgar Dean Glossup)	Jul 9, 1907	Posey, TX	Mar 4, 1999
Dearing, Edgar	May 4, 1893	Ceres, CA	Aug 17, 1974
de Cordoba, Pedro	Sep 28, 1881	New York, NY	Sep 17, 1950
de Cordova, Leander	Dec 3, 1878	Jamaica	Sep 19, 1969
Defreest, Babe (Thelma Elder)	Sep 2, 1907	Placer City, CA	Mar 1986
Dehner, John (John Forkum)	Nov 23, 1915	New York, NY	Feb 4, 1992
de la Cruz, Joe	Mar 19, 1892	Mexico	Dec 14, 1961
Dell, Claudia	Jan 10, 1909	San Antonio, TX	Sep 5, 1977
DeMain, Gordon (Gordon Wood)	Sep 28, 1886	IA	Mar 5, 1954
Demetrio, Anna	Nov 8, 1900	Italy	Nov 8, 1959
DeMille, Katherine	Jun 29, 1911	Canada	Apr 27, 1995
deNormand, George	Sep 22, 1903	New York, NY	Dec 23, 1976

NAME	BIRTH DATE	PLACE	DEATH DATE
Dent, Vernon	Feb 16, 1895	San Jose, CA	Nov 4, 1963
Depp, Harry	Feb 22, 1883	St. Louis, MO	Mar 3, 1960
Desmond, William	Jan 23, 1878	Ireland	Nov 2, 1949
DeStefani, Joseph	Oct 3, 1879	Italy	Oct 26, 1940
de Valdez, Carlos	Aug 7, 1888	Chile	Oct 30, 1939
Devine, Andy	Oct 27, 1905	Flagstaff, AZ	Feb 18, 1977
Dew, Eddie	Jan 29, 1909	Sumner, WA	Apr 6, 1972
Dillard, Art	Feb 20, 1907	TX	Mar 30, 1960
Dillard, Bert	1909		Jun 19, 1960
Dilson, John	Feb 18, 1891	Brooklyn, NY	Jun 1, 1944
Dix, Billy	Sep 4, 1911	Miami, OK	Mar 22, 1973
Dix, Dorothy (Marie Thye)	Jun 13, 1908	IL	Jun 23, 2000
Dix, Richard (Ernest Brimmer)	Jul 18, 1893	St. Paul, MN	Sep 20, 1949
Dixon, Denver	Jan 4, 1890	New Zealand	Nov 9, 1972
(Victor Adamson)			
Dixon, Joan	1931		Feb 20, 1992
Dodd, Jimmie	Mar 28, 1910	Cincinnati, OH	Nov 10, 1964
Dodson, Bert	1916		Oct 2, 1995
Dominguez, Joe	Mar 19, 1894	Mexico	Apr 11, 1970
Donnell, Jeff (Jean)	Jul 10, 1921	S. Windham, MA	Apr 11, 1985
Dorr, Lester	May 8, 1893	MA	Aug 25, 1980
Doucette, John	Jan 21, 1921	Brockton, MA	Aug 16, 1994
Downs, Johnny	Oct` 10, 1913	Brooklyn, NY	Jun 6, 1994
Doyle, Maxine	Jan 1, 1915	San Francisco, CA	May 7, 1973
Dresden, Curley (Albert)	Jul 17, 1900	Chicago, IL	Jun 7, 1953
Drexel, Nancy	Apr 6, 1912	New York, NY	Nov 19, 1989
(Dorothy Kitchen)			
Driver, Ada Bell	1874		1952
Dumbrille, Douglas	Oct 13, 1889	Canada	Apr 2, 1974
Duna, Steffi	Feb 8, 1913	Hungary	Apr 22, 1992
Duncan, Bob	Dec 7, 1906	Topeka, KS	Mar 13, 1967
Duncan, Kenne	Feb 19, 1902	Canada	Feb 7, 1972
(Kenneth MacLachlen)			
Duncan, William	Dec 16, 1874	Scotland	Feb 8, 1961
Dundee, Jimmie	Dec 19, 1900	MO	Nov 20, 1953
Dunham, Phil	Apr 23, 1885	England	Sep 5, 1972
Dunn, Bobby	Aug 28, 1890	Milwaukee, WI	Mar 24, 1937
Dunn, Eddie	Mar 31, 1896	Brooklyn, NY	May 5, 1951
Dunn, Ralph	May 23, 1902	Titusville, PA	Feb 19, 1968
DuPuis, Art	Mar 29, 1901	Canada	Apr 18, 1952
Durand, Dave	Sep 29, 1921	Los Angeles, CA	Jul 25, 1998
Durkin, James	May 21, 1879	Canada	Mar 12, 1934
Du Val, Juan	Apr 28, 1899	Spain	Apr 1, 1954
Dwire, Earl	Oct 3, 1883	Rockport, MO	Jan 16, 1940
Dyer, William	Mar 11, 1881	Atlanta, GA	Dec 22, 1933
Eagles, James	Sep 10, 1907	Norfolk, VA	Dec 15, 1959
Earle, Edward	Jul 16, 1882	Canada	Dec 15, 1972
Ebsen, Buddy (Christian)	Apr 2, 1908	Belleville, IL	Jul 6, 2003

NAME	BIRTH DATE	PLACE	DEATH DATE
Eburne, Maude	Nov 10, 1875	Canada	Oct 15, 1960
Eckhardt, Oliver	Sep 14, 1873	MO	Sep 15, 1952
Edwards, Cliff "Ukelele Ike"	Jun 14, 1895	Hannibal, MO	Jul 17, 1971
Edwards, Penny (Millicent)	Aug 24, 1928	Jackson Heights, NY	Aug 26, 1998
Edwards, Sarah	Oct 11, 1881	South Wales	Jan 7, 1965
Eggenton, Joseph	Feb 29, 1871	Ponfert, CT	Jul 3, 1946
Eilers, Sally	Dec 11, 1908	New York, NY	Jan 5, 1978
Eldredge, George	Sep 10, 1888	San Francisco, CA	Mar 12, 1977
Eldredge, John	Aug 30, 1904	San Francisco, CA	Sep 23, 1961
Elliott, Bill (Gordon Nance)	Oct 16, 1904	Pattonsburg, MO	Nov 26, 1965
Elliott, Dick	Apr 30, 1886	MA	Dec 22, 1961
Elliott, John	Jul 5, 1876	Pella, IA	Dec 12, 1950
Ellis, Edward	Nov 12, 1870	Coldwater, MI	Jul 26, 1952
Ellis, Frank	Feb 26, 1897	OK	Feb 23, 1969
Ellis, Robert	Jun 27, 1892	New York, NY	Dec 29, 1974
Ellison, James (James Smith)	May 4, 1910	Guthrie Ctr., IA	Dec 23, 1993
Emmett, Fern	Mar 22, 1896	Oakland, CA	Sep 3, 1946
Emory, Richard (Emory Johnson)	Jan 27, 1899	Santa Barbara, CA	Mar 4, 1994
Engle, Billy	May 28, 1889	Austria	Nov 28, 1966
Erickson, Leif (William Anderson)	Oct 27, 1911	Alameda, CA	Jan 29, 1986
Ethier, Alphonse	Dec 10, 1874	Virginia City, NV	Jan 4, 1943
Evans, Dale (Frances Octavia Smith)	Oct 31, 1912	Uvalde, TX	Feb 7, 2001
Evans, Douglas	Jan 26, 1904	VA	Mar 25, 1968
Evans, Gene	Jul 11, 1922	Holbrook, AZ	Apr 1, 1998
Evans, Jack	Mar 5, 1893	NC	Mar 14, 1950
Evans, Muriel	Jul 10, 1910	Minneapolis, MN	Oct 26, 2000
Everton, Paul	Sep 19, 1868	New York, NY	Feb 26, 1948
Faire, Virginia Brown	Jun 26, 1904	Brooklyn, NY	Jun 30, 1980
Farley, Dot	Feb 5, 1881	Chicago, IL	May 21, 1971
Farley, James	Jan 8, 1882	Waldron, AZ	Oct 2, 1947
Farnum, Franklyn	Jun 5, 1876	Boston, MA	Jul 4, 1961
Farnum, William	Jul 4, 1876	Boston, MA	June 5, 1953
Farr, Hugh	Dec 6, 1903	Llano, TX	Mar 17, 1980
Farr, Karl	Apr 25, 1909	Rochelle, TX	Sep 20, 1961
Farrell, Tommy	Oct 7, 1921	Hollywood, CA	May 9, 2004
Faust, Martin	Jan 16, 1886	Germany	Jul 20, 1943
Fawcett, Jimmy (James)	Sep 9, 1896	New York, NY	Jun 9, 1942
Fawcett, William	Sep 8, 1894	High Forest, MN	Jan 25, 1974
Fay Dorothy (Southworth)	Apr 4, 1915	Prescott, AZ	Nov 5, 2003
Featherstone, Eddie	Sep 9, 1896	NY	Jun 12, 1965
Felix, Art			Jun 9, 1980
Fenton, Frank	Apr 9, 1906	Hartford, CT	Jul 24, 1957
Ferguson, Al	Apr 19, 1888	Ireland	Dec 4, 1971
Ferguson, Frank	1906	Ferndale, CA	Sep 12, 1978
Fernandez, Emilio	Mar 26, 1903	Mexico	Aug 6, 1986

NAME	BIRTH DATE	PLACE	DEATH DATE
Fields, Stanley (Walter Agnew)	May 20, 1884	Allegheny, PA	Apr 23, 1941
Findlay, Ruth	1904	New York, NY	Jul 13, 1949
Finley, Evelyn	Mar 11, 1916	Douglas, AZ	Apr 7, 1989
Fisher, Shug (George)	Sep 26, 1907	Spring Creek, OK	Mar 16, 1984
Fiske, Richard (Tom Potts)	Nov 20, 1915	Shelton, WA	Aug 10, 1944
Fiske, Robert	Oct 30, 1889	Griggsville, MO	Sep 12, 1944
Fix, Paul	Mar 13, 1901	Dobbs Ferry, NY	Oct 14, 1983
Flavin, James	May 14, 1904	Portland, ME	Apr 23, 1976
Fleishmann, Harry	Jan 7, 1899	Segerstown, PA	Nov 28, 1943
Fleming, Alice	Aug 9, 1882	Brooklyn, NY	Dec 6, 1952
Fleming, Bob	Feb 19, 1878	Canada	Oct 4, 1933
Fletcher, Tex (Geremino Bisceglia)	Jan 17, 1909	Harrison, NY	Mar 14, 1987
Flint, Sam	Oct 19, 1882	Gwinette County, GA	Oct 24, 1980
Foo, Lee Tung	Apr 23, 1875	CA	May 1, 1966
Foran, Dick (Nicholas)	Jun 18, 1910	Flemington, NJ	Aug 10, 1979
Ford, Francis (Francis O'Ferna)	Aug 15, 1882	Portland, ME	Sep 5, 1953
Ford, Ross	1923		Jun 22, 1988
Forman, Carol (Carolyn Sawls)	Jun 19, 1918	Epes, AL	Jul 9, 1997
Forman, Tom (Thomas Farmer)	Oct 29, 1891	MN	Nov 16, 1951
Forrest, William	Oct 10, 1902	Cambridge, MA	Jan 29, 1989
Foster, Helen	May 23, 1906	Independence, KS	Dec 25, 1982
Foulger, Byron	Aug 27, 1899	Ogden, UT	Apr 4, 1970
Fowler, Art	1902		Apr 4, 1953
Fox, Jimmy	Mar 22, 1891	PA	Jun 16, 1974
Fowley, Douglas	May 30, 1911	New York, NY	May 21, 1998
Francis, Noel	Nov 21, 1910	Temple, TX	Oct 30, 1959
Francis, Olin	Sep 13, 1891	Mooresville, MS	Jun 30, 1952
Franey, Billy (William)	Jun 23, 1889	Chicago, IL	Dec 9, 1940
Frank, Christian	Mar 13, 1890	New York, NY	Dec 10, 1967
Fraser, Robert	Jun 29, 1889	Worcester, MA	Aug 17, 1944
Frazee, Jane (Jane Frehse)	Jul 15, 1918	Duluth, MN	Sep 6, 1985
French, Charles K.	Jan 17, 1860	Columbus, OH	Aug 2, 1952
French, Ted	Apr 2, 1903		Jul 3, 1978
Frey, Arno	Oct 11, 1900	Germany	Jun 26, 1961
Friedkin, Joel	May 15, 1885	Russia	Sep 9, 1954
Fritchie, Barbara	Apr 24, 1915	Kansas City, MO	Apr 18, 1989
Frost, Terry	Oct 26, 1906	Bemidji, MN	Mar 1, 1993
Fuller, Clem	Jul 6, 1908	CA	May 24, 1961
Fung, Willie	Mar 3, 1896	China	Apr 16, 1945
Furey, Barney	Sep 7, 1886	Boise, ID	Jan 18, 1938
Furness, Betty (Elizabeth)	Jan 3, 1916	New York, NY	Apr 2, 1994
Gale, June	Jul 6, 1918	San Francisco, CA	Nov 13, 1996
Galindo, Nacho	Nov 7, 1908	Mexico	Jun 22, 1973
Gallager, Ray	Apr 17, 1885	San Francisco, CA	Mar 6, 1953

NAME	BIRTH DATE	PLACE	DEATH DATE
Gallander, John	1903		1983
Gamboa, Elias	Jul 20, 1895	Mexico	Dec 9, 1959
Gan, Chester	Jul 4, 1908	San Francisco, CA	Jun 30, 1959
Garcia, Allan	Mar 11, 1887	San Francisco, CA	Sep 4, 1938
Gargan, Edward	1902		Feb 19, 1964
Garralaga, Martin	Nov 10, 1894		Jun 12, 1981
Geary, Bud (Maine)	Feb 15, 1898	Salt Lake City, UT	Feb 22, 1946
Geraghty, Carmelita	Mar 21, 1901	Rushville, IN	Jul 7, 1966
Gerad, Joseph	Apr 2, 1871	Williamsport, PA	Aug 21, 1949
Gerwin, George	1902		Jan 9, 1979
Gibson, Helen (Helen Wegner)	Aug 27, 1892	Cleveland, OH	Oct 10, 1977
Gibson, Hoot (Edmund)	Aug 6, 1892	Tekamah, NE	Aug 23, 1962
Gilbert, Jody	Mar 18, 1916	Ft. Worth, TX	Feb 3, 1969
Gilman, Fred	1902		Mar 30, 1988
Giraud, Octavio	Apr 1, 1880	Cuba	Jun 3, 1958
Glass, Ned	Apr 1, 1906	Poland	Jun 15, 1984
Glendon, J. Frank	Oct 25, 1886	Choteau, MO	Mar 17, 1937
Gomez, Augie	Aug 10, 1889	Philadelphia, PA	Jan 1, 1966
Goodwin, Harold	Dec 1, 1902	Peoria, IL	July 13, 1987
Gordon, Edward	1886		Nov 10, 1938
Gordon, Mary	May 16, 1882	Scotland	Aug 23, 1963
Gordon, Roy	Oct 18, 1884	OH	Jul 23, 1972
Gould, William			Mar 29, 1960
Graham, Fred	1908		Oct 10, 1979
Granger, Dorothy	Nov 21, 1911	New London, OH	Jan 4, 1995
Grant, Frances (Stella Fortier)	Feb 15, 1910	Roxbury, MA	Feb 22, 1982
Grant, Kirby (Kirby Hoon)	Nov 24, 1911	Butte, MT	Oct 30, 1985
Grapewin, Charles	Dec 20, 1876	Xenia, OH	Feb 2, 1956
Gray, Don	1901		Jul 24, 1966
Gray, Roger	May 26, 1887	Omaha, NE	Jan 20, 1959
Grayson, Donald (Carl Graub)	Jul 23, 1908	Canton, OH	Apr 16, 1958
Green, Duke (William Green)	Nov 30, 1900	Los Angeles, CA	Nov 22, 1984
Greene, Harrison	Jan 18, 1894	Portland, OR	Sep 28, 1945
Grey, Shirley (Agnes Zetterstand)	Apr 11, 1910	Naugtuck, CT	Aug 21, 1981
Grey, Virginia	Mar 22, 1917	Los Angles, CA	July 31, 2004
Gribbon, Edward	Jan 3, 1890	New York, NY	Sep 28, 1965
Griffith, Gordon	Jul 4, 1907	Chicago, IL	Oct 12, 1958
Griffith, James	Feb 13, 1919	Los Angeles, CA	Sep 17, 1993
Griffith, William	Dec 18, 1897	IN	Jul 21, 1960
Guard, Kit (Christen Klitgaard)	May 5, 1884	Denmark	Jul 18, 1961
Guilfoyle, Paul	Jul 14, 1902	Jersey City, NJ	Jun 27, 1961
Guizar, Tito (Frederico Tolentino)	Apr 8, 1908	Mexico	Dec 24, 1999
Gulliver, Dorothy	Sep 8, 1908	Salt Lake City, UT	May 23, 1997
Gunn, Earl	May 8, 1901	MI	Apr 14, 1963
Gwynne, Anne	Dec 10, 1918	Waco, TX	Mar 3, 2003
Haade, William	Mar 2, 1903	New York, NY	Nov 15, 1966

NAME	BIRTH DATE	PLACE	DEATH DATE
Hack, Herman	Jun 15, 1899	IL	Oct 19, 1967
(Herman Hackenjos)			
Hackathorne, George	Feb 13, 1896	Pendleton, OR	Jun 25, 1940
Hackett, Karl (Carl Germain)	Sep 5, 1893	Carthage, MO	Oct 24, 1948
Hadley, Reed (Reed Herring)	Jun 25, 1911	Petrolia, TX	Dec 11, 1974
Haggerty, Don	1914		Aug 19, 1988
Hagney, Frank	Mar 20, 1884	Australia	Jun 25, 1973
Hale, Jonathan	Mar 21, 1891	Canada	Feb 28, 1966
(Jonathan Hatley)			
Hall, Arch	Dec 21, 1908	MO	Apr 28, 1978
Hall, Ben	Mar 18, 1899	Brooklyn, NY	May 20, 1985
Hall, Ellen	Apr 18, 1922	Los Angeles, CA	Mar 24, 1999
Hall, Henry	Nov 5, 1876	MO	Dec 11, 1954
Hall, Ruth	Dec 29, 1912	Jacksonville, FL	Oct. 9, 2003
Hall, Thurston	May 10, 1882	Boston, MA	Feb 20, 1958
Hamblen, Stuart	Oct 20, 1908	Kellysville, TX	Mar 9, 1989
Hamilton, John	Jan 19, 1887	Shippensburg, PA	Oct 15, 1958
Hannan, Chick (Chester)	May 24, 1901	Iron River, MI	Aug 14, 1980
Harding, Tex (John Thye)	Jan 4, 1918	Spokane, WA	Apr 1981
Harlan, Kenneth	Jul 26, 1895	Boston, MA	Mar 6, 1967
Harlan, Otis	Dec 29, 1865	Zanesville, OH	Jan 20, 1940
Harmon, Pat (Plummer Harmon)	Feb 3, 1886	Lewiston, IL	Nov 26, 1958
Harr, Silver	Sep 21, 1892	ID	Sep 19, 1968
Harrison, James	May 26, 1908	Milwaukee, WI	Nov 9, 1977
Hart, Gordon	Nov 26, 1884	England	Dec 27, 1963
Hart, Mary, *see Lynne Roberts*			
Hart, Neal	Apr 7, 1879	Richmond, NY	Apr 2, 1949
Harvey, Don	Dec 12, 1911	KS	Apr 24, 1963
Harvey, Harry, Jr.	Oct 9, 1929	OK	Dec 8, 1978
Harvey, Harry, Sr.	Jan 10, 1901		Nov 27, 1985
Harvey, Jack (John M.)	Sep 16, 1881	Cleveland, OH	Nov 10, 1954
Harvey, Paul	Sep 10, 1882	IL	Dec 14, 1955
Haskell, Al	Dec 4, 1886	CA	Jan 6, 1969
Hatton, Raymond	Jul 7, 1887	Red Oak, IA	Oct 21, 1971
Hayden, Harry	Nov 8, 1882	Canada	Jul 23, 1955
Hayden, Russell (Pate Lucid)	Jun 12, 1910	Chico, CA	Jun 9, 1981
Haydon, Julie	Jun 10, 1910	Oak Park, IL	Dec 19, 1994
(Donella Donaldson)			
Hayes, Bernadene	Mar 15, 1903	Chicago, IL	Aug 29, 1987
Hayes, Gabby (George)	May 7, 1885	Wellsville, NY	Feb 9, 1969
Hayes, Linda	Oct 11, 1918	Sac City, IA	Dec 19, 1995
Hayworth, Rita	Oct 17, 1918	Brooklyn, NY	May 14, 1987
(Margarita Cansino)			
Hearn, Edward	Sept 6, 1888	Dayton, WA	Apr 15, 1963
Helton, Percy	Jan 31, 1894	New York, NY	Sep 11, 1971
Hendricks, Ben, Jr.	Nov 2, 1893	New York, NY	Aug 15, 1938
Hendricks, Noah "Shorty"	Dec 20, 1889	MO	Mar 4, 1973
Hendrix, Jack	1874		Feb 26, 1949

NAME	BIRTH DATE	PLACE	DEATH DATE
Henry, Bill (William)	Nov 10, 1914	Los Angeles, CA	Aug 10, 1982
Henry, Buzz (Robert)	Sep 4, 1931	CO	Sep 30, 1971
Henry, Carol	Jul 14, 1918	OK	Sep 17, 1987
Herman, Al	Feb 25, 1887	Scotland	Jul 2, 1967
Heyburn, Weldon	Sep 19, 1910	Washington, DC	May 18, 1951
Hewston, Alfred	Sep 12, 1882	San Francisco, CA	Sep 6, 1947
Heyes, Herbert	Aug 3, 1889	Vader, WA	May 30, 1958
Heywood, Herbert	Feb 1, 1881	IL	Sep 15, 1964
Hickman, Howard	Feb 9, 1890	Columbia, MO	Dec 31, 1949
Hill, Al	Jul 14, 1892	New York, NY	Jul 14, 1954
Hill, Doris	Mar 21, 1905	Roswell, NM	Mar 3, 1976
Hill, Josephine	Oct 3, 1899	San Francisco, CA	Dec 17, 1989
Hill, Robert F.	Apr 14, 1886	Canada	Mar 18, 1966
Hillie, Verna	May 5, 1914	Hancock, MI	Oct 3, 1997
Hinds, Samuel	Apr 4, 1875	Brooklyn, NY	May 2, 1967
Hodgins, Earle	Oct 6, 1893	UT	Apr 14, 1964
Hoey, Dennis	Mar 30, 1893	England	Jul 25, 1960
Hoffman, Gertrude (Gertrude Anderson)	1898		Jun 3, 1955
Hoffman, Gertrude	May 17, 1871	Germany	Oct 21, 1966
Hoffman, Otto	May 2, 1879	NY	Jun 23, 1944
Hogan, Dick	Nov 27, 1918		Aug 18, 1995
Holland, John	Jun 11, 1900	Kenosha, WI	May 21, 1993
Holloway, Sterling	Jan 4, 1905	Cedartown, GA	Nov 22, 1992
Holman, Harry	Mar 15, 1862	Lebanon, MO	May 2, 1947
Holmes, Pee Wee (Gilbert)	Jun 15, 1895	Miles City, MT	Aug 17, 1936
Holmes, Jack	Jul 21, 1889	PA	Feb 27, 1950
Holmes, Stuart	Mar 10, 1884	Chicago, IL	Dec 29, 1971
Holt, Jack (Charles John, Jr.)	May 31, 1888	Winchester, VA	Jan 18, 1951
Holt, Jennifer (Elizabeth)	Nov 19, 1920	Los Angeles, CA	Sep 21, 1997
Holt, Tim (Charles John, III)	Feb 5, 1919	Beverly Hills, CA	Feb 15, 1973
Homans, Robert	Nov 8, 1875	Malden, MA	Jul 28, 1947
Hoose, Fred	Mar 4, 1868	VT	Mar 12, 1952
Hopton, Russell	Feb 18, 1900	New York, NY	Apr 7, 1945
Horvath, Charles	Oct 27, 1921	PA	Jul 23, 1978
House, Newton	Nov 1, 1911	Holly, CO	July 23, 1987
Houston, George	Jan 11, 1896	Hamilton, NJ	Nov 12, 1944
Howard, Booth	1873		Oct 27, 1958
Howard, Edward	Sep 2, 1910	Tuscaloosa, AL	Sep 16, 1946
Howes, Reed	Jul 5, 1900	Washington, DC	Aug 6, 1964
Howlin, Olin	Feb 19, 1896	Denver, CO	Sep 20, 1959
Hoxie, Al	Oct 7, 1901	Lewis County, ID	Apr 5, 1982
Hoxie, Jack	Jan 11, 1885	Kingfisher, OK	Mar 28, 1965
Hudman, Wesley	1916		Feb 29, 1964
Hughes, Carol	Jan 27, 1915	Chicago, IL	Aug 8, 1995
Hughes, Kay (Catherine Rhoads)	Jan 16, 1914	Los Angeles, CA	Apr 4, 1998
Hughes, Mary Beth	Nov 13, 1919	Alton, IL	Aug 17, 1995

NAME	BIRTH DATE	PLACE	DEATH DATE
Hugo, Mauritz	Jan 12, 1909	Sweden	Jun 16, 1974
Hull, Warren	Jan 17, 1903	Gasport, NY	Sep 14, 1974
Hunnicutt, Arthur	Feb 17, 1911	Gravelly, AR	Sep 26, 1979
Hunt, Eleanor	Jan 10, 1910	New York, NY	Jun 12, 1981
Hunter, Richard	Apr 21, 1875	CA	Dec 22, 1962
Hurst, Paul	Oct 15, 1888	Traver, CA	Feb 27, 1953
Hymer, Warren	Feb 25, 1906	New York, NY	Mar 25, 1948
Ince, John	Aug 29, 1878	New York, NY	Apr 10, 1947
Ingraham, Lloyd	Nov 30, 1874	Rochelle, IL	Apr 4, 1956
Ingram, Jack	Nov 15, 1902	Chicago, IL	Feb 20, 1969
Jackson, "Pineapple" Eugene	Dec 25, 1916	Buffalo, NY	Oct 26, 2001
Jackson, Selmer	May 7, 1888	Lake Mills, IA	Mar 30, 1971
Jackson, Warren	Feb 12, 1892	Paris, TX	May 10, 1950
Jagger, Dean	Nov 7, 1903	Lima, OH	Feb 5, 1991
James, Alf	Oct 12, 1865	Australia	Oct 9, 1946
James, John	1914		May 20, 1960
James, Walter	Jun 3, 1882	Chattanooga, TN	Jun 27, 1946
Jamison, Bud	Feb 15, 1894	Vallejo, CA	Sep 30, 1944
Jaquet, Frank	Mar 16, 1885	WI	May 11, 1958
Jarrett, Art	Feb 5, 1884	Marysville, CA	Jun 12, 1960
Jenks, Frank	Nov 4, 1907	Des Moines, IA	May 13, 1962
Jenks, Si (Howard Jenkins)	Sep 23, 1876	Morristown, PA	Jan 6, 1970
Jennings, Al	Nov 25, 1863	VA	Dec 26, 1961
Jiminez, Soledad	Mar 10, 1884	Spain	Oct 17, 1966
Johnson, Ben	Jun 13, 1918	Foraker, OK	Apr 8, 1996
Johnson, Chubby (Charles)	Aug 13, 1903	Terre Haute, IN	Oct 31, 1974
Johnson, June	May 28, 1918	St. Louis, MO	Jul 14, 1987
Johnson, LeRoy	1919		Oct 1995
Johnson, Noble	Apr 18, 1881	Colorado Spgs, CO	Jul 23, 1987
Jolley, I. Stanford	Oct 24, 1900	Elizabeth, NJ	Dec 6, 1978
Jones, Buck (Charles Gebhard)	Dec 12, 1891	Vincennes, IN	Nov 30, 1942
Jones, Gordon	Apr 5, 1912	Alden, IA	Jun 20, 1963
Jordan, Sid	Aug 12, 1889	Muskogee, OK	Sep 30, 1970
Jory, Victor	Nov 23, 1902	Dawson City, AK	Dec 12, 1982
Judd, John	1893		Oct 7, 1950
Judge, Neoma	Sep 27, 1910	SD	Jun 7, 1968
Kaaran, Suzanne	Mar 21, 1912	Brooklyn, NY	Aug 27, 2004
Kane, Eddie	Aug 12, 1889	St. Louis, MO	Apr 30, 1969
Keane, Edward	May 28, 1884	New York, NY	Oct 12, 1969
Keane, Robert	Mar 4, 1883	New York, NY	Jul 2, 1981
Keckley, Jane	Sep 10, 1876	Charleston, SC	Aug 14, 1963
Keefe, Cornelius	Jul 13, 1900	Boston, MA	Dec 11, 1972
Keene, Tom (George Duryea)	Dec 20, 1896	Rochester, NY	Aug 4, 1963
Keith, Donald	Sep 6, 1903	Boston, MA	Aug 1, 1969
Keith, Ian (Keith Ross)	Feb 9, 1898	Boston, MA	Mar 26, 1960
Kellogg, Bruce	Apr 13, 1916	Thermopolis, OH	May 22, 1967

NAME	BIRTH DATE	PLACE	DEATH DATE
Kellogg, John	Jun 3, 1916		Feb 22, 2000
Kelly, Lew	Aug 24, 1879	St. Louis, MO	Jun 10, 1944
Kelly, Paul	Aug 9, 1899	Brooklyn, NY	Nov 6, 1956
Kelsey, Fred	Aug 20, 1884	Sandusky, OH	Sep 2, 1961
Kendall, Cy (Cyrus)	Mar 10, 1898	St. Louis, MO	Jul 22, 1953
Kennedy, Bill	Jun 27, 1908	Cleveland Heights, OH	Jan 27, 1997
Kennedy, Douglas (Keith Douglas)	Sep 14, 1915	New York, NY	Aug 10, 1973
Kennedy, Edgar	Apr 26, 1890	Monterey, CA	Nov 9, 1948
Kennedy, Jack			Nov 6, 1960
Kennedy, Merna	Sep 7, 1908	Kankakee, IL	Dec 20, 1944
Kennedy, Tom	Jul 15, 1885	New York, NY	Oct 6, 1965
Kenney, Jack	Nov 16, 1886	IL	May 26, 1964
Kent, Robert	Dec 3, 1908	Hartford, CT	May 4, 1955
Kerr, Donald	Aug 5, 1891	Eagle Grove, IA	Jan 25, 1977
Kerrigan, J. M.	Dec 16, 1884	Ireland	Apr 29, 1964
Keyes, Stephen	Jun 3, 1916	Sherman, TX	May 25, 2003
Kibbe, Guy	Mar 6, 1882	Sante Fe, NM	May 24, 1956
Kibbee, Milton	Jan 27, 1896	Santa Fe, NM	Apr 17, 1970
King, Brad	Nov 23, 1918		Jan 1, 1991
King, Charles	Oct 31, 1889	New York, NY	Jan 11, 1944
King, Charles L. "Charlie"	Feb 21, 1895	Hillsboro, TX	May 7, 1957
King, Jack	1883		Oct 8, 1943
King, Joe	Feb 9, 1883	Austin, TX	Apr 11, 1951
King, John "Dusty" (Miller McLeod)	Jul 11, 1909	Cincinnati, OH	Nov 11, 1987
King, Marjorie	1911		Jan 3, 1998
King, Pee Wee (Julius Kuczynski)	Feb 8, 1914	Abrams, WI	Mar 7, 2000
Kirby, Jay (Bill George)	Jan 28, 1920	Durango, CO	Jul 30, 1964
Kirk, Jack (Jack Kirkhuff)	1895	Nickerson, KS	Sep 3, 1948
Kirke, Donald	May 17, 1901	Jersey City, NJ	May 18, 1971
Kirkwood, James	Feb 22, 1885	Grand Rapids, MI	Aug 24, 1963
Kitchen, Dorothy, *see Nancy Drexel*			
Knapp, Evalyn	Jun 17, 1908	Kansas City, MO	Jun 10, 1981
Knight, Fuzzy (John Forrest Knight)	May 9, 1901	Fairmont, WV	Feb 23, 1976
Knott, Lydia	Oct 1, 1866	Tyner, IN	Mar 30, 1955
Kohler, Fred, Jr.	Jul 8, 1912	Scottsdale, AZ	Jan 9, 1993
Kohler, Fred, Sr.	Apr 21, 1888	Dubuque, IA	Oct 28, 1938
Kortman, Bob	Dec 24, 1887	NY	Mar 13, 1967
Lackteen, Frank	Aug 29, 1895	Lebanon	Jul 8, 1968
Laidlaw, Ethan	Nov 25, 1899	Butte, MT	May 25, 1963
Lambert, Jack	May 13, 1920	New York	Feb 18, 2000
LaMont, Harry	Jun 17, 1882	New York, NY	May 8, 1957
Landis, Carole	Jan 1, 1919	Fairchild, WI	Jul 5, 1948
Lane, Allan "Rocky" (Harry Albershart)	Sep 22, 1909	Mishawaka, IN	Oct 27, 1973

NAME	BIRTH DATE	PLACE	DEATH DATE
Lane, Nora	Sep 12, 1905	Chester, IL	Oct 16, 1948
Lane, Richard	May 28, 1899	Rice Lake, WI	Sep 5, 1982
Lansford, T. C. "Sonny"			Aug 7, 1989
LaRoux, Carmen	Sep 4, 1909	Mexico	Aug 24, 1942
LaRue, Frank	Dec 5, 1878	OH	Sep 26, 1960
LaRue, Jack	May 3, 1903	New York, NY	Jan 11, 1984
(Gaspare Biondolillo)			
LaRue, Lash	Jun 14, 1917	MI	May 21, 1996
(surname was Wilson)			
Laughton, Eddie (Edward)	Jun 20, 1902	England	Mar 21, 1952
Launders, Perc	Oct 11, 1904	CA	Oct 2, 1952
Laurenz, John	1909		Nov 7, 1958
Lauter, Harry	Jun 19, 1914	White Plains, NY	Oct 30, 1990
Lawler, Anderson	May 5, 1902	Russellville, AL	1959
Lawrence, Jay	1924		Jun 18, 1987
Lawrence, William	Aug 22, 1896	Brooklyn, NY	Nov 28, 1947
Leary, Nolan	Apr 26, 1891		Dec 12, 1987
Lease, Rex	Feb 11, 1903	Central City, WV	Jan 3, 1966
Lee, Billy	Sep 12, 1929	Nelson, IN	Nov 17, 1989
Lee, Duke	May 13, 1881	VA	Apr 1, 1959
Lee, Mary (Mary Lee Wooters)	Oct 24, 1924	Centralia, IL	Jun 6, 1996
Lee, Pinky (Pinkaus Leff)	May 2, 1907	St. Paul, MN	Apr 3, 1993
Leiber, Fritz	Jan 31, 1882	Chicago, IL	Oct 14, 1949
LeMoyne, Charles	Jun 27, 1889	IL	Sep 13, 1956
(Charles Lemon)			
Leonard, David	Sep 5, 1891	New York, NY	Apr 2, 1967
Leonard, Sheldon	Feb 22, 1907	New York, NY	Jan 10, 1997
(Sheldon L. Bershad)			
LeSaint, Edward	Dec 13, 1870	Cincinnati, OH	Sep 10, 1940
Leslie, Nan	Jun 4, 1926	Los Angeles, CA	Jul 27, 2000
Lewis, George J.	Dec 10, 1903	Guadalajara, Mexico	Dec 8, 1995
Lewis, Mitchell	Jun 26, 1880	Syracuse, NY	Aug 24, 1956
Lewis, Ralph	Oct 28, 1872	Englewood, IL	Dec 4, 1937
Lewis, Sheldon	Apr 20, 1869	Philadelphia, PA	May 7, 1958
Lewis, Texas Jim	Oct 15, 1909	Meigs, GA	Jan 23, 1990
Lincoln, Caryl	Nov 16, 1903	Oakland, CA	Feb 20, 1983
Lincoln, Elmo	Feb 6, 1889	Rochester, IN	Jun 27, 1952
(Otto Elmo Linkenhelt)			
Lindley, Bert	Dec 3, 1873	Chicago, IL	Sep 12, 1953
Littlefield, Lucien	Aug 16, 1895	San Antonio, TX	Jun 4, 1960
Livingston, Bob	Dec 9, 1904	Quincy, IL	Mar 7, 1988
(Robert Randall)			
Lloyd, George	Nov 5, 1892	Edinburgh, IL	Aug 15, 1967
(Lloyd Langford)			
Loft, Arthur	May 15, 1897	Ouray, CO	Jan 1, 1947
London, Tom	Aug 24, 1889	Louisville, KY	Dec 5, 1963
(Leonard Clapham)			
Long, Jack			Aug 7, 1938
Long, Walter	Mar 5, 1879	Nashua, NH	Jul 4, 1952

NAME	BIRTH DATE	PLACE	DEATH DATE
Lorch, Theodore	Sep 29, 1880	Springfield, IL	Nov 11, 1947
Lorraine, Louise	Oct 1, 1901	San Francisco, CA	Feb 2, 1981
(Louise Escovar)			
Lowery, Robert	Oct 17, 1913	Kansas City, MO	Dec 26, 1971
(Robert Lowery Hanks)			
Loy, Myrna (Myrna Williams)	Aug 2, 1905	Helena, MT	Dec 14, 1993
Lucas, Wilfred	Jan 30, 1871	Canada	Dec 13, 1940
Luden, Jack	Feb 8, 1902	Reading, PA	Feb 15, 1951
Lund, Lucille	Jun 3, 1912	Buckley, WA	Feb 16, 2002
Lyden, Pierce	Jan 8, 1908	Hildreth, NE	Oct 10, 1998
Lynn, Emmett	Feb 14, 1897	Muscatine, IA	Oct 20, 1958
Lyons, Cliff	Jul 4, 1901	SD	Jan 6, 1974
MacDonald, Edmund	May 7, 1908	MA	Sep 2, 1951
MacDonald, J. Farrell	Apr 14, 1875	Waterbury, CT	Aug 2, 1952
MacDonald, Kenneth	Sep 8, 1901	Portland, IN	May 5, 1972
(Kenneth Dollins)			
MacDonald, Wallace	May 5, 1891	Nova Scotia	Oct 30, 1978
Mack, Betty (Idalene Thurber)	Nov 30, 1901	IL	Nov 5, 1980
Mack, Cactus	Aug 8, 1899	Weed, NM	Apr 17, 1962
(Taylor McPeters)			
MacLane, Barton	Dec 25, 1902	Columbia, SC	Jan 1, 1969
MacLaren, Mary	Jan 19, 1900	Pittsburgh, PA	Nov 9, 1985
MacQuarrie, Frank	Jan 27, 1875	San Francisco, CA	Dec 25, 1950
McAuliffe, Leon	Jan 3, 1917	Houston, TX	Aug 22, 1988
McCall, William	May 19, 1870	DeLavin, IL	Jan 10, 1938
McCarroll, Frank	Sep 5, 1892	MN	Mar 8, 1954
McCarty, Patti	1921		Jul 7, 1985
McClary, Clyde	Jul 10, 1888	Minneapolis, MN	Jun 30, 1939
McClure, Bud	Feb 17, 1883	CA	Nov 2, 1942
McCollough, Philo	Jun 16, 1893	San Bernadino, CA	Jun 5, 1981
McCormick, Merrill (William)	Feb 5, 1891	Denver, CO	Aug 19, 1953
McCoy, Tim	Apr 10, 1891	Saginaw, MI	Jan 29, 1978
McCullough, Ralph	Sep 2, 1895	Laramie, WY	Dec 25, 1943
McDaniel, Etta	Dec 1, 1890	Wichita, KS	Jan 13, 1946
McDaniel, Sam	Jan 29, 1886	Wichita, KS	Sep 24, 1962
McDonald, Francis	Aug 22, 1891	Bowling Green, OH	Sep 18, 1968
McDowell, Nelson	Aug 8, 1870	Greenfield, MO	Nov 3, 1947
McGlynn, Frank, Jr.	Jul 9, 1904	Marin, CA	Mar 29, 1939
McGowan, John P.	Feb 24, 1880	Australia	Mar 26, 1952
McGrail, Walter	Oct 19, 1888	Brooklyn, NY	Mar 19, 1970
McGuinn, Joe	Jan 21, 1904	Brooklyn, NY	Sep 22, 1971
McIntyre, Christine	Apr 16, 1911	Nogales, AZ	Jul 8, 1984
McKay, Wanda	Jun 22, 1923	Ft. Worth, TX	Apr 11, 1996
(Dorothy Quackenbush)			
McKee, Lafe (Lafayette)	Jan 23, 1872	Morrison, IL	Aug 10, 1959
McKenzie, Robert	Sep 22, 1880	Ireland	Jul 8, 1949
McKim, Sammy	Dec 20, 1924	Canada	Jul 9, 2004
McLeod, Catherine	Jul 2, 1925	Santa Monica, CA	May 11, 1997

NAME	BIRTH DATE	PLACE	DEATH DATE
McMahon, Leo	Nov 11, 1913	Sonora, CA	Oct 31, 1995
McTaggert, Bud (Malcolm)	May 23, 1910	NE	May 29, 1949
Magrill, George	Jan 5, 1900	Brooklyn, NY	May 31, 1952
Mahoney, Jock	Feb 7, 1919	Chicago, IL	Dec 14, 1989
(Jacques O'Mahoney)			
Mallinson, Rory	Oct 27, 1913	GA	Mar 26, 1976
Mann, Hank	May 28, 1887	New York, NY	Nov 25, 1971
Manners, Sheila (see Sheila Bromley)			
Many Treaties, Chief	Apr 4, 1874	MT	Feb 29, 1948
(William Hazlett)			
Mapes, Ted	Nov 25, 1901	St. Edward, NE	Sep 9, 1984
Marcus, James	Jan 21, 1867	New York, NY	Oct 15, 1937
Maris, Mona	Nov 7, 1903	Argentina	Mar 29, 1991
Marlowe, Frank	Jan 20, 1904	MA	Mar 30, 1964
Marshall, Tully	Apr 10, 1864	Nevada City, CA	Mar 9, 1943
(William Phillips)			
Martin, Chris-Pin	Nov 19, 1893	Tucson, AZ	Jun 27, 1953
(Ysabel Ponciana Praz)			
Martin, Richard	Dec 12, 1917	Spokane, WA	Sep 4, 1994
Marion, Beth	Jun 11, 1912	Clinton, IA	Feb 18, 2003
Mason, James	Feb 3, 1889	France	Nov 7, 1959
(not the British actor)			
Mason, LeRoy	Jul 2, 1903	Larimore, ND	Oct 13, 1947
Mathews, Carl	Feb 19, 1899	OK	May 3, 1959
Matthews, Forrest	Sep 24. 1908		Nov 22, 1951
Matts, Frank	Apr 20, 1920		Nov 13, 1990
Mayer, Ray	Apr 24, 1901	Lexington, NE	Nov 21, 1948
Maynard, Ken	Jul 21, 1895	Vevey, IN	Mar 23, 1973
Maynard, Kermit	Sep 20, 1897	Vevey, IN	Jan. 16, 1971
Mayo, Frank	Jun 28, 1889	New York, NY	Jul 9, 1963
Meehan, Lew	Sep 7, 1890	MN	Aug 10, 1951
Meeker, George	Mar 5, 1903	Brooklyn, NY	Aug 19, 1984
Mehaffey, Blanche	Jul 28, 1908	Cincinnati, OH	Mar 31, 1968
Meredith, Iris	Jun 3, 1915	Sioux City, IA	Jan 22, 1980
Merton, John	Feb 18, 1901	WA	Sep 19, 1959
(Myrtland F. La Varre, Sr.)			
Messinger, Gertrude	Apr 28, 1912	Spokane, WA	Nov 8, 1995
Middleton, Charles	Oct 7, 1874	Elizabethtown, KY	Apr 22, 1949
Miles, Betty	Jan 11, 1910	Santa Monica, CA	Jun 6, 1992
Miljan, John	Nov 8, 1893	Lead City, SD	Jan 24, 1960
Miller, Charles	Mar 16, 1891	CA	Jun 5, 1955
Miller, Ivan	Nov 13, 1888	NE	Sep 27, 1967
Miller, Lorraine	Jan 5, 1922	Flint, MI	Feb 6, 1978
Miller, Walter	Mar 9, 1892	Dayton, OH	Mar 30, 1940
Millett, Arthur	Apr 21, 1874	Pittsfield, ME	Feb 24, 1952
Mitchell, Bruce	Nov 16, 1880	Freeport, IL	Sep 26, 1952
Mitchell, Ewing	1910		Sep 2, 1988
Mitchell, Frank "Cannonball"	May 13, 1905	New York, NY	Jan 21, 1991

NAME	BIRTH DATE	PLACE	DEATH DATE
Mitchum, Robert	Aug 6, 1917	Bridgeport, CT	Jul 1, 1997
Mix, Art (George Kesterson)	Jun 18, 1896	IL	Dec 7, 1972
Mix, Ruth	Jul 13, 1912	Dewey, OK	Sep 21, 1972
Mix, Tom	Jan 6, 1880	DuBois, PA	Oct 12, 1940
Moehring, Kansas (Carl)	Jul 9, 1897	OH	Oct 3, 1968
Monroe, Tom	Sep 2, 1919	Waco, TX	Dec 4, 1993
Montague, Monte (Walter)	Apr 23, 1891	Somerset, KY	Apr 6, 1959
Montana, Montie (Owen Harlan Mickel)	May 10, 1910	Wolf Point, MT	May 20, 1998
Montgomery, George (George Letz)	Aug 29, 1916	Brady, MT	Dec 12, 2000
Montgomery, Jack	Nov 14, 1891	Omaha, NE	Jan 21, 1962
Montoya, Alex	Oct 19, 1907	TX	Sep 25, 1970
Moore, Clayton	Sep 12, 1914	Chicago, IL	Dec 28, 1999
Moore, Dennis (Denny Meadows)	Jan 26, 1908	Ft. Worth, TX	Mar 1, 1964
Moore, Pauline	Jun 14, 1914	Harrisburg, PA	Dec 7, 2001
Moran, Peggy	Oct. 23, 1918	Clinton, IA	Oct. 25, 2002
Morante, Milburn	Apr 6, 1887	San Francisco, CA	Jan 28, 1964
Morgan, Boyd "Red"	Oct 24, 1915	Waurika, OK	Jan 8, 1991
Morgan, Buck (Louis Chirco)	Jun 20, 1907	MO	Aug 27, 1981
Morgan, Lee	Jun 12, 1902	TX	Jan 30, 1967
Moreland, Mantan	Sep 3, 1902	Monroe, LA	Sep 28, 1973
Morin, Alberto	Nov 26, 1902	Puerto Rico	Apr 7, 1989
Morrell, George	Apr 10, 1872	CA	Apr 28, 1955
Morris, Adrian	Jan 12, 1903	Mt. Vernon, NY	Nov 30, 1941
Morris, Wayne (Bert DeWayne)	Feb 17, 1914	Los Angeles, CA	Sep 14, 1959
Morrison, Pete	Aug 8, 1890	Denver, CO	Feb 5, 1973
Morton, Charles	Jan 28, 1908	IL	Oct 26, 1966
Morton, James	Aug 25, 1884	Helena, MT	Oct 24, 1942
Moulton, Edwin "Buck"	Apr 8, 1891	New York, NY	May 7, 1959
Mower, Jack	Sep 5, 1890	Honolulu, HI	Jan 6, 1965
Muir, Esther	Mar 11, 1903	Andes, NY	Aug 1, 1995
Mulhall, Jack	Oct 7, 1887	Wappingeers Falls, NY	Jun 1, 1979
Murdock, Perry	Sep 18, 1901	OK	Apr 19, 1988
Murphy, Charles	Dec 12, 1881	Independence, MO	Jun 11, 1942
Murphy, Horace	Jun 3, 1880	Finley, TN	Jan 20, 1975
Murray, Zon	Apr 13, 1910	MO	Apr 30, 1979
Naish, J. Carroll	Jan 21, 1900	New York, NY	Jan 24, 1973
Nash, George	1873	Philadelphia, PA	Dec 31, 1944
Nazarro, Cliff	Jan 31, 1904	New Haven, CT	Feb 18, 1961
Nestell, Bill	Mar 3, 1893	CA	Oct 18, 1966
Newill, James	Aug 12, 1911	Pittsburgh, PA	Jul 15, 1975
Nigh, Jane	Feb 25, 1925	Hollywood, CA	Oct 5, 1993
Nolan, Bob (Robert Nobles)	Apr 1, 1908	Canada	Jun 16, 1980
Nolan, Jim (James)	Mar 29, 1916	San Francisco, CA	Jul 9, 1985
Norman, Lucille (Lucille Boileau)	Jun 15, 1921	Lincoln, NE	Apr 1, 1998
Norris, Edward	Mar 10, 1911	Philadelphia, PA	Dec 18, 2002

NAME	BIRTH DATE	PLACE	DEATH DATE
Novello, Jay	Aug 22, 1904	Chicago, IL	Sep 2, 1982
Nye, Carol	Oct 4, 1901	Canton, OH	Mar 17, 1974
Oakman, Wheeler	Feb 21, 1890	Washington, DC	Mar 19, 1949
O'Brien, Dave (David Poole Fronabarger)	May 31, 1912	Big Springs, TX	Nov 8, 1969
O'Brien, George	Apr 19, 1899	San Francisco, CA	Jul 4, 1985
O'Connor, Frank	Apr 11, 1882	NY	Nov 22, 1959
O'Day, Nell	Sep 22, 1910	Prairie Hill, TX	Jan 3, 1989
O'Dell, Doye	1912	Gustine, CO	Jan 3, 2000
O'Dell, Georgia	1893		Sep 6, 1950
Oliver, Guy	Sep 25, 1878	Chicago, IL	Sep 1, 1932
O'Malley, Pat	Sep 3, 1890	Forest City, PA	May 21, 1966
Ortego, Artie	Feb 9, 1890	San Jose, CA	Jul 24, 1960
Osborne, Bud (Lennie)	Jul 20, 1884	Claymore, OK	Feb 2, 1964
O'Shea, Jack (John Rellaford)	Apr 6, 1906	San Francisco, CA	Oct 1, 1967
Otho, Henry (H. O. Wright)	Feb 6, 1888	Brooklyn, NY	Jun 7, 1940
Padden, Sarah	Oct 16, 1881	England	Dec 4, 1967
Padjan, Jack	Dec 14, 1887	MT	Feb 1, 1960
Page, Bradley	Sep 8, 1901	Seattle, WA	Dec 18, 1985
Page, Dorothy (Dorothy Stofflett)	Mar 4, 1904	Northampton, PA	Mar 26, 1961
Palmer, Tex (Luther W. Palmer)	Jul 31, 1904	Xenia, OH	Mar 22, 1982
Park, Post	Nov 4, 1899	MO	Sep 18, 1955
Parker, Cecilia	Apr 26, 1914	Canada	Jul 25, 1993
Parker, Eddie	Dec 12, 1901	MI	Jun 20, 1960
Parkinson, Cliff	Sep 3, 1898	KS	Oct 1, 1950
Parrish, Helen	Mar 12, 1924	Columbus, GA	Feb 22, 1959
Patrick, Dorothy	Jun 3, 1922	Canada	May 31, 1987
Patrick, Gail	Jun 20, 1911	Birmingham, AL	Jul 16, 1980
Patrick, Gil	Aug 5, 1896	MN	Feb 21, 1971
Patterson, Hank (Elmer)	Oct 9, 1888	AL	Aug 25, 1975
Patterson, Shirley	Dec 26, 1922	Winnepeg, Canada	Apr 4, 1995
Patton, Bill	Jun 2, 1894	Amarillo, TX	Dec 12, 1951
Pawley, Edward	1903		Jan 27, 1988
Pawley, William	Jul 21, 1905	Kansas City, MO	Jun 15, 1952
Payne, Sally	Sep 5, 1912	Chicago, IL	May 8, 1999
Payton, Claude	Mar 30, 1882	Centerville, IA	Mar 1, 1955
Pearce, George	Jun 26, 1865	New York, NY	Aug 12, 1940
Pegg, Vester	Mar 23, 1889	Appleton City, MO	Feb 19, 1951
Peil, Ed, Sr.	Jan 18, 1882	Racine, WI	Dec 29, 1958
Pendleton, Steve (Gaylord)	1908		Oct 3, 1984
Penn, Leonard	Nov 13, 1907	Springfield, MA	May 20, 1975
Pepper, Barbara	May 31, 1915	New York, NY	Jul 18, 1969
Perrin, Jack	Jul 25, 1896	Three Rivers, MI	Dec 17, 1967
Perry, Joan	Jul 7, 1911	Pensacola, FL	Sep 15, 1996
Perry, Pascale (Harvey Poirier)	Oct 22, 1895	Tucson, AZ	Jul 11, 1953
Perryman, Lloyd	Jan 29, 1917	Ruth, AR	May 31, 1977

NAME	BIRTH DATE	PLACE	DEATH DATE
Peters, Ralph	May 19, 1903	Canada	Apr 12, 1959
Phelps, Lee	May 15, 1893	PA	Mar 19, 1953
(Napoleon Bonaparte Ku-Kuck)			
Phelps, Willie		VA	Mar 1, 2004
Philbrook, James	Oct 22, 1924		Oct 24, 1982
Phillips, Eddie	Aug 14, 1899	Philadelphia, PA	Feb 22, 1965
Pickard, John	Jun 25, 1913	Lascassas, TN	Aug 4, 1993
Pickens, Slim	Jun 29, 1919	Kingsburg, CA	Dec 12, 1983
(Louis Bert Lindley, Jr.)			
Pierce, Jim	Aug 8, 1900	IN	Nov 12, 1983
Platt, Edward	Feb 4, 1916	Staten Island, NY	Mar 19, 1974
Plues, George	Jun 12, 1895	WA	Aug 16, 1953
Plummer, Rose	Jan 19, 1876	CA	Mar 3, 1955
Pollard, Snub (Harold Frazier)	Nov 9, 1889	Australia	Jan 19, 1962
Porter, Ed	May 26, 1881	Columbus, IN	Jul 29, 1939
Potel, Victor	Oct 12, 1889	Lafayette, IN	Mar 8, 1947
Powell, Lee	May 15, 1908	Long Beach, CA	Jul 20, 1944
Powell, Russ	Sep 16, 1875	Indianapolis, IN	Nov 28, 1950
Powers, John	1885		Sep 25, 1951
Powers, Lucille	Nov 18, 1911	San Antonio, TX	Sep 11, 1981
Prather, Lee (Oscar)	May 5, 1888	NE	Jan 3, 1958
Price, Hal (Harry Price)	Jun 24, 1886	Waukegon, OH	Apr 15, 1964
Price, Stanley	Dec 31, 1892	KS	Jul 13, 1955
Prickett, Maudie	Oct 25, 1915		Apr 14, 1976
Prosser, Hugh	Mar 2, 1907		Nov 8, 1952
Puig, Eva	Feb 3, 1894	Mexico	Oct 6, 1968
Purcell, Dick	Aug 6, 1905	Greenwich, CT	Apr 10, 1944
Pyle, Denver	May 11, 1920	Bethune, CO	Dec 25, 1997
Quantaro, Nena	Mar 17, 1908	Mt. Vernon, NY	Nov 23, 1985
Ragan, Mike, *see Holly Bane*			
Raines, Steve	Jun 17, 1916		Jan 4, 1996
Randall, Jack (Addison)	May 12, 1906	San Fernando, CA	Jul 16, 1945
Randall, Stuart	Jul 24, 1909	Brazil, IN	Jun 22, 1988
Rankin, Arthur (Arthur Davenport)	Aug 30, 1896	New York, NY	Mar 23, 1947
Rawlins, Monte	1907		July 13, 1988
Rawlinson, Herbert	Nov 15, 1885	England	Jul 12, 1953
Redwing, Rodd	Aug 24, 1904	New York, NY	May 30, 1971
Reed, Donald	Jul 23, 1901	Mexico	Feb 28, 1973
Reed, Marshall	May 28, 1917	Englewood, CO	Apr 15, 1980
Reed, Phillip	Mar 25, 1908	New York, NY	Dec 4, 1996
Reed, Walter (Walter Smith)	Feb 10, 1916	Bainbridge WA	Aug 20, 2001
Reeves, George	Jan 6, 1913	Woodstock, IA	Jun 16, 1959
(George Bessolo)			
Reeves, Robert	Jan 28, 1892	Marlin, TX	Apr 13, 1960
Regas, George	Nov 9, 1890	Greece	Dec 13, 1940
Regas, Pedro	Apr 18, 1897	Greece	Aug 10, 1974
Reicher, Frank	Dec 2, 1875	Germany	Jan 19, 1965
Remley, Ralph	May 24, 1885	Cincinnati, OH	May 26, 1939

NAME	BIRTH DATE	PLACE	DEATH DATE
Renaldo, Duncan	Apr 23, 1904		Sep 3, 1980
Revier, Dorothy (Doris Velegra)	Apr 18, 1904	Oakland, CA	Nov 19, 1993
Reynolds, Craig (Hugh Enfield)	Jul 15, 1907	Anaheim, CA	Oct 22, 1949
Reynolds, Marjorie (Marjorie Goodspeed)	Aug 12, 1917	Buhl, ID	Feb 1, 1997
Rice, Frank	May 13, 1892	Muskegon, MI	Jan 9, 1936
Richards, Addison	Oct 20, 1902	Zanesville, OH	Mar 22, 1964
Richards, Frank	Sep 15, 1909		Apr 15, 1992
Richards, Keith	Jul 18, 1914	Pittsburgh, PA	Mar 23, 1987
Richardson, Jack	Nov 18, 1884	New York, NY	Nov 17, 1957
Richmond, Kane (Frederick Bowditch)	Oct 10, 1906	Minneapolis, MN	Mar 22, 1973
Richmond, Warner	Jan 11, 1886	Racine, WI	Jun 19, 1948
Ricks, Archie	Feb 29, 1896	CA	Jan 10, 1962
Rickson, Joseph	Sep 6, 1880	Clearcreek, MT	Jan 8, 1958
Ridgely, John	Sep 6, 1909	Chicago, IL	Jan 17, 1968
Risdon, Elisabeth	Apr 6, 1888	England	Dec 20, 1958
Ritter, Tex (Woodward Maurice)	Jan 12, 1905	Murval, TX	Jan 2, 1974
Rivero, Julian	Jul 15, 1890	San Francisco, CA	Feb 24, 1976
Roadman, Betty	Dec 5, 1889	MO	Mar 24, 1975
Robards, Jason, Sr.	Dec 31, 1892	Hillsdale, MI	Apr 4, 1963
Robbins, Skeeter Bill (Roy)	Jul 16, 1887	Glen Rock, WY	Nov 28, 1933
Roberson, Chuck (Charles)	May 10, 1919		Jun 8, 1988
Roberts, Lynne (Theta May)	Nov 22, 1922	El Paso, TX	Apr 1, 1978
Robertson, Willard	Jan 1, 1886	Runnels, TX	Apr 5, 1948
Robinson, Frances	Apr 26, 1916	Wadsworth, NY	Aug 16, 1971
Robinson, Rad	Nov 11, 1910	Bountiful, UT	Sep 20, 1988
Robinson, Ruth	Aug 18, 1887	KS	Mar 17, 1966
Robyns, William	1855	St. Louis, MO	Jan 22, 1936
Rochelle, Claire	1910	MO	May 23, 1981
Rockwell, Jack (John Trowbridge)	Oct 6, 1890	Mexico	Nov 10, 1947
Rodriguez, Estelita	Jul 2, 1928	Cuba	Mar 12, 1966
Rogers, Jean (Eleanor Lovegren)	Mar 25, 1916	Belmont, MA	Feb 24, 1991
Rogers, Jimmie	Jul 25, 1915	New York, NY	Apr 28, 2000
Rogers, Roy (Leonard Sly)	Nov 5, 1911	Cincinnati, OH	Jul 6, 1998
Rogers, Ruth	Oct 4, 1918	Tracy, CA	Oct 9, 1953
Roland, Gilbert (Luis de Alonso)	Dec 11, 1905	Mexico	May 15, 1994
Roman, Ric			Aug 11, 2000
Romero, Cesar	Feb 15, 1907	New York, NY	Jan 1, 1994
Roosevelt, Buddy (Kent Sanderson)	Jun 25, 1898	Meeker, CO	Oct 6, 1973
Roper, Jack	Mar 25, 1904	MS	Nov 28, 1966
Roquemore, Henry	Mar 13, 1886	Marshall, TX	Jun 30, 1943
Roscoe, Al (Allan)	Aug 23, 1888	Memphis, TN	Mar 8, 1933
Rosener, George	May 23, 1879	Brooklyn, NY	Mar 29, 1945
Ross, Betsy King	Mar 14, 1922	St. Paul, MN	Oct 4, 1989
Ross, Earle	Mar 29, 1888	IL	May 21, 1961

NAME	BIRTH DATE	PLACE	DEATH DATE
Roth, Gene (Gene Stutenroth)	Jan 8, 1903	SD	Jul 19, 1976
Roubert, Matty	Jan 22, 1907	New York, NY	May 17, 1973
Roux, Tony	May 7, 1901	Mexico	Nov 9, 1976
Rowland, Henry	Dec 28, 1913	Omaha, NE	Apr 26, 1984
Royce, Frosty	Dec 20, 1910	OK	May 5, 1965
Royle, William	Mar 22, 1887	Rochester, NY	Aug 9, 1940
Ruhl, William	Oct 25, 1901	OR	Mar 12, 1956
Russell, Reb (Lafayette)	May 31, 1905	Osawatomie, KS	Mar 16, 1978
Rutherford, Jack (John)	Apr 13, 1893	England	Aug 21, 1982
Ryan, Sheila (Katherine McLaughlin)	Jun 8, 1921	Topeka, KS	Nov 5, 1975
Ryan, Tim	Jul 27, 1899	Bayonne, NJ	Oct 22, 1956
St. John, Al "Fuzzy"	Sep 10, 1892	Santa Ana, CA	Jan 21, 1963
St. Polis, John	Nov 24, 1873	New Orleans, LA	Oct 8, 1946
Sais, Marin	Aug 2, 1890	San Rafael, CA	Dec 31, 1971
Sale, Virginia (Wren)	Aug 20, 1889	Urbana, IL	Aug 23, 1992
Sanders, Hugh	Mar 13, 1911	IL	Jan 9, 1966
Sanford, Ralph	May 31, 1899	Springfield, MA	Jun 20, 1963
Santachi, Tom	Oct 24, 1880	MO	Apr 9, 1931
Sarracino, Ernest	Feb 12, 1914		May 20, 1998
Saum, Clifford	Dec 18, 1882	Columbus, MS	Mar 5, 1943
Sawyer, Joe (Joseph Sauers)	Aug 29, 1901	Canada	Apr 4, 1982
Sayers, Loretta	Feb 23, 1911	Seattle, WA	Sep 14, 1999
Sayles, Francis	Nov 22, 1891	Buffalo, NY	Mar 19, 1944
Saylor, Syd (Leo Sailor)	May 24, 1895	Chicago, IL	Dec 21, 1962
Schildkraut, Joseph	Mar 22, 1895	Austria	Jan 21, 1964
Scott, Fred	Feb 2, 1902	Fresno, CA	Dec 16, 1991
Scott, Randolph	Jan 23, 1898	Orange, VA	Mar 2, 1987
Sears, Alan	Mar 9, 1887	TX	Aug 18, 1942
Sears, Fred	Jul 7, 1912	Boston, MA	Nov 30, 1957
Seay, James	Sep 30, 1914		Oct 10, 1992
Sebastian, Dorothy	Apr 26, 1905	Birmingham, AL	Apr 8, 1957
Semels, Harry	Nov 30, 1887	New York, NY	Mar 2, 1946
Sepulveda, Carl	Feb 5, 1897	UT	Aug 24, 1974
Seward, Billie	Nov 23, 1912	Philadelphia, PA	Mar 20, 1982
Shannon, Frank	Jul 27, 1884	Ireland	Feb 1, 1959
Shannon, Harry	Jun 13, 1890	Saginaw, MI	Jul 27, 1964
Shannon, Jack	Aug 31, 1892	OH	Dec 27, 1968
Sharpe, David	Feb 2, 1910	St. Louis, MO	Mar 30, 1980
Shaw, Janet (see Ellen Clancy)			
Shayne, Robert (Robert Shaen Dawe)	Oct 4, 1900	Yonkers, NY	Nov 29, 1992
Sheldon, Jerry (Charles Patton)	Mar 6, 1901	MO	Apr 11, 1962
Sheldon, Kathryn	Sep 22, 1879	Cincinnati, OH	Dec 25, 1975
Shilling, Marion	Sep 12, 1909	Denver, CO	Nov 6, 2004
Shooting Star	1890		Jun 4, 1966
Shrum, Cal	Jul 4, 1910	Mountain Home, AR	Mar 11, 1996
Shuford, Andy	Dec 16, 1917	Helena, AR	May 19, 1995

NAME	BIRTH DATE	PLACE	DEATH DATE
Shumway, Lee	Mar 4, 1884	Salt Lake City, UT	Jan 4, 1959
Shumway, Walter	Aug 26, 1884	Cleveland, OH	Jan 13, 1965
Silverheels, Jay (Harold J. Smith)	Sep 26, 1912	Canada	Mar 5, 1980
Simpson, Mickey	Dec 3, 1913	Rochester, NY	Aug 23, 1985
Simpson, Russell	Jun 17, 1889	San Francisco, CA	Dec 12, 1959
Smith, Albert J.	Feb 15, 1894	Chicago, IL	Apr 12, 1939
Smith, Arthur "Fiddlin"	1900		Feb 24, 1973
Smith, Jack C.	Nov 16, 1896	Seattle, WA	Jan 14, 1944
Smith, Tom	Sep 10, 1892	OK	Feb 23, 1976
Snowflake (Fred Toones)	Jan 5, 1906	Raleigh, NC	Feb 13, 1962
Soderling, Walter	Apr 13, 1872	CT	Apr 10, 1948
Soldani, Charles	Jun 1, 1893	OK	Sep 10, 1968
Sondergaard, Gale	Feb 15, 1899	Litchfield, MN	Aug 14, 1985
Sothern, Hugh (Roy Sutherland)	Jul 20, 1881	Anderson County, KY	Apr 13, 1947
Sowards, George	Nov 27, 1888		Dec 20, 1975
Space, Arthur	Oct 12, 1908	New Brunswick, NJ	Jan 13, 1983
Spencer, Tim (Vernon)	Jul 13, 1908	Webb City, MO	Apr 26, 1974
Spiker, Ray	Jan 6, 1902	WI	Feb 23, 1964
Standing Bear, Chief	1860	Ft. Robinson, NE	Feb 20, 1939
Stanley, Edwin	Nov 22, 1880	Chicago, IL	Dec 24, 1944
Stanley, Louise (Louise Keyes)	Jan 28, 1915	Springfield, MO	Dec 28, 1982
Starrett, Charles	Mar 28, 1903	Athol, MA	Mar 22, 1986
Steele, Bob	Jan 23, 1907	Portland, OR	Dec 21, 1988
(Robert Adrian Bradbury)			
Steele, Tom (Tom Skeoch)	Jun 12, 1907	Scotland	Nov 4, 1990
Steele, William	Mar 28, 1889	San Antonio, TX	Feb 13, 1966
Steers, Larry	Feb 14, 1888	Chicago, IL	Feb 15, 1951
Stein, Sammy	Apr 1, 1906	New York, NY	Mar 30, 1956
Stephens, Harvey	Aug 21, 1901	Los Angeles, CA	Dec 22, 1986
Stephenson, James	Apr 14, 1889	England	Jul 29, 1941
Stevens, Charles	Mar 3, 1893	Solomonsville, AZ	Aug 22, 1964
Stevens, Landers	Feb 17, 1877	San Francisco, CA	Dec 19, 1940
Stevens, Onslow	Mar 29, 1902	Los Angeles, CA	Jan 5, 1977
Stevens, Robert	Aug 25, 1880		Dec 19, 1963
Stewart, Donald	1911	PA	Mar 1, 1966
Stewart, Roy	Oct 17, 1883	San Diego, CA	Apr 26, 1933
Stirling, Linda (Louise Schultz)	Oct 11, 1921	Long Beach, CA	Jul 20, 1997
Stockdale, Carl	Feb 19, 1874	Worthington, MN	Mar 15, 1953
Stockman, Boyd	Feb 12, 1915		Mar 10, 1998
Stone, Arthur	Nov 28, 1883	St. Louis, MO	Sep 4, 1940
Stone, George	May 18, 1903	Poland	May 26, 1967
Stone, Milburn	Jul 5, 1904	Burton, KS	Jun 12, 1980
Stone, Paula	Jan 20, 1916	New York, NY	Dec 23, 1997
Stoney, Jack	Oct 1, 1897	PA	Jan 29, 1978
Storey, June	Apr 20, 1918	Canada	Dec 18, 1991
Storm, Jerome	Nov 11, 1890	Denver, CO	Jul 10, 1958
Strang, Harry	Dec 13, 1892	VA	Apr 10, 1972

NAME	BIRTH DATE	PLACE	DEATH DATE
Strange, Glenn	Aug 16, 1899	Weed, NM	Sep 20, 1973
Strange, Robert	Nov 26, 1881	New York, NY	Feb 22, 1952
Strauch, Joe, Jr. "Tadpole"	May 18, 1929	Chicago, IL	May 31, 1986
Stroud, Claude	Mar 26, 1907	Kauffman, TX	Oct 16, 1985
Stuart, Nick (Nicholas Pratza)	Apr 10, 1903	Romania	Apr 7, 1973
Sullivan, Charles	Apr 24, 1899	LA	Jun 25, 1972
Sully, Frank	Jun 17, 1908	St. Louis, MO	Dec 17, 1975
Summerville, Slim (George)	Jun 10, 1892	Albuquerque, NM	Jan 6, 1946
Sutton, Grady	Apr 5, 1908	Chattanooga, TN	Sep 17, 1995
Sutton, Paul	May 14, 1912	Albuquerque, NM	Jan 31, 1970
Swickard, Josef	Jun 26, 1866	Germany	Feb 29, 1940
Switzer, Carl "Alfalfa"	Aug 7, 1927	Paris, IL	Jan 21, 1959
Sylvester, Henry	Sep 2, 1881	MO	Jun 8, 1961
Taggart, Ben	Apr 5, 1889	New York, NY	May 17, 1947
Talbot, Lyle (Lilse Henderson)	Feb 8, 1902	Pittsburgh, PA	Mar 3, 1996
Taliaferro, Hal	Nov 13, 1895	Sheridan, WY	Feb 12, 1980
(Floyd Taliaferro Alderson—aka Wally Wales)			
Tannen, Charles	Oct 22, 1915	New York, NY	Dec 28, 1980
Tannen, William	Nov 17, 1911	New York, NY	Dec 2, 1976
Tansey, Emma	Sep 12, 1870	Louisville, KY	Mar 23, 1942
Tansey, Sherry (James Sheridan)	Mar 3, 1904	New York, NY	Apr 12, 1961
Taylor, Al	Aug 29, 1887	MA	Mar 2, 1951
Taylor, Dub	Feb 26, 1907	Richmond, VA	Oct 3, 1994
(Walter) "Cannonball"			
Taylor, Duke (Ruel F. Taylor)	Nov 13, 1897	OK	Aug 21, 1982
Taylor, Ferris	Mar 25, 1888	TX	Mar 6, 1961
Taylor, Forrest	Dec 29, 1883	Bloomington, IL	Feb 19, 1965
Taylor, Kent (Louis Weiss)	May 11, 1907	Nashua, IA	Apr 9, 1987
Teal, Ray	Jan 12, 1902	Grand Rapids, MI	Apr 2, 1976
Tearle, Conway	May 17, 1878	New York, NY	Oct 1, 1938
Tenbrook, Harry	Oct 9, 1887	Norway	Sep 14, 1960
Terhune, Max	Feb 12, 1891	Franklin, IN	Jun 5, 1973
Terrell, Kenneth	Apr 29, 1904	GA	Mar 8, 1966
Terry, Al	May 22, 1893	New York, NY	Jul 15, 1967
Terry, Don	Aug 8, 1902	Natick, MA	Oct 6, 1988
Terry, Sheila (Kay Clark)	Mar 5, 1910	Warroad, MA	Jan 18, 1957
Terry, Tex	Aug 22, 1902	Coxville, IN	May 18, 1985
Thomas, Frank	Feb 13, 1889	St. Joseph, MO	Nov 25, 1989
Thomas, Lyn	1929	Ft. Wayne, IN	Aug 26, 2004
Thompson, Nick	Sep 11, 1890	Galveston, TX	Apr 22, 1980
Thomson, Kenneth	Jan 7, 1899	Pittsburgh, PA	Jan 26, 1967
Thorne, William	Oct 14, 1878	Fresno, CA	Mar 10, 1948
Thorpe, Jim	May 28, 1886	Prague, OK	Mar 28, 1953
Thundercloud, Chief	Apr 12, 1899	Santa Rita, AZ	Nov 30, 1955
(Victor Daniels)			
Todd, Harry	Dec 13, 1863	Allegheny, PA	Feb 15, 1935
Toler, Sidney	Apr 28, 1873	Warrensburg, MO	Feb 12, 1947
Tombes, Andrew	Jun 29, 1891	Ashtabula, OH	Mar 1976

NAME	BIRTH DATE	PLACE	DEATH DATE
Toney, Jim	Jan 1, 1884		Sep 19, 1973
Toomey, Regis	Aug 13, 1902	Pittsburgh, PA	Oct 12, 1991
Toones, "Snowflake" Fred	Jan 5, 1906	NC	Feb 13, 1962
Towne, Aline	Nov 30, 1930	Canada	Feb 2, 1996
Travis, Merle	Nov 29, 1917	Rosewood, KY	Oct 19, 1983
Trent, Jack	Aug 24, 1896	TX	Aug 1, 1961
Trowbridge, Charles	Jan 10, 1882	Mexico	Oct 30, 1967
Turich, Felipe	Dec 5, 1898	Mexico	Mar 9, 1992
Turich, Rosa	Jun 9, 1903	Tucson, AZ	Nov 20, 1998
Turner, George	Apr 27, 1877	Leavenworth, KS	Oct 3, 1947
(not the Republic serial star)			
Turner, Martin	Dec 20, 1882	TX	May 14, 1957
Tuttle, Wesley	Dec 10, 1917	Lamarr, CO	Sep 29, 2003
Twelvetrees, Helen	Dec 25, 1908	Brooklyn, NY	Feb 13, 1958
(Helen Marie Jurgens)			
Twitchell, Archie (Michael Brandon)		OR	Jan 31, 1957
Tyler, Harry	Jun 13, 1888	New York, NY	Sep 15, 1961
Tyler, Tom (Vincent Markowski)	Aug 9, 1903	Port Henry, NY	May 1, 1954
Tyrrell, John	Dec 7, 1900	New York, NY	Sep 19, 1949
Urecal, Minerva	Sep 22, 1884	Eureka, CA	Feb 26, 1966
Usher, Guy	May 9, 1883	Mason City, IA	Jun 16, 1944
Vallin, Rick	Sep 24, 1919	Russia	Aug 31, 1977
Vallon, Michael	Jul 21, 1897	Dover, MN	Nov 13, 1973
Van Sickel, Dale	Nov 29, 1907	GA	Jan 25, 1977
Van Sloan, Edward	Nov 1, 1882	San Francisco, CA	Mar 8, 1964
Van Zandt, Phil	Oct 12, 1904	Holland	Feb 16, 1958
Vaughan, Dorothy	Nov 5, 1889	St. Louis, MO	Mar 15, 1955
Vaughn, Alberta	Jun 27, 1904	Ashland, KY	Apr 26, 1992
Venable, Evelyn	Oct 18, 1913	Cincinnati, OH	Nov 16, 1993
Vernon, Dorothy	Nov 11, 1875	Germany	Oct 28, 1970
Vernon, Wally	May 27, 1904	New York, NY	Mar 7, 1970
Villegas, Lucio	Feb 25, 1883	Chile	Jul 20, 1968
Visaroff, Michael	Nov 18, 1892	Russia	Feb 27, 1951
Vogan, Emmett	Sep 27, 1893	Cleveland, OH	Nov 13, 1969
von Brincken, William	May 27, 1881	Germany	Jan 18, 1946
(Wilhelm)			
Vosper, John	Jul 3, 1902	Chicago, IL	Apr 6, 1954
Wagner, Max	Nov 28, 1901	Mexico	Nov 16, 1975
Wakely, Jimmy (James)	Feb 16, 1914	Mineola, AR	Sep 23, 1982
Wales, Ethel	Apr 4, 1878	Passiac, NJ	Feb 15, 1952
Walker, Cheryl	Aug 1, 1918	South Pasadena, CA	Oct 24, 1971
Walker, Ray	Aug 10, 1904	Newark, NJ	Oct 6, 1980
Walker, Robert	Jun 18, 1888	Bethlehem, PA	Mar 4, 1954
(not the MGM star)			
Wallace, Morgan	Jul 26, 1881	Lom Poc, CA	Dec 12, 1953
Waller, Eddy	Jun 14, 1889	Chippewa Falls, WI	Aug 19, 1977
Walling, William	Jun 2, 1872	Sacramento City, IA	Mar 5, 1932
Walters, Luana	Jul 22, 1912	Los Angeles, CA	May 19, 1963

NAME	BIRTH DATE	PLACE	DEATH DATE
Ward, Black Jack (Jerome)	May 3, 1891	LA	Aug 29, 1954
Warde, Anthony	Nov 4, 1908	PA	Jan 8, 1975
Warren, E. Alyn	Jun 2, 1874	Richmond, VA	Jan 22, 1940
Warren, James (James Wittlig)	Feb 14, 1913	Marietta, OH	Mar 28, 2001
Warwick, Robert	Oct 9, 1878	Sacramento, CA	Jun 6, 1964
Washburn, Bryant	Apr 28, 1889	Chicago, IL	Apr 30, 1963
Washington, Edgar "Blue"	Feb 12, 1898	Los Angeles, CA	Sep 15, 1970
Watkin, Pierre	Dec 29, 1887	Sioux City, IA	Feb 3, 1960
Watson, Minor	Dec 22, 1889	Marianna, AR	Jul 28, 1965
Wayne, John (Marion Robert Morrison)	May 26, 1907	Winterset, IA	Jun 11, 1979
Weaver, Leon "Abner"	Aug 12, 1882	Ozark, MO	May 27, 1950
Weaver, Marjorie	Mar 2, 1913	Crossville, TN	Nov 1994
Weeks, Barbara	Mar 3, 1914	Somerville, MA	Jun 24, 2003
Welch, Niles	Jul 29, 1888	Hartford, CT	Nov 21, 1976
Welden, Ben	Jun 12, 1901	Toledo, OH	Oct 17, 1997
Wells, Jacqueline (see Julie Bishop)			
Wells, Ted (John Oscar)	Jan 11, 1899	Midland, TX	Jun 7, 1948
Welsh, William	Feb 9, 1870	Philadelphia, PA	Jul 16, 1946
Wentworth, Martha	Jun 2, 1889	New York, NY	Mar 8, 1974
Wenzel, Arthur	May 5, 1907	WI	Feb 10, 1961
Wescoatt, Norman "Rusty"	1911		Sept 3, 1987
Wessel, Richard	Apr 20, 1911	WI	Apr 20, 1965
West, Wally (Theo Wynn)	Oct 11, 1903	Gough, TX	May 16, 1984
Whitaker, Charles "Slim"	Jul 29, 1893	Kansas City, MO	Jun 27, 1960
White, Dan	Mar 25, 1908	Falmouth, FL	Jul 7, 1980
White, Lee "Lasses"	Aug 28, 1888	Wills Point, TX	Dec 16, 1949
Whiteford, Blackie (John)	Apr 27, 1889	New York, NY	Mar 21, 1962
Whitespear, Greg	Apr 18, 1889	OK	Feb 20, 1956
Whitley, Ray	Dec 5, 1901	Atlanta, GA	Feb 21, 1979
Whitlock, Lloyd	Jan 2, 1891	Springfield, MO	Jan 8, 1966
Whitney, Claire	May 6, 1890	New York, NY	Aug 27, 1969
Wilcox, Frank	Mar 13, 1907	DeSoto, MO	Mar 3, 1974
Wilde, Lois	Sep 20, 1907	MN	Feb 16, 1995
Wiley, Jan	Feb 23, 1916	Marion, IN	May 27, 1993
Wilke, Bob (Robert)	May 18, 1914	Cincinnati, OH	Mar 28, 1989
Wilkerson, Guy	Dec 21, 1899	Katy, TX	Jul 8, 1971
Wilkerson, William	Sep 18, 1902	OK	Mar 3, 1966
Williams, Bill (Herman Katz)	May 15, 1914	Brooklyn, NY	Sep 21, 1992
Williams, Charles	Sep 27, 1898	Albany, NY	Jan 4, 1958
Williams, Guinn "Big Boy"	Apr 26, 1899	Decatur, TX	Jun 6, 1962
Williams, Maston	Apr 15, 1879	Corsicana, TX	Jul 15, 1978
Williams, Robert	Sep 23, 1904	IL	Jun 17, 1978
Williams, Roger	Feb 8, 1898	CO	Dec 18, 1964
Williams, Spencer	Jul 14, 1893	Vidalia, LA	Dec 13, 1969
Williams, Tex (Sollie)	Aug 23, 1917	Ramsey, IL	Oct 11, 1985
Willing, Foy (Foy Willingham)	1915	Bosque County, TX	Jul 24, 1978

NAME	BIRTH DATE	PLACE	DEATH DATE
Willis, Matt	Oct 16, 1914		Mar 30, 1989
Willis, Norman	May 27, 1903	Chicago, IL	Jan 27, 1988
Wills, Bob	Mar 6, 1906	Limestone Co., TX	May 13, 1975
Wills, Chill	Jul 18, 1902	Seagoville, TX	Dec 15, 1978
Wills, Henry	1921	Florence, AZ	Jan 1, 1997
Wills, Walter	Aug 22, 1881	New York, NY	Jan 18, 1967
Wilsey, Jay "Buffalo Bill, Jr."	Feb 6, 1896	Hillsdale, MO	Oct 25, 1961
Wilson, Charles	Jul 29, 1894	New York, NY	Jan 7, 1948
Wilson, Clarence	Nov 17, 1876	Cincinnati, OH	Oct 5, 1941
Wilson, Dorothy	Nov 4, 1909	Minneapolis, MN	Jan 7, 1998
Wilson, Harry	Nov 22, 1897	England	Sep 6, 1978
Wilson, Lois	Jun 28, 1896	Pittsburgh, PA	Mar 3, 1988
Wilson, Tom	Aug 27, 1880	Helena, MT	Feb 19, 1965
Wilson, Whip (Roland Charles Meyers)	Jun 15, 1911	Granite, IL	Oct 23, 1964
Winkler, Robert	1927		Dec 28, 1989
Withers, Grant	Jan 17, 1905	Pueblo, CO	Mar 27, 1959
Withers, Isabel	Jan 20, 1896	Frankton, IN	Sep 3, 1968
Wolfe, Bill	Aug 14, 1894	New York, NY	Feb 16, 1975
Wolfe, Ian	Nov 4, 1896	Canton, IL	Jan 23, 1992
Wood, Britt	Sep 27, 1893	TN	Apr 14, 1965
Woodbury, Joan	Dec 17, 1915	Los Angeles, CA	Feb 22, 1989
Woods, Donald (Ralph Zink)	Dec 2, 1904	Brandon, CO	Mar 15, 1998
Woods, Harry	May 5, 1889	Cleveland, OH	Dec 28, 1968
Woodward, Bob	Mar 5, 1909	OK	Feb 7, 1972
Worden, Hank (Norton)	Jul 23, 1901	Rolfe, IA	Dec 6, 1992
Wright, Mack	1895	Princeton, IN	Aug 14, 1941
Wright, Wen (Harry Wendell)	1916		Jun 17, 1954
Wrixon, Maris	Dec 28, 1916	Pasco, WA	Oct 6, 1999
Wyatt, Al	Mar 7, 1920	Mayfield, KY	Aug 12, 1992
Yaconelli, Frank	Oct 2, 1898	Italy	Nov 19, 1965
York, Duke	Oct 17, 1908	Danby, NY	Jan 24, 1952
Young, Carleton	Oct 21, 1905	New York, NY	Nov 7, 1994
Young, Clara Kimball	Sep 6, 1890	Chicago, IL	Oct 15, 1960
Young, Clifton	Sep 15, 1917	New York, NY	Sep 10, 1951
Young, Polly Ann	Oct 25, 1908	Denver, CO	Jan 14, 1997
Yowlachie, Chief (Daniel Simmons)	Aug 5, 1891	WA	Mar 7, 1966
Yrigoyen, Bill			1976

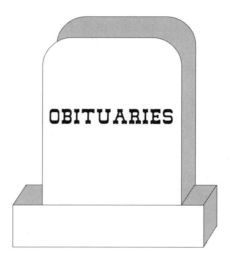

OBITUARIES

While the obituaries make for interesting reading, they must not be taken for fact. Some of the publicity created by the Hollywood studios crept over into the performer's death reports. Note: See first part of book for dates of deaths.

ART ACORD
Called Suicide

Ex-Cowboy Film Star, Working at Mining in Mexico, Takes Poison

MEXICO CITY, Jan. 4 (AP) — Dispatches from Chihuahua to the newspaper Excelsior say that Art Acord, former movie actor in Hollywood, swallowed poison and died today.

He had been working there in the mining business for several months.

The dispatches said Acord had lived in Chihuahua City for several months, during which time his affairs apparently had gone from bad to worse and he developed deep melancholy. He was found suffering in his hotel room at 10 o'clock this morning, and a doctor was summoned, who took him to a hospital.

Acord, according to the dispatches, told the physician he had taken poison and wanted to die. Despite efforts to resuscitate him, he died early this afternoon.

Art Acord, former cowboy film star, was with Buffalo Bill's Wild West Show before entering the motion-picture business. He was a crack rider, having won honors at big Wild West events all over the United States. He received the Croix de Guerre for his exploits in hand-to-hand fighting in the World War, serving with the Thirty-ninth Infantry.

Hollywood Cowboy Legend BOB ALLEN Dies Oct. 9

NEW YORK — They say he lived the part. Bob "Tex" Allen, silverscreen legend who starred in more than 40 movies and made his name as one of the first Hollywood cowboys, was the same dignified gentleman off-camera as he played under the hot lights.

With his crystal blue eyes, jaunty smile and snow-white Stetson hat, Allen — whose real name was Theodore Baehr — was an original: virtuous, honorable and a good guy to the end, said his family.

At age 92, Allen died in his sleep on Friday, Oct. 9, in Oyster Bay, N.Y., after a four-week battle with cancer.

His death came only three months after Roy Rogers passed away at age 86, and just a week after singing cowboy legend Gene Autry died at 91. The three were icons of a past era, a time when determination went hand-in-hand with the certainty that the black-cloaked villains always finished last.

"There was something about those old days in Hollywood — the characters were too good to be true," said Theodore Baehr, Jr., the actor's son, who now lives in Camarillo, Calif. "My father was just as good off-screen as he was on. He wasn't self-righteous. He was naturally kind and gentle."

Gene Autry

Singing Cowboy GENE AUTRY Dies at 91

Actor-Businessman's Financial Empire Included Broadcast Outlets, Baseball Team

by Claudia Levy
Washington Post Staff Writer

Gene Autry, 91, who parlayed his movie and record earnings as Hollywood's first singing cowboy into a financial empire that included the California Angels baseball team, died Oct. 2 at his home

in the Studio City neighborhood of Los Angeles. He had been ill for some time, but the cause of death was not reported.

Mr. Autry was the only entertainer with five stars on Hollywood's Walk of Fame, one each for radio, records, movies, television and live theater. He stopped performing in the 1950s, after 95 films, nearly 30 years in pictures, and a television program that lasted for six seasons.

Mr. Autry helped spark a national interest in country music and helped define the Western style of singing. He cut 635 records, including mellow renditions of "Back in the Saddle Again," "You Are My Sunshine" and "Rudolph the Red-Nosed Reindeer" that made his radio program a national favorite for decades.

"Back in the Saddle" was back on the charts five years ago as part of the soundtrack of the movie "Sleepless in Seattle." A three-CD

42

box set of his songs, "Sing, Cowboy, Sing!," was re-released last year. In all, he won nine gold-record awards and a platinum record.

On the screen, Mr. Autry rode hard, strummed his guitar prettily and promoted gentle virtues. He told young fans he believed in "Ten Cowboy Commandments"— including values such as respect, tolerance of others, honesty and truth, not taking unfair advantage of anyone and helping people in distress.

He was ranked the top cowboy movie star from 1937 to 1943, heyday of the Western. This placed him in a friendly rivalry with the other singing cowboy, Roy Rogers, who died three months ago. Other popular cowboy stars in this period were Hopalong Cassidy (William Boyd) and John Wayne.

Mr. Autry and his chestnut "wonder horse" Champion began withdrawing from show business in the mid-1950s. He became a full-time businessman, with four radio stations, interests in newspapers, oil wells, ranches and hotels such as the Mark Hopkins Hotel in San Francisco.

This made him an immensely rich man, and he was ranked for years among the top 400 wealthiest Americans by Forbes magazine. One dream went unfulfilled, however: The Angels never won the American League pennant, for which he had long yearned.

Former president and ex-movie star Ronald Reagan issued a statement with his wife, Nancy,

saying that Mr. Autry had "delighted and touched millions through many careers, as cowboy, singer, actor, radio star, baseball owner, art collector, philanthropist, businessman and good and caring citizen...."

"So often, we've caught ourselves humming 'Back in the Saddle Again,' a song that will always bring back warm memories of Gene," the Reagans said.

Orvon Gene Autry was born in Tioga, Tex., into a family that descended from early settlers of the state, including an ancestor who died at the Alamo.

Gene Autry got his first guitar, from the Sears, Roebuck and Co. catalogue, when he was 12, and he was performing locally by the time he was 15. He worked for the railroad as an apprentice and telegraph operator until he was discovered in 1927, strumming a guitar in a telegraph office in Chelsea, Okla., by humorist and actor Will Rogers, then one of the most popular entertainers in the world.

It was the year that sound had come to film. Rogers encouraged him to pursue his career. He made his first record two years later, a version of his idol Jimmie Rodgers' "Blue Yodel No. 5." In 1931, he sold 500,000 copies of his break-through record, "That Silver-Haired Daddy of Mine." Sales had reached a million by the next year, and because of the record's success, the notion of awarding a gold-plated copy was institutionalized.

Mr. Autry was hired as the yodeling cowboy for "National Barn Dance," a widely popular radio program broadcast from Chicago. The radio station was owned by Sears, Roebuck, which began featuring Mr. Autry's records, songbooks and guitar in its catalogues. Mr. Autry became a national singing sensation.

One historian later noted that "the time was right for a man gentle with children, romantic enough to serenade a lady and courageous enough to defend what is right with his wit, his fists, or—rarely—his guns. He was the perfect hero for the Depression."

Mr. Autry's first film was "In Old Santa Fe." He sang in only one scene, but it was the most popular of the movie.

He helped "codify a romantic, albeit unrealistic, image of cowboy culture," as one critic put it, "as well as popularize what we now call country." It was the success of his group, the Singing Cowboys, that led the music trade papers to change the designation of rural white music from "hillbilly" to "country and western."

At the start of World War II, when he was one of the top 10 box office attractions in the nation, Mr. Autry temporarily left show business to serve in the Army Air Forces. He flew supply planes in the Far East.

When he returned from the war, he began solidifying his business interests. But the kind of "B" movies he had made were fading in popularity, and he failed to re-gain his status as one of the top 10 moneymakers. By the early 1950s, he owned broadcasting stations, a studio and his own television production company.

In 1949, he made his biggest single musical hit, "Rudolph," a Johnny Marks song he recorded reluctantly, in a single take, as the flip side of another song. That year, he recorded another song that would become a Western classic, "Ghost Riders in the Sky."

His own 200 compositions included "Here Comes Santa Claus."

Mr. Autry, who had once played minor league baseball with the Tulsa Oilers, became owner of the Angels when the team was formed as an expansion franchise in 1961.

Three years ago, the Walt Disney Co. bought an interest in the team and then took operating control. Now called the Anaheim Angeles, the team was in the running for the playoffs this year but lost the American League West division lead in the last week of the regular season.

Disney has an agreement to acquire Mr. Autry's remaining share.

Mr. Autry was also founder in Los Angeles 10 years ago of the Gene Autry Western Heritage Museum, built largely with funds from his foundations. It features Western memorabilia and art.

"I felt that I owed something. The West has been very kind to me over the years," Mr. Autry said at the time. He said the museum was a gift to the world rather than a monument to himself. It houses a

1870s-era steam fire engine from Nevada, guns owned by Annie Oakley and Wyatt Earp, and costumes of TV's Lone Ranger and Tonto.

In the late 1980s, Mr. Autry and his former movie sidekick, Pat Buttram, hosted 93 episodes of the 90-minute "Melody Ranch Theatre" show on The Nashville Network, spotlighting the telecasting of his old Republic and Columbia movies. The show was one of the highest-rated programs on TNN.

Mr. Autry was vice president of the American League and active in the Masons. He was inducted into the Country Music Hall of Fame, the Nashville Songwriters' Hall of Fame, the National Cowboy Hall of Fame, and the National Association of Broadcasters Hall of Fame. He received the Songwriters' Guild Life Achievement Award and the Hubert Humphrey Humanitarian of the Year Award.

He was honored by his songwriting peers with a lifetime achievement award from ASCAP.

His first wife, Ina Spivey, died in 1980. Survivors include his wife, Jackie Autry, and a sister.

(The Associated Press contributed to this report.)

BOB BAKER

Former Western Star Dies at 64

Stanley Leland Weed, 64, better known to his host of friends as "Tumbleweed," died at Whipple Veterans Hospital, Prescott, at 7:20 a.m., Saturday, Aug. 30, 1975.

Funeral services were at Wescott Funeral Home in Cottonwood at 10 a.m. Thursday, with graveside services conducted by the Fort Verde Chapter of the Disabled American Veterans, at Clear Creek Cemetery immediately following.

A memorial service was held at the Flagstaff Lodge No. 7, F and A.M. Wednesday night at 7:30 p.m.

Tumbleweed, a resident of Camp Verde since 1959, was well-known in the motion picture industry as Bob Baker. He was popular in films during the era of the B-Western movie, starring in such pictures as "Courage of the West," "The Singing Outlaw," "Border Wolves" and "Black Bandit." He was a saddle maker by trade and had a shop in Camp Verde for many years.

Survivors include his wife, Evelyn; one daughter, Barbara May Brown, El Paso, Tex.; three sons, Kenneth, Cottonwood, Tom, Portland, Ore., and Walter, Camarillo, Calif.; one brother, Robert; and four sisters, Gretchen McDermott and Lori Jean Weis, California, Jean Alger, Kansas, and Miriam Grabeel, Prescott.

Pallbearers are Wade Bounds, Nelson Harris, Melvin Rask, Eugene Mulholland, Cecil Morris and Ted Morris. Honorary pallbearers are Frank Matheny, Minard Coons, Robert (Bud) Taylor, Elbert

Walker, L. H. (Slim) Kite, C.C. Tuffy Peach, Ray Meyer and Norman York.

Members of the Color Guard of the D.A.V. were Al Long, commander; Floyd Wilson, Ed Naui and Wava Golliher.

The family asks that in lieu of flowers, donations may be made to the Cancer Research Society.

Ballew retired from both careers during World War II to take up aircraft factory work on the West Coast. He came to Fort Worth to work at General Dynamics 32 years ago.

Besides his daughter, he is survived by two brothers, W.V. "Smoke" Ballew of Dallas and Charles Robert Ballew of Bellevue, WA.

SMITH BALLEW, Band-Leader, Movie Star

Smith Ballew, nationally known band-leader and cowboy movie star of the 1930s who had been a Fort Worth resident since 1952, died May 2 in a Longview hospital. He was 82.

Ballew broke his hip in a fall at his Westcliff apartment in Fort Worth and had gone to Longview to be cared for by his daughter, Justine Mercer.

He sang the vocals for his Smith Ballew Orchestra, which made records during the early 1930s.

In the mid-1930s, Ballew found a new career as a singing cowboy in movie westerns. His films for 20th Century-Fox included *Roll Along Cowboy, Western Gold, Panamint's Bad Man, Hawaiian Buckaroo* and *Gaucho Serenade,* with Gene Autry.

JAMES S. BANNON

Cremation services for James S. Bannon, age 73, of Ojai were held Monday under the direction of the Clausen Funeral Home.

Mr. Bannon died Saturday, July 28, 1984 at an Ojai convalescent hospital following a brief illness. He was born April 9, 1911 in Kansas City, Missouri and had lived in the Ojai Valley for the past 4 months having moved here from Plano, Texas.

Mr. Bannon was an actor having worked in both radio & in movies. He was also an avid golfer.

He is survived by:

SON: Jack Bannon, Van Nuys, California

DAUGHTER: Margaret Kilfoil, Tarzana, California

BROTHER: Fr. John Francis Bannon S.J., St. Louis, Missouri

3 Grandchildren

DONALD (RED) BARRY, 69

Film Actor, Is a Suicide

The New York Times, July 17, 1980

HOLLYWOOD (UPI) July 18 — Donald (Red) Barry, the actor who rode across movie screens as the Red Ryder in the 1940's serial and went on to appear in a host of television shows, shot and killed himself last night following an argument with his estranged wife. He was 69 years old.

Capt. Dan Cooke, spokesman for the Los Angeles police, said officers were called to Mr. Barry's home in North Hollywood at about 9:30 p.m. to quiet a family dispute.

"The officers thought the dispute was settled," Captain Cooke said, "but as they were getting in their car to go, Barry walked out of the house, put a .38-caliber revolver to his head and fired."

Mr. Barry was pronounced dead a short time later at Riverside Hospital in Los Angeles.

The actor's wife of more than 20 years, Barbara, recently moved out of their home with the couple's two daughters, Christina 15, and Deborah 10, and rented a nearby apartment.

A family friend said the younger daughter was staying with Barry and called her mother when she noticed her father acting strangely. When Mrs. Barry arrived, the friend said Mr. Barry attempted to strangle her, and she fled and called the police.

Mr. Barry, who was born in Houston, made his first movie appearance in "Night Waitress" in 1936. He also appeared in "The Woman I Love," "Sinners in Paradise" and "The Crowd Roars," before he adapted the cartoon character Red Ryder for the popular movie serial.

He later appeared in "I'll Cry Tomorrow," "Jesse James' Women" and a number of television shows.

Lieut. Gov. REX BELL of Nevada, Ex-Cowboy Screen Star, Dies

The New York Times, July 5, 1962

LAS VEGAS, Nev., July 4, 1962 (UPI) — Lieut. Gov. Rex

Bell of Nevada, former silent Western screen star and husband of actress Clara Bow, died tonight of a coronary occlusion at Sunrise Hospital after attending a political meeting to boost his candidacy for Governor. He was 58 years old.

This afternoon, Mr. Bell had addressed a Fourth of July picnic for the Republican Party. Dressed in cowboy boots and other western attire, he had appeared in good health as he introduced Paul Laxalt, his running mate for lieutenant governor.

Cattleman in Real Life

Mr. Bell, who was a cattleman on screen and off it for much of his life, was raised in the city.

He was born George Belden, in Chicago, where he attended grade school until his family moved to Hollywood. There, after his graduation from high school, he became a movie extra, working with such cowboy stars as Tom Mix and Buck Rogers, and rose to star in horse operas himself.

He and Miss Bow were married in Las Vegas in 1931. Mr. Bell occasionally appeared in films with Miss Bow, but devoted more and more time to running a large ranch they had bought at Searchlight, Nev., extending into California.

Mr. Bell was elected lieutenant governor in 1954 and re-elected in 1958, when he was the only Republican to survive a Democratic sweep. He had been expected to win the gubernatorial nomination without opposition.

Miss Bow, the one time "It Girl" of the films, has been in ill health for about twenty years and is confined to a Culver City, Calif., rest home, but she sometimes makes trips to the Bell home in Nevada. They have two sons, Rex Anthony, and George Robert. A broker also survives.

BILL "COWBOY RAMBLER" BOYD

Bill Boyd, 67, country and western singer, died Dec. 7, 1977 in a Dallas hospital. He spent his youth on his father's cattle ranch, combining singing and guitar playing with cowboy chores. A Dallas resident for 48 years, he fronted his own band, the Cowboy Ramblers, on WRR Dallas in a daily radio show, "Western Roundup," from 1929 until 1973, when he suffered a stroke.

In the 1930-40s, he played club dates throughout the U.S. with his band and singing brother, Jim Boyd. Boyd had recorded more than 300 records on RCA-Victor label until retiring in 1973. He also starred in six musical western feature films as "Bill (Cowboy Rambler) Boyd," to avoid confusion with another western film star, the late William (Hopalong Cassidy) Boyd. His first starring role was in "Texas Manhunt," which preemed in 1941 at the Capitol Theatre in Dallas.

Survived by his wife, two daughters, two brothers, three sisters and four grandchildren.

WILLIAM BOYD, 'Hopalong Cassidy,' Dies

The New York Times

HOLLYWOOD, Sept. 13 (AP) — William Boyd, who rose to stardom as Hopalong Cassidy, died last night at a South Laguna Beach, Calif., hospital of complications from Parkinson's disease and congestive heart failure. He was 74 years old.

Mr. Boyd's portrayal of Hopalong—a "good guy" who wore a black hat but was a paragon of virtue—was the longest-running characterization in Hollywood history. He rode the range on his horse, Topper, for a quarter of a century in movies and on television.

Hoppy, a character half conceived by writers, half by Boyd, didn't smoke, drink or swear. He captured villains rather than shoot them. The responsibility of being a children's hero transformed Mr. Boyd, a one-time playboy, into a philanthropist devoted to strengthening the fiber of American youth.

"When you've got kids look-ing up to you," he would say, "when you've got parents saying what a wonderful guy Hoppy is, what do you do? You have to be a wonderful guy."

Born in Hendrysburg, Ohio to a poor farm laborer, Mr. Boyd quit school after the sixth grade and went to work. He came to Hollywood as a young man and appeared in films such as "The Volga Boatman," "King of Kings" and "Two Arabian Nights." He became a romantic idol of the '20s, in a class with such stars as Wallace Reid and Rod LaRocque.

He spent freely, gambled heavily and lived lavishly. He bought a Beverly Hills mansion, a Malibu beach house and a ranch. He married and divorced three actresses, Ruth Miller, Elinor Fair and Dorothy Sebastian. Miss Miller bore him a son, who lived only nine months.

Then, in 1932, the good life came to a halt. A Broadway actor named William Boyd, now dead, was arrested at a drinking and gambling party. In the morning papers in Hollywood, Mr. Boyd's picture was published in error. An apology was printed later, but his career plunged downhill.

He was a has-been in 1935 when a Paramount producer offered to star him in a series of cowboy films. Mr. Boyd asked for a few changes in his role, then made the first "Hopalong Cassidy" movie.

Movie executives said that Mr. Boyd, who couldn't ride a horse, had made Hopalong too much of a gentleman. But he persisted, became a good rider and adopted Topper who would be his mount for 19 years.

The movies were popular and he quietly bought up all television rights to the idea. In 1948 the first Hoppy show appeared on television. Viewers' reaction told the story—Mr. Boyd had hit a jackpot.

In 1937 he had married Grace Bradley, and he credited her with his success. He remained devoted to her until his death.

Mr. Boyd founded a club called Hoppy's Troopers, which rivaled the Boy Scouts in membership. It had a Hopalong Code of Conduct, which preached loyalty, honesty, ambition, kindness and other virtues.

He donated money to children's hospitals and homes, saying: "The way I figure it, if it weren't for the kids, I'd be a bum today. They're the ones who've made my success possible. They're the ones that should benefit from it."

He retired in 1953 after making 106 Hoppy shows. He and his wife bought real estate and moved to Palm Desert where they lived quietly.

In 1968 he underwent surgery for removal of a cancerous tumor from a lymph gland. From then on Mr. Boyd refused all interviews and photographs.

The character of Hopalong Cassidy had been conceived many years before Mr. Boyd first took the part, by Clarence E. Mulford, then a Brooklyn license clerk, who had been turning out Western fiction on the East Coast since 1904.

Mr. Mulford's Hopalong was a standard rough-talking hard-drinking gambling gunslinger. His nickname came from a knee injury in a gunfight that gave him an irregular gait off his horse.

But Mr. Boyd succeeded in imposing his own vision of the Hopalong character on the series of films produced by Harry Sherman. He had had his fill of playing heavies, and soon Hopalong was a kind of middle-aged Galahad in shining black cowboy suit and boots.

Mr. Mulford, who died in 1956, did not take this amiss: he accepted the idea that the old-time Hopalong was for adults, while the new, shinier model was for children.

"I have a great deal of admiration for Boyd's accomplishments," he said. "Let Bill have his Hopalong, I have mine...."

JOHNNY MACK BROWN, 70, Dies; Cowboy Star and Football Hero

The New York Times, November 16, 1974

WOODLAND HILLS, Calif., Nov. 15 (UPI) — Johnny Mack Brown, who went from All-America college-football player and Rose Bowl hero to become the star of hundreds of Saturday-matinee Western movies in the nineteen thirties and forties, died yesterday. He was 70 years old.

Mr. Brown died of kidney failure, according to a spokesman for the Motion Picture Country Home and Hospital, where he had been under treatment for a month.

He was a halfback on the University of Alabama team that beat the University of Washington, 20 to 19, in the Rose Bowl in 1926, in which Mr. Brown went on to become an actor and once said he had appeared in more than 300 pictures, mostly B-grade Westerns with his horse, Reno.

Money-Making List

His first Western was "Billy the Kid" with Wallace Beery in 1930. From 1942 to 1950 he was consistently named to The Motion Picture Herald's list of the 10 top money-making Western actors. Almost all of his films were aimed at the Saturday-afternoon children's market.

He retired in the fifties and was host and manager of a restaurant in the San Fernando Valley.

Mr. Brown was born in Dothan, Ala., and had his first brush with the movies while still a college football player. It led eventually to his acting career. Movie crew members on location in Birmingham in the early filming of "Men of Steel" with Victor McLaglen, attended a football game and were introduced to the players afterward.

George Fawcett, a character actor, remembered Mr. Brown especially after his Rose Bowl exploits. He returned to California in 1927 as an assistant football coach from the University of Alabama and looked up Mr. Fawcett.

Met Von Stroheim

Mr. Fawcett introduced Mr. Brown to Erich Von Stroheim, the director, who, according to one story, cupped Mr. Brown's face in his hands, gazed into his face and said, "You could be an actor."

The Rose Bowl game in 1926 was the highlight of Mr. Brown's football career, he said in later years, because "we were the first Southern team ever to participate. We were supposed to be kind of lazy down South—full of hookworms and all. Nevertheless, we came out here and beat one of the finest teams in the country, making it a kind of historic event for Southern football. We didn't play just for Alabama, but for the whole South."

Mr. Brown is survived by his widow, Cornelia, and four children.

Funeral held for actor
ROD CAMERON

GAINESVILLE, Ga. (UPI) — A private funeral was held Thursday for veteran film and television actor Rod Cameron who was once rejected by the Canadian Northwest Mounted Police only to become a Hollywood cowboy. He was 73.

The rugged Canadian-born actor died Wednesday at Lanier Park Hospital following an extended illness.

Cameron got his start in films in 1940 and appeared in dozens of movies and television shows over the next few decades.

He began his career as an understudy for Fred MacMurray, landed a role in the 1943 film "Gung Ho," then starred with such actresses as Yvonne DeCarlo and Maria Montez in "Pirates of Monterey" and "Frontier Gal."

Cameron went on to appear in numerous Westerns, including "Boss of Boomtown," "Trigger Trail" and "Riders of the Santa Fe."

"I got on a horse and that was my big mistake," Cameron said in a 1979 interview. "I didn't even know how to ride a horse when I came to Los Angeles. Even after I did 400 episodes on three different detective series, 'Coronado Nine,' 'City Detective' and 'State Trooper,' casting directors would say 'Oh yes, Rod Cameron, the cowboy.'"

Cameron, born Roderick Cox on Dec. 7, 1910, in Calgary, Alberta, Canada, moved to the United States after being rejected by the Northwest Mounted Police because of an injury.

He moved to New York, got a job building the Holland Tunnel between New York and New Jersey, and worked just long enough to buy a train ticket to California to make a name for himself in movies.

HARRY CAREY, Star of Stage, Screen

Veteran Actor Who Won Fame as Cowboy Hero Dies at 69—Scored in 'Trader Horn'

The New York Times, Monday, September 22, 1947

HOLLYWOOD, Calif., Sept. 21 (AP) — Harry Carey, veteran screen actor and leading man of silent films, died today at the age of 69 in his home at near-by Brentwood after a brief illness. He was a Western picture hero for more than a decade, and became a rancher in real life, owning more than 1,500 acres at one time.

In recent years, after a return to the stage, he came back as a character actor in motion pictures.

Played Roles in Westerns

Harry Carey, appeared in more than 300 motion pictures and several New York plays, customarily portrayed a two-fisted gun-playing, muscular son of the West in the films. In silent pictures he epitomized the Western hero. He himself lived for many years on a homespun ranch where he raised turkeys.

Still straight, lean and strong in his sixties, Mr. Carey played many roles other than Westerns as a character actor and star in the last years of his career. He was in the movies thirty-two years before he made his legitimate Broadway debut. A fine actor, he was frequently highly praised by critics.

Born in New York on Jan. 16, 1878, he was the son of Mr. and Mrs. Henry De Witt Carey and was christened Henry De Witt Carey II. His father was a Special Sessions judge and later operated a horse-car line.

Mr. Carey grew up in City Island, the Bronx, and as a boy learned from mounted police the horseback riding that later helped him so much in the movies. He played tackle on New York University's football team, made his stage debut in stock in the Yorkville Theatre, New York, in the early Nineteen Hundreds and studied law at New York Law School.

Stricken with pneumonia when he was filling in as an emergency horse-car driver in a snowstorm, Mr. Carey gave up his law studies and wrote a melodrama, "Montana," although he had not been West. He toured in the play as its star from 1904 to 1908.

Made First Film in 1908

In 1908 Mr. Carey acted in his first motion pictures, three Westerns produced on Staten Island. He went to Hollywood in 1911 and from then on that center of the picture industry was usually his headquarters.

Through the long years of the silent films Mr. Carey went on with his great success as a Western star. With the beginning of talkies in the Nineteen Twenties Mr. Carey's services were no longer in demand, so he turned to making personal appearances in the nation's theatres.

In 1929, however, he was sent to Africa for the better part of a year to play the lead in the film "Trader Horn." His reputation enhanced by that film, he again became one of the screen's leading character actors.

His pictures in the Nineteen Thirties included "Slide, Kelly, Slide," "A Little Journey," "Satan Town," "The Frontier Trail," "Border Devils," "Cavalier of the West," "The Last Outlaw," "Valiant is the Word for Carrie," "Kid Galahad," "Born Reckless," "Souls at Sea," "King of Alcatraz" and "Mr. Smith Goes to Washington." In the last named he played the role of Vice President of the United States and won the praise of John N. Garner, then Vice President.

In the early Nineteen Forties Mr. Carey starred in "The Shepherd of the Hills" and appeared in "Among the Living," "Parachute Battalion," "Sundown" and "Air Force."

Mr. Carey made his first appearance in a Broadway play in 1940 in "Heavenly Express." THE NEW YORK TIMES said he played the role of an aged locomotive engineer "with seasoned authority." The following year he was again seen on the stage in a revival of "Ah, Wilderness!" In 1944 he appeared in "—But Not Goodbye."

The Careys had a son and a daughter.

SUNSET CARSON, Cowboy Movie Star, Dies

Knoxville News-Sentinel, May 2, 1990
by Associated Press

RENO, Nev. — Sunset Carson, a 1940s cowboy movie hero, died in Reno on Tuesday, one day after winning a settlement in a 3-year-old lawsuit over money earned from some of his old pictures.

Mr. Carson, 63, died at Washoe Medical Center after apparently suffering a heart attack in his room at the Ponderosa Hotel.

He was scheduled to be buried in Jackson, Tenn., where he had lived since 1988, said Jack Smith of George A. Smith & Sons funeral parlor in Jackson.

Mr. Carson, who was a rodeo star at 17, appeared in more than 40 Westerns including "Bandits of the Badlands," "Oregon Trail" and "Bells of Rosarita."

In 1978, he put together a series of 78 classic Westerns featuring himself and other Western stars, including Ken Maynard and Roy Rogers.

He filed suit in 1987 complaining the South Carolina Educational Television Producers Inc. and Ken Heard Releasing Inc., who helped in the production of the "Six Gun Heroes" series but failed to pay him for videocassette sales and promotional materials sold on the show since 1982.

Mr. Carson's Reno attorney, Larry Dunn, said the suit was settled out of court in Mr. Carson's favor on Monday. Dunn would not give a money amount.

Mr. Carson spent recent years crusading against drugs and against violence, sex and crude language in movies and on television.

He is survived by his wife of one year, Jeanne, a son and a daughter.

BILL CODY

Bill Cody, 57, silent film cowpoke star, died Jan. 24, 1948 in Santa Monica, after several months' illness. His biggest hits were gallopers for Pathe and Universal. He later starred on the road in the Downie Bros.' "Bill Cody's Ranch Wild West Show." His last stint was a bit in "Joan of Arc."

Wife and two sons survive.

RAY CORRIGAN

Ray Corrigan, 73, onetime Hollywood western film performer and owner of Corriganville, for many years a favorite film location near Hollywood, died Aug. 10 of a heart attack at his Brookings Harbor, Ore., home. He had been an Oregon resident since selling property in 1965 to Bob Hope for a reported $2,800,000, and in recent years had been active in real estate development and motion picture production.

A physical culture enthusiast, he served as a photographic double for Johnny Weissmuller in the "Tarzan" series and was at Metro for four and one-half years during the 1930s, where he appeared in 31 films, before swinging over to Universal to star in "Night Life of the Gods," in the role of Apollo. He did six other features, then Republic inked him to star in a serial, "Undersea Kingdom," in which his character name was Crash Corrigan. Born Ray Benard, he adopted the name that remained with him throughout his career.

Following another serial, "The Painted Stallion," Corrigan was cast with Bob Livingston and Max Terhune in "The Three Mesquiteers" series of westerns. The trio made 16 films together, and when Livingston left he was replaced by John Wayne, who bowed out after eight features and with his success in John Ford's "Stagecoach" still ringing in his ears.

Wayne's exit also marked Corrigan's departure from the series. He took Terhune with him for a series tagged "The Range Busters" at Monogram, where the third in a new trio was a singer named John "Dusty" King.

Corrigan bought 17,000 acres, which had been used as a dump in the San Fernando Valley in 1937, for $10,000 and spent five years cleaning up the property. He built what became known as Corriganville, site of countless locations for Hollywood producers.

Surviving are his wife, Irene; son, Robert, and daughter, Patricia Ann, both by a previous marriage.

Actor BUSTER CRABBE Dies

SCOTTSDALE, Ariz. (AP) — Buster Crabbe, a former Olympic swimming champion who went on to star in movies as Tarzan and Flash Gordon, died Saturday at his home in this Phoenix suburb. He was 75.

He had "had a little heart problem over the years," but five minutes before he died he was making plans to attend an arthritis telethon in Nashville, Tenn., and "didn't have any pain any place," said his wife, Virginia.

Crabbe, who called himself "King of the Serials," once remarked that he made only one A picture, "King of the Jungle," in which he portrayed the Lion man. He said the rest were sub-Bs or serials, including his movie roles as "Buck Rogers" and "Flash Gordon."

"I made nine of them, more than anyone else in talkies," Crabbe once boasted of his serials. "Only William Desmond made more — 10 silent serials. I did three 'Flash Gordons,' two 'Tarzans,' a 'Buck Rogers,' plus 'Pirates of the High Seas,' 'Red Barry' and 'Sea Hound.'

"We knocked off 13 chapters in five to six weeks and didn't allow for much dramatic skill. Some say that my acting rose to the point of incompetence and then leveled off."

Crabbe said in a 1980 interview that neither he nor the legendary Johnny Weismuller, moviedom's first talking Tarzan, ever gave a successful rendition of Tarzan's jungle call.

"At first it was three voices," he said of the Tarzan yell. "The studio put together a baritone, a bass and a hog caller... Finally they settled on a version by Tom Held, a film cutter who happened to be my father-in-law."

Crabbe began his movie career in 1933 after winning an Olympic gold medal in the 400-meter swimming event in the 1932 Summer Games in Los Angeles and a bronze medal at the 1928 Games in Amsterdam.

During the 1932 Games a talent scout from Paramount Pictures selected 40 athletes for screen tests. Crabbe was the only one to make it to the screen.

Crabbe starred in "Tarzan the Fearless" in 1933, his only full-length screen appearance as Tarzan. Other movies include "Nevada" 1936, "Queen of Broadway" 1943, "Caged Fury" 1948, "Gunfighters of Abilene" 1959, Arizona Raiders" 1965 and many more.

One of his final appearances on television was as an aging astronaut on the NBC series "Buck Rogers in the 25th Century." Gil Gerard played Buck Rogers in the series, which ran from 1979-81.

His real name was Clarence Linden Crabbe, but he was called Buster since a child and was also known as Larry. Crabbe was born Feb. 7, 1908 in Oakland, Calif.

He devoted his later career to helping Americans keep fit.

Mrs. Crabbe said she and her husband celebrated their 50th wedding anniversary last week. Survivors also include a son, Cullen; daughter, Susan Fletcher, and seven grandchildren.

KEN CURTIS
Actor who played Festus in 'Gunsmoke' dies

From wire reports
Died on April 29, 1991

FRESNO, Calif. — Ken Curtis, who as a boy helped out in his father's jail in Colorado and as a character named Festus Haggen performed similar work for Marshal Matt Dillon in the long-running television western "Gunsmoke," has died at age 74.

Film producer A.C. Lyles said yesterday that his friend was found dead by his wife when she awoke in their Fresno-area home Sunday morning.

The onetime big-band vocalist had been in apparent good health, Lyles said and attended a rodeo in nearby Clovis on Saturday. The cause of death has not been determined.

In addition to his television roles, Curtis acted with John Wayne in some of Hollywood's classic films, including "The Searchers" and "The Quiet Man."

Born Curtis Gates in Bent County, in the dry lands of Colorado where his father was sheriff, he worked on the family ranch and at the town jail and studied saxophone in high school.

He went to Los Angeles in 1938 and became a staff singer on NBC radio, where he was heard by composer Johnny Mercer and singer Jo Stafford.

They recommended him to Tommy Dorsey, who changed his name to Ken Curtis. He replaced Frank Sinatra in the Tommy Dorsey band after Sinatra left to become a solo artist. Curtis later went on to Shep Field's Orchestra.

Some of his featured songs included "Love Sends a Little Gift of Roses," "This is Worth Fighting For" and "Breathless."

After serving in the infantry in the U.S. Army during World War II, Curtis resumed a singing career on Johnny Mercer's radio show and recorded the popular "Tumbling Tumbleweeds."

Columbia Pictures heard the song and signed Curtis as a singing cowboy. He appeared in a series of low-budget Westerns with Guinn "Big Boy" Williams.

Curtis then joined the singing group Sons of the Pioneers. Director John Ford hired those vocalizing cowboys for the soundtrack of his 1950

"Wagonmaster" and Curtis afterward became a stock player with Ward Bond, Ben Johnson and Harry Carey, Jr. in the legendary Ford-John Wayne collaboration.

Curtis — whose first wife was Ford's daughter Barbara — soon began appearing in television Westerns, including "Have Gun Will Travel," "Rawhide" and "Gunsmoke."

His seedy, drawling, unwashed "Gunsmoke" character with the squinty eyes and drooping hat became so beloved that when Dennis Weaver left the role of Chester Goode in 1964, Curtis signed on as his replacement for the remaining 11 years of what proved the most enduring Western series in TV history.

With Milburn Stone, who portrayed Galen "Doc" Adams, Curtis formed a dancing and singing act in which Festus and Doc entertained at rodeos.

Curtis also starred briefly in the 1961-63 adventure series "Ripcord" and for a single season, 1983-84, in the Western soap opera "The Yellow Rose."

Other movies he appeared in included "The Alamo," "How the West Was Won," "Mr. Roberts" and "Cheyenne Autumn."

He retired about 10 years ago, Lyles said, but appeared in "Once Upon a Texas Train," a TV movie, in 1988.

Survivors include his second wife, Torrie, and her two children by a previous marriage.

Silent Film Cowboy Star 'BOB CUSTER'

TORRANCE, Calif., Dec. 30 (AP) — Raymond Glenn, 76, who played the silent screen cowboy Bob Custer, died Friday at his home. The cause of death was not known immediately.

Mr. Glenn made more than 100 feature films in the pre-talkie days.

An engineering graduate of the University of Kentucky, Mr. Glenn became superintendent of building and safety for the city of Newport Beach after leaving the entertainment business.

He is survived by his wife, Mildred, and a son, Raymond Jr. of Longview, Tex.

Taking the name Bob Custer, Mr. Glenn made eight Western films for Syndicated Pictures, Corp. in 1929 and 1930 and then made such films as "Law of the Mounted,' "The Last Roundup," "Riders of the Rio Grande" and "Code of the West."

ART DAVIS

ART DAVIS (1/16/87, age 74): Country/Western performer who played supporting roles with Jack Luden, Bill Elliott and Tim McCoy. Later he co-starred with Bill Boyd and Lee Powell in the Frontier Marshall series for PRC.

In 1939, Art supported Monte 'Alamo' Rawlins in THE ADVENTURES OF THE MASKED PHANTOM (Equity Pictures), in which he was billed as Larry Mason.

EDDIE DEAN, 91; First of Singing Cowboys to Star in Color Movies

by Elaine Woo
Times Staff Writer

Eddie Dean, one of the last singing cowboy stars of the 1940s, died Thursday of heart and lung disease in Thousand Oaks. He was 91.

Known as the golden-throated cowboy for an exceptionally melodious voice, Dean appeared in more than 30 Western movies starting in 1936. In the 1940s he was among the 10 most popular cowboy stars and was the first singing cowboy to do movies in color.

"That is really what sold my pictures—the color," he told author David Rothel in the 1978 book "The Singing Cowboys." "Because they had singing cowboys out there (in Hollywood) like crazy. You could go around every corner and run into a singing cowboy."

Judging from the critics' comments, it certainly was not Dean's acting that made his films memorable. They described his performances with terms such as "so-so," "self-conscious" and "indifferent."

Most critics agreed that Dean's singing was the best part of his movies. He possessed, in the words of one critic, "one of the better sets of pipes among cowboy Carusos." The late Gene Autry, with whom Dean appeared in several movies, once said he had the best voice of all the cowboy singers.

"He was a singer first and foremost," said James Nottage, curator at the Autry Museum of Western Heritage, which honored Dean, Gene Autry, Dale Evans, Monte Hale and other singing cowboys at a three-day festival in 1992.

Dean performed well into his 80s, often appearing at the Palomino Club in North Hollywood. In addition to singing Country and Western tunes, he was a skillful impressionist. His depiction of Elvis Presley, Nottage said, was masterful.

Dean also composed about 100

songs, including the Country and Western classic "One Has My Name, the Other Has My Heart" and "I Dreamed of a Hillbilly Heaven." Many of the songs were co-written with his wife of 68 years, Dearest, who survives him.

Born Eddie Dean Glosup in Posey, Texas, Dean started in show business as a vaudeville singer. In 1930 he landed his first radio show in Tulsa, Okla., and soon moved on to the "National Barn Dance" program. Later, he won a singing role on the popular "Judy Canova Show."

He segued into films around 1936 with bit parts in Westerns such as Tex Ritter's "Golden Trail."

His big break came in 1944 in "The Harmony Trail" with Ken Maynard. He made 18 more films in rapid succession over the next several years.

In his later years he acted in bit parts in films and on television. He had a standing part as the yo-deling cop in "The Beverly Hill-billies" television series.

He will receive a star on the Palm Springs Walk of Fame on March 20.

In addition to his wife, survi-vors include a daughter, Donna Knorr of Costa Mesa; a son, Edgar Dean Glosup of Shingle Springs, Calif.; a sister, Lorene Lacuata of Phoenix, eight grandchildren, nine great grandchildren and one great great grandchild.

He will be buried Monday at Valley Oaks Memorial Park in Westlake Village.

"WILD" BILL ELLIOTT of Westerns Dies

Cowboy Star, 62, Was Hero of More Than 60 Films

LAS VEGAS, Nev., Nov. 27, 1965 (AP) — Wild Bill Elliott, the Western movie and television ac-tor, who was once voted one of the 10 leading money-makers in West-erns, died yesterday of cancer. He was 62 years old.

Also Played Red Ryder

William Elliott, who had starred in more than 60 sagebrush sagas, was nicknamed "Wild Bill" after he was cast as Wild Bill Hickok in a 1939 movie serial. It was estimated that he disposed of more badmen than all the frontier marshals together. He also ap-peared as Red Ryder in a series that began in 1943.

Square-jawed, rangy, laconic Wild Bill was a natural recruit for his roles on the range. He could ride a horse, was fast on the draw and seemed equally adept at throwing lead or punches. He departed from what had become the standard type of the movie cowboy, however, by never carrying a guitar or bursting into song. He also frequently kissed his leading ladies with ardor.

"I guess," he once remarked, "I helped invent the adult Western. But, luckily, the kids never noticed."

A perfectionist, he practiced riding tricks, fancy shooting and roping.

Mr. Elliott was born on a ranch near Pattonsburg, Mo., learned riding and roping at the stockyards in Kansas City, where his father worked and later entered rodeos there.

He studied acting at the Pasadena (Calif.) Playhouse and early in his career appeared in non-Western dramatic films.

His picture credits included "In Old Sacramento," "The Plainsman and The Lady," "Wyoming," "The Fabulous Texan" and "Old Los Angeles."

He is survived by his widow, the former Dolly Moore, who was a model, and a daughter, Barbara, by his first marriage to Mrs. Helen Elliott, which ended in divorce.

TEX FLETCHER

TEX FLETCHER/Jerry Bisceglia (3/14/87, age 77): Early in his career, he was known as Slim Fletcher, later changing to the more Western sounding Tex. He spent many years in radio, beginning in 1931 on WNAX, in Yanktown, South Dakota. Moving to New York, he joined WOR Radio and for many years had a successful radio show on that station.

In 1939, Fletcher starred in his one and only Western feature, SIX GUN RHYTHM (Arcadia Pictures/Grand National). He served in WW2 and after discharge, he returned to radio and eventually moved into television, where he appeared on "The Bobby Benson Show," and on "Frontier Diary."

Fletcher made many recordings for Decca, Grand Award and Dakota Records. During his early days, he'd worked with the Rex Cole Mountaineers and with Judy Canova, long before she went on to become a popular screen comedienne.

Tex Fletcher was born in Harrison, New York.

DICK FORAN

Dick Foran, a veteran actor in western movies who appeared with Gene Autry, Roy Rogers and, more recently, John Wayne, died Friday at Panorama City Hospital in California at the age of 69.

First seen in the 1934 musical, *Stand Up and Cheer,* under the name Nick Foran, Mr. Foran's first name was changed to Dick when he later signed with Warner Brothers during the 1930's.

A man of rugged, athletic build, Mr. Foran had curly red hair and stood six feet, three inches tall. He was an excellent horseman and enjoyed singing.

Mr. Foran helped write the music for *My Little Buckaroo,* and earlier, sang on the George Burns and Gracie Allen radio show.

Introduced 'April' Songs

To movie audiences, he introduced songs that were to become classics off the screen, *I'll Remember April,* and *April in Paris.*

Mr. Foran's last feature film appearance was in the independently produced *Brighty of the Grand Canyon,* released in 1967. In recent years he had worked almost exclusively in television commercials.

He appeared in nearly 200 movies during his 45 year career and was best known for his roles in *The Petrified Forest, The Fighting 69th, My Little Chickadee, Fort Apache* and *Donovan's Reef.*

He was born John Nicholas Foran, in New Jersey, the son of a state senator. He attended Princeton University but left school never to return after a summer spent in California where he was signed as an actor with Fox Studios.

Friend of Fonda and Stewart

He shared an apartment with the actors, Henry Fonda and James Stewart, the latter sometimes playing the guitar for Mr. Foran at his singing auditions.

For his 1936 role in *The Petrified Forest,* which starred Bette Davis, Leslie Howard and Humphrey Bogart, Mr. Foran was nominated for an Academy Award.

He was married three times.

HOOT GIBSON, Film Cowboy, Dies; Made His First Movie in 1915

Special to The New York Times

HOLLYWOOD, Calif., Aug. 23 — Hoot Gibson, one of Hollywood's most famous cowboy stars, died early this morning of cancer at the Motion Picture Country House and Hospital, in Woodland Hills, Calif. He was 70 years old.

Mr. Gibson, whose real name was Edmund Richard Gibson, had been ill for a long time and had re-entered the home on Sunday. His last film appearance was in 1959 in a bit part in John Wayne's "The Horse Soldiers."

He is survived by his widow, the former Dorothy Dunstan, a singer he married in 1941; a daughter, Mrs. Lois Flanders; three sisters, Mrs. Jessie Gassaway, Mrs. Bettie Bedoian and Mrs. Jeanette Shaeffer, and a brother, Leon.

Gun-Toting Immortal

Hoot Gibson rode through the cinematic sagebrush for nearly fifty years — chasing villains, dispatching Indians and rescuing sloe-eyed ranch girls. He was one of that rapidly vanishing breed of screen cowboys who made the Western the only indigenous American motion-picture form.

Along with such gun-toting immortals as Tom Mix, Ken Maynard, William S. Hart and Col. Tim McCoy, Mr. Gibson thrilled several generations of Saturday matinee gum-chewers with his straight-shooting.

When Hoot Gibson rode across the gullies and arroyos of the Wild West, his thousands of fans were assured it was their hero behind the pommel for he was one of Hollywood's few genuine horsemen.

He was born in Tekamah, Neb., where his father had a ranch. It was here that he learned to ride, rope and wrangle, although he once jokingly said, "If you don't know how to ride a horse, you can be a cowboy actor and it doesn't make a difference."

Once asked if he would risk a spectacular fall from a horse for an extra $5, he told the director:

"Make it ten bucks and I'll let him kick me to death."

In 1920, Mr. Gibson was signed by Universal Pictures to star in a number of five-reel silent Westerns. His director was John Ford, who also had just been promoted. Mr. Ford also directed the cowboy star in "The Horse Soldiers."

Mr. Gibson's film career blossomed in 1925 and for about five years he was one of Hollywood's leading stars. His salary during these golden days was $14,500 a week and he was surrounded by fast cars, race horses and planes.

It was during this period that the intrepid film cowboy appeared in films with such typical Western titles as "Smilin' Gun," "The Long, Long Trail," "Trigger Tricks" and "Spurs."

In 1933, Mr. Gibson was seriously injured while piloting an airplane in a special match race against Ken Maynard at the National Air Races in Los Angeles. He suffered three fractured vertebrae and broken ribs and physicians feared his film career had ended.

Like the heroes of his Western epics, however, Mr. Gibson refused to let his injuries end his performing. Although he never again attained the film heights and always walked with a slight limp, he returned to ride horses after many months in the hospital.

Ran a Dude Ranch

He retired in 1944 after starring in about 200 silent movies and seventy-five talkies.

Although Mr. Gibson made a fortune during his movie career his recent years were spent in something less than the opulence he knew when he was one of Hollywood's top stars. A series of bad business investments left him almost penniless. But he never lost his courage.

"I don't cry," he said while in a hospital in 1960. "I guess we'll eat."

Mr. Gibson married three times. His first wife was Helen Johnson, a singer. They were divorced in 1927. In 1930 he married Sally Eilers, who appeared with him in several films before and during their marriage, which ended in divorce in 1933.

KIRBY GRANT, Star of 'Sky King' Killed in Accident

Lexington Herald-Leader, Lexington, KY
Thursday, October 31, 1985

COCOA, Fla. — Kirby Grant, who entertained millions as the star of the popular "Sky King" radio and television series, was killed in a traffic accident near Titusville yesterday as he drove to view the launch of the space shuttle at Kennedy space Center.

Grant, 73, was pronounced dead on arrival at Jess Parrish Memorial Hospital in Titusville less than an hour after the 8 a.m. accident on State Road 50 about four miles west of Titusville, Florida Highway Patrol Capt. Mike Kirby said.

Grant, of Winter Springs, a city 15 miles north of Orlando, Fla., was driving in traffic on the two-lane road when he attempted to pass another automobile. The car pulled into his path and Grant swerved across the road and into a ditch to avoid it, Kirby said.

The impact flung Grant from the car into about 3 feet of standing water. A passing motorist, Roy Walters of Orlando, pulled the former television hero out "almost immediately" but he could not be revived, Kirby said.

Kirby said that state troopers have no information on the other vehicle involved in the accident and that an investigation is continuing. Grant was alone in his car.

An autopsy will be performed to determine the cause of death, he said.

Arnold Richmond, the chief of visitor services at the space center, said Grant had been invited by a friend to watch the shuttle launch from the VIP stands.

Grant starred in "Sky King"

from 1951 to 1954, and the show appeared in reruns from 1959 to 1966. He played the lead role of Sky King, a good man who wore a cowboy hat, always did right, and traveled about in a twin-engine airplane called Songbird. The show originated on radio, where it was heard from 1946 to 1954, with a different set of actors supplying the voices.

Born Kirby Grant Hoon Jr. in Butte, Mont., on Nov. 24, 1911, Grant first made his acting reputation in film in the late 1930s.

Before playing Sky King, he played leads in low-budget Westerns and other action pictures, often as a Canadian Mountie in such movies as "Trail of the Yukon," "Call of the Klondike," "Northwest Territory," "Yukon Gold" and "Northern Patrol."

Grant was educated at the University of Washington in Seattle, Whitman College in Walla Walla, Wash., and the American Conservatory of Music. He was considered a child prodigy as a violinist. Also an accomplished singer, Grant was a radio and supper club entertainer before entering films.

Grant and his wife, Carolyn, moved to Florida in 1971. He said right away "I fell in love with the place."

In 1976 he started the Sky King Youth Ranch for troubled teenage boys. But the state forced the Central Florida ranch to close in July 1977 after it ran into financial problems.

Grant is survived by his wife, daughters Kendra and Kristin, and son Kirby III.

WILLIAM S. HART, 75, Film Veteran, Dies

'Wild West' Idol During Era of Silent Screen Was Figure on Stage for Many Years

AN EASTERN-BORN COWBOY

Considered Good Horseman— Contributed Old Pictures to Museum, Estate to Public

LOS ANGELES, June 24, 1946 (AP) — William S. Hart, Eastern-born "wild west" movie actor of a quarter of a century ago, died here late last night in a hospital. His age was 75.

At the bedside was his son, William S. Hart Jr., who last Thursday was appointed co-guardian, with George Frost, of the actor's person. Young Hart's mother, Winifred Westover, from whom the actor was divorced twenty years ago, had been almost constantly at Mr. Hart's side.

Major Idol of Silent Screen

William S. Hart was known to a generation of motion-picture fans as the long-faced, iron-jawed he-man of the West, but he was also remembered by patrons of the "legitimate" theatre in the parts he took in "Ben-Hur," "The Virginian" and many other plays, including several Shakespearean dramas.

As the strong and silent cowboy hero he became one of the major idols of the screen and he amassed a fortune during the golden years, earning $1,000 a day for grinning into an unloaded .45 and galloping across the wide plains near Hollywood.

He was the hero of thousands of eager boys the world over, and he was the ideal of thousands of women. It was said that at one time in his motion-picture career he received as many as 200 love letters a day.

Mr. Hart did not marry until he was nearly 50, but his matrimonial venture was not successful. He and his wife were separated five months after marriage and after long-drawn divorce proceedings the marriage was dissolved. His wife, who gave birth to a son, William S. Hart Jr., was Winifred Westover, a motion-picture actress of San Francisco.

Later in life Mr. Hart tried his hand at writing. He turned out a couple of books for boys and an autobiography, "My Life East and West," but the main successes in his career were in Hollywood as the two-gun terror of bad men and savior of maidens in distress.

He was born at Newburgh, N.Y. on Dec. 6, 1870, but his parents moved West when he was still an infant. His father was a builder of flour mills, and the family lived in Minnesota and Dakota until the lad was 15 years old. They moved to New York, where William began his career as a clerk in the post office at Park Row.

Made Stage Debut in 1889

Sorting mail, however, was irksome work, and he spent much time going to theatres and became infatuated with the stage. He applied for a part in a play for some time in vain, but finally made his debut at the People's Theatre, New York, on Jan. 21, 1889, in "Austerlitz," with Daniel Bandmann. Subsequently, he played many parts with Lawrence Barrett.

After that he joined R. D. McLean and Marie Prescott and appeared at the Union Square Theatre in November, 1891, as Phesarius in "The Gladiator," and also in "Antony and Cleopatra," "The Merchant of Venice," "Othello" and other classical plays.

He then toured with Ada Rehan, playing Shakespeare in "When Bess Was Queen." For some time he was associated with Mme. Modjeska, taking such parts as Armand Duval in Dumas' "Camille," Julian Grey in "The New Magdalen," Benedick in "Much Ado About Nothing," Macbeth and Mark Antony in "Antony and Cleopatra."

Mr. Hart appeared at the Garrick Theatre in New York with Mme. Modjeska as Angelo in "Measure for Measure," Armand Duval, and the Duke of Malmsbury in "Mistress Betty." In 1897 he toured in "Under the Polar Star," and the next year, at the

People's Theatre in New York, he played the dual parts in "The Man With the Iron Mask."

In 1899 he played Romeo to Julia Arthur's Juliet, and in November of that year he created the role of Messala in "Ben-Hur," a part he played for two years. In 1903, at the Broadway Theatre, he took the part of Patrick Henry in "Hearts Courageous."

He had been unwilling to leave the legitimate stage until 1914, when he turned his attention to the cinema. From early parts, for which he earned $75 a week, he quickly became a favorite of the screen, and he was presently as much discussed as Charlie Chaplin, Mary Pickford and other stars of the day. His first picture was "The Bargain," and this was followed by "The Disciple."

Was an Excellent Horseman

Mr. Hart was an excellent horseman. With his long, imperturbable but almost sinister face, he made a first-class Western hero of the plains. Always calm and showing the utmost sang-froid, he was exceptionally suited to the pantomine of the silent pictures.

Some of the films which he created were "The Toll Gate," "Square Deal Sanderson," "Wagon Tracks," "Sand," "White Oak," "Tumbleweeds" and "Singer Jim McKee." His pinto pony Paint became almost as famous as he himself.

Many of the pictures were made by Mr. Hart. He had his own studio in Hollywood and was generally surrounded by motion-picture cowboys and cowgirls.

"Tumbleweeds" Last Film

Mr. Hart's last motion picture, "Tumbleweeds," was produced in 1926. He was not satisfied with the exploitation given to that silent film by the United Artists Corporation. He and his sister, Miss Mary E. Hart, acting as the William S. Hart Company, began litigation against United Artists.

RUSSELL HAYDEN

Russell Hayden, 71, veteran character actor, died June 10, 1981 of viral pneumonia at Desert Hospital in Palm Springs, Calif.

Best known for his performances as "Lucky" in 45 Hopalong Cassidy pictures with William Boyd, Hayden, whose real name was Pate Lucid, began in the sound recording and cutting departments of Paramount before becoming an actor in 1937. His first picture was "The Hills of Old Wyoming," after which he appeared in some 60 other films, aside from the Hopalong Cassidy series. Under contract to Columbia and Universal subsequent to his stint at Paramount, he was named one of the top 10 moneymaking western stars by the Motion Picture Herald poll in 1943-44.

After World War II service as a naval aerial combat photographer, he founded M.H. Productions and owned the 32,000 acre Pioneer Town ranch, where numerous western and TV series, including "Judge Roy Bean," his own "Cowboy G-Men" show with Jackie Coogan and "26 Men" were shot.

He is survived by his wife, former actress Lillian (Mousy) Porter.

JACK HOLT, 62, Dies; Veteran Film Star

Western Hero in Movies for Many Years Succumbs on Coast of Heart Ailment

LOS ANGELES, Jan. 18, 1951 (AP) — Jack Holt, veteran motion-picture actor, died tonight in the veterans' hospital in West Los Angeles. His age was 62. He was stricken with a heart attack before the holidays and again several days ago.

His son, Tim, also a Western star, was almost constantly at his side.

Mr. Holt was under a physician's care at his hotel apartment in Santa Monica before he was taken to the veteran's hospital. Only last night he was reported improving.

Both Hero and Villain

For many years both hero and villain on the screen, Mr. Holt was born a minister's son with an incurable wanderlust. Born on May 31, 1888 in Winchester, Va., he was a great-great-grandson of Chief Justice John Marshall. His father was the Rev. Charles John Holt, a Protestant Episcopal minister.

From the first, Mr. Holt, who later became one of the great motion-picture cowboy figures, loved horses and horseback riding, and much of his early youth was spent in the saddle in the Virginia town. It was said that he learned to walk and ride at the same time.

Before he reached school age the family, including six children, moved to the Bronx. Young Jack attended Trinity School for several years before his father's failing health forced the family to return to Virginia, where a career in law was planned for the young horseman.

But now Jack wanted to be a soldier, and at the age of 16 he entered the Virginia Military Institute. The next year, he was suspended from the school for a year for painting the statue of George Washington green and orange, his class colors. Later, he returned to complete a course in civil engineering.

After graduation, he took a job in New York directing a gang of laborers in the airlocks of the Pennsylvania Railroad tunnel. He

68

tired of this work, and flipped a coin to decide whether to seek his fortune in the Panama Canal Zone or in Alaska. Alaska won and he took a job with the Donahue Exploration Company as an engineer on their copper claims in the northern regions.

For six years, Mr. Holt remained in Alaska as a surveyor, laborer, miner and teamster. For a time he drove a mail sled over a 300-mile route. Then he tired of Alaska and he set out for Oregon, where he lived in a friend's tent in the middle of a fruit orchard.

Returned to First Love

Here he came back to horseback riding and he learned the cowboy tricks of horsemanship which played such an important part in his later career. He wandered to San Francisco, where he heard that movie companies were searching for stunt men who had a way with a horse.

And so Mr. Holt went to San Rafael, Calif., where expert riders were needed for the shooting of "Salomy Jane." For $10 he jumped a horse from a thirty-five-foot cliff into a pool of water, and broke two ribs in the bargain.

After three months of work as an extra the young horseman began to play character roles for some of the early movie companies: Bishop, Reliance, Liberty and Universal. His early appearances were in "The Shrine of Our Lady of Sorrows," "The Specialist's Fee" and "The Honey-

Bee's Prisoner," the last written and directed by Jack Hawks.

At Universal Mr. Holt received his first big part, that of the Captain of the Guard in "The Dumb Girl of Portici," which starred Pavlova, along with Douglas Gerard and Rupert Julian.

The actor began to play the role of the villain, but leading men objected to his ability at winning sympathy of audiences and soon Mr. Holt became a hero. He was signed by Paramount and played in 'The Little American," with Mary Pickford; "The Road Through the Dark," "Conrad's Victory" and "The Life Line."

Opposite Clara Kimball Young

Mr. Holt's role in "The Woman Thou Gavest Me," in which he was featured with Clara Kimball Young, brought him to the public eye in earnest. He followed with "Crooked Streets," "Held by the Enemy" and "After the North," a western film which portended his career as a cowboy hero.

Subsequently Mr. Holt alternated between a western hero and a drawing room Romeo. He played in "Bought and Paid For," "Gentleman of Leisure," "Making a Man," "Nobody's Money" and "The Tiger's Claw." But the West won out and Mr. Holt became the prototype of the man on horseback.

Mr. Holt was an impeccable Englishman in "The Tigress," a spy in "The Warning," a Yankee captain of the Civil War in "Court Martial" and a daredevil diver in

"Submarine."

He continued his movie career in a great variety of character roles through most of 1950. Mr. Holt in collaboration with Carolyn Coggins wrote in 1949 a children's book, "Lance and His First Horse."

TIM HOLT, Western Film Star Who Made 149 Pictures, Dead

SHAWNEE, Okla., Feb. 15 (AP) — Tim Holt, a popular star in Western movies before and after World War II, died today at the Shawnee Medical Center Clinic. He was 54 years old.

Mr. Holt was a rancher and sales manager for radio station KEBC-FM in Oklahoma City.

He is survived by his widow, Birdie, and three children.

A Son's Role at 10

Tim Holt, during a film career that started when he was 16 years old, appeared in 149 motion pictures, most of them Westerns. The son of another noted actor, Jack Holt, a star of silent pictures, the younger Holt was born in Beverly Hills, Calif., on Feb. 5, 1919. He attended Culver Military Academy and began his screen career in 1935. His first screen appearance, however, was in 1929, when he was 10 years old, playing Jack Holt's son.

Toward the end of World War II, Mr. Holt, then a lieutenant in the Army Air Corps, flew as bombardier on a B-29 named The Reluctant Dragon in raids over Tokyo.

In 1952, at the height of his career, he was one of the top 10 Western actors selected by a poll of movie-theater owners on the basis of film popularity. He placed fifth behind Roy Rogers, Gene Autry, Rex Allen and Bill Elliott.

In the Orson Welles 1942 version of Booth Tarkington's "The Magnificent Ambersons," Mr. Holt played George Amberson Minafer. A New York Times reviewer wrote "Tim Holt draws out all of the meanness in George's character, which is precisely what the part demands."

GEORGE F. HOUSTON
Opera Singer, 47

Head of Pasadena, Calif., Unit Dies on Eve of Guild Tour—Began Here in 1927

The New York Times,
Tuesday, November 14, 1944

HOLLYWOOD, Calif., Nov. 13 (UP) — George Fleming Houston, opera singer and Hollywood actor, died last night of a heart ailment on the eve of a nationwide operatic tour sponsored by the Theatre Guild of New York. His age was 47.

Mr. Houston, husband of Virginia Card, light opera singer, who is now appearing in the hit musical "Oklahoma" in Chicago, was head of the American Music Theatre of Pasadena, Calif., a group presenting opera in English.

Friends said Mr. Houston was preparing to take the opera company on a tour of the nation when he was stricken. He succumbed on his way to a hospital after collapsing on a Hollywood street.

Mr. Houston served in the French Army from 1915 to 1918 and then entered Rutgers University, where he was a football star. Subsequently he started a career in opera.

Mr. Houston, son of a New Jersey clergyman, first became known to the opera going public in 1927 as a member of the Rochester American Opera Company, a development of the Eastman School of Music in Rochester, N.Y.

On his first New York appearance with this organization, at the Guild Theatre, April 4, 1927, as Ohmin in Mozart's "The Abduction From the Seraglio," Olin Downes wrote in The New York Times:

"The leading member of the cast in the point of artistic achievement was Mr. Houston, who has a bass or bass-baritone of sonorous, manly quality, who uses his voice effectively and enters into a comedy part with gusto and without undue exaggeration."

When Mr. Houston sang Mephistopheles in New York nearly a year later the same critic noted that he had grown as a singer and actor and gave promise of still further advances. His Escamillo in "Carmen" did not meet with the same approval.

Early in his career Mr. Houston was with Earl Carroll productions for five years, and in "The New Moon." In 1938 he was the Mephisto of Max Reinhardt's production of "Faust" in the Pilgrimage Theatre, Hollywood.

JACK HOXIE

Jack Hoxie was promoted to "glory." The funeral service was held at the First Methodist Church in Keyes, Oklahoma, where Jack had been a member since his baptism there on September 1, 1962. His pastor, Leroy Sebastian, conducted the service. Jack was laid to rest in the Willowbar Cemetery in Keyes, where his headstone is engraved with a cowboy hat raised overhand, rearing on a mounted horse. Beneath the figure is the inscription: *HOXIE, A Star in Life— A Star in Heaven, Jack HOXIE, January 11, 1885—March 27, 1965.*

Buck Jones

BUCK JONES
Is Dead
of Injuries in Fire

Cowboy Movie Star Succumbs Along With Most of Those At Party in His Honor

Wife Too Late To See Him
Actor 53, Was in the Films for Twenty Years—
He Served in France in the World War

BOSTON, Nov. 30 (U.P.)— Charles (Buck) Jones, cowboy motion picture star, died at a hospital late today of burns suffered in the Coconut Grove fire. Mr. Jones was the guest of honor at a party when the fire broke out. Attending physicians said they "had abandoned all hope for Jones' recovery immediately after examining his burns."

Mr. Jones, a 53-year-old native of Vincennes, Ind., and a long-time favorite of American boy movie fans, was the 481st person to die in the disaster.

A check-up showed that of about two dozen guests at the Jones testimonial dinner, thirteen were known dead, seven, mostly women, were recorded as missing and presumably dead, and the others were in hospitals with burns or injuries which may prove fatal.

Wife on Her Way to Him

The doctors reported that Mr. Jones died "from smoke inhalation and burned lungs, and from third and second degree burns on the face and neck."

Idol of millions of movie fans, Mr. Jones died alone, although his wife was reported speeding to his bedside when death came.

In another ward of the crowded Massachusetts General Hospital Mr. Jones' Boston representative, Martin Sheridan, lay in critical condition. Mr. Sheridan's wife, who also attended the Jones party, was dead.

Scott R. Dunlap, one of Hollywood's leading producers of Westerns and Mr. Jones' personal manager, was near death late today.

Other guests at the Jones party who perished included Edward A. Ansin, president of the Interstate Theatres Corporation, which operates a New England movie chain; Philip Seletsky, chief film booker for the M. & P. Theatres of Boston; Charles Sterns, manager of United Artists Corporation; Fred P. Sharby Sr. and his son, Fred, Jr., showmen of Keene, N.H.; Eugene Goss of Cambridge, a one-time associate of Cecil B. De Mille; Harry Asher of Boston, president of Producers Releasing Corporation; Moses Grassgreen of Universal Pictures and Bernard Levin of Columbia Pictures.

Life Like That of Film Hero

The career of Charles (Buck) Jones, veteran screen cowboy and early contemporary of such famous stars as Bronco Billy Anderson, William S. Hart and Tom Mix, was not unlike that of one of the dashing heroes of the Western films in which he starred for more than twenty years.

Born Charles Frederick Gebhard in Vincennes, Ind., on Dec. 4, 1889, he was educated in the public schools of Indianapolis, but very soon started a life of roving which took him to Montana, where he worked as a cowhand.

Then he joined the United States Cavalry for service in the Philippines and after this was engaged as an expert rider with the Miller Brothers 101 Ranch Wild West Show.

During the World War he served in France with the First Air Squadron of the United States Army. After the war he remained in Europe as a trick rider with various traveling shows. One of his exhibitions brought him to the attention of William Fox, who signed him to Hollywood. There he played in more than 100 silent and talking films over a period of twenty years being one of the few actors to continue in popularity so long.

Disliked Singing Cowboys

In the wide span of his career, Mr. Jones worked for several studios, including Fox, Universal, Columbia and most recently, Monogram. Some of his recent films were "Ghost Town Law," "Below the Border," "Forbidden Trails" and "Gunman From Bodie."

In an interview about a year ago he bewailed the general invasion of Western films by crooners and singing cowboys.

"They use 'em to save money on horses and riders and ammunition," he said.

His constant boast was that he had remained "an old-time cowboy, the sort the kids used to want to grow up to be like."

Mr. Jones' name was changed

legally in 1937. He was married to the former Odele Osborne. They had one daughter, Maxine, who is the wife of Noah Beery, Jr.

He was in Boston to end a personal appearance tour of ten principal cities on behalf of the war bond drive and Navy recruiting.

Scott R. Dunlap, producer of the Monogram series of "Rough Rider" films in which Buck Jones was starred, entered the motion-picture business in 1915 and worked in virtually every capacity connected with the production of films.

He formerly was vice president in charge of production at Monogram Studio.

He was born in Chicago on June 20, 1892, and was educated in the public schools of that city.

In addition to the recent Buck Jones films he also produced the "Mr. Wong" series and many other low-budget films.

TOM KEENE, Actor, of Films and Stage

GLENDALE, Calif., Aug. 6, 1963 (UPI) — Tom Keene, a former cowboy actor in films, died Sunday night of cancer. He was 65 years old.

Mr. Keene appeared in numerous Westerns in the nineteen-thirties and was on Broadway in "Abie's Irish Rose."

Survivors include his widow, Florence, and a stepson, Robert Ramsey.

Mr. Keene was one—although not the first—of those who played "Abie" in the play's long run in New York and on the road in the twenties. He used his own name, George Duryea at the time.

He also had a leading role in the long run of "White Cargo" in New York and on tour.

Born in New York State, Mr. Keene came West as a young man and did ranch work before returning East to the stage. After several plays here he was signed for films by the late Cecil B. De Mille, and changed his name.

His Westerns included "Ghost Valley," "Partners," "Saddle Buster," "Sundown Trail" and "Beyond the Rockies."

He was also in "Honky Tonk," "Tol'able David," "Tide of Empire" and "Thunder."

JOHN "DUSTY" KING

The last of the Range Busters is gone. John "Dusty" King, who starred in 20 of the 24 Buster films, passed away on November 11, at the age of 78. King, Ray "Crash" Corrigan, and Max Terhune were the original Range Busters, and they were the primary performers throughout the series. David Sharpe and Dennis Moore also participated in the series. King was preceded in death by Terhune who died on June 5, 1973, and by

Corrigan who passed away on August 10, 1976. King was born Miller McLeod Everson on July 11, 1909, in Cincinnati, Ohio. He worked as a radio broadcaster and a big band vocalist prior to entering films.

ALLAN (ROCKY) LANE

Allan (Rocky) Lane, 64, one of the top western stars of the 1950s, died from a bone marrow disorder at Motion Picture Country Hospital, Woodland Hills, Calif., Oct. 27, 1973. Under contract at Republic, he was a straight oater performer while Gene Autry and Roy Rogers shared their thesping with song, and in 1951 and 1953 was one of the 10 top moneymaking western stars in a national poll.

Following attendance at Notre Dame he played professional football, was a photographic illustrator and on the stage before turning to the screen. He also was the voice for "Mr. Ed" in the TV series.

Mother survives.

Cowboy Star LASH LaRUE Dies; Famed for Bullwhip "B" Movies

Norfolk, VA Pilot, May 31, 1996
Associated Press

LOS ANGELES — Lash LaRue, a bullwhip-cracking star of low-budget 1940s Westerns whose movie career quickly faded with the onset of the TV age, died last week. He was believed to be 78.

Moviegoers in the years after World War II knew LaRue for his handiwork with a whip and his trademark black outfits, but he never achieved the enduring fame of such cinema cowboys as Gene Autry and Roy Rogers.

He died May 21 at Providence St. Joseph Medical Center in Burbank, hospital spokeswoman Michelle Meier said Thursday. She said she could not release any information on the cause of death.

LaRue's films included "Song of Old Wyoming" and "The Caravan Trail," 1945; "Law of the Lash," "Heartaches," "Border Feud," 1947; "Mark of the Lash,' "The Enchanted Valley," "The

Fighting Vigilantes," 1948; and "Son of Billy the Kid" and "Dead Men's Gold," 1949.

LaRue's date of birth in Gretna, La., was listed as June 15, 1917, but Phil Smoot, a North Carolina film producer, said the actor told him he was actually several years older.

"Lash was a real cowboy in his heart," Smoot said. "He really was Lash LaRue."

"How could any kid who grew up wanting to be a cowboy not enjoy being Lash LaRue? It was a dream come true," LaRue himself said in an interview nearly 20 years ago.

With his Hollywood career over, LaRue, whose real first name was Al, performed in touring shows, later trying his hand at evangelizing.

He claimed to have been married and divorced 10 times and had a series of personal and legal troubles.

In 1957 he was tried and acquitted in Memphis, Tenn., where he was charged with buying and concealing stolen property — sewing machines taken from a car parked at the Memphis fairgrounds where his Wild West show was appearing. LaRue burst into tears at the jury's verdict.

He reportedly took a dozen sleeping pills in 1958 in a suicide attempt in Long Beach, when he was sued for divorce on grounds of extreme cruelty. His apartment manager called an ambulance and he was saved.

The next year, his wife and sister-in-law clobbered him during a domestic brawl at a friend's home in Garden Grove. After receiving five stitches in his scalp, LaRue was booked for investigation of assault, battery and disturbing the peace.

In the 1970s, when he became a traveling evangelist, he was convicted of possessing marijuana. A judge put him on probation.

LaRue was one of a number of colorful stars who were a staple of Westerns from the early years of the 20th century to the 1940s: Other big names included Hoot Gibson, Buck Jones, Tom Mix, Sunset Carson and Yakima Canutt.

In the 1950s, TV Westerns ended the era of "B" Westerns in theaters.

Some, like Rogers, made the transition to TV. But LaRue's series, "Lash of the West," was short-lived. It aired in 1952-53, containing recycled footage of his old movies.

ROBERT LIVINGSTON, 83 An Actor in 100 Films

Robert Livingston, an actor who played the Lone Ranger and was in many Hollywood Westerns, died Monday of emphysema at his home in Tarzana, Calif. He was 83 years old.

Mr. Livingston appeared in more than 100 films between 1926

and 1975, including many silent-era slapstick comedies such as a series called "The Collegians" and a 29-film series of Westerns for Republic Pictures called "The Three Mesquiteers." He played Zorro in "The Bold Caballero" (1936). His best-known role was in "The Lone Ranger Rides Again" (1939), when he became the only Lone Ranger ever to remove his mask. However, according to Samuel Sherman, his publicist, Mr. Livingston felt that his career was handicapped by being typecast as a cowboy actor.

His other films included "Mutiny on the Bounty" (1935), "Pistol Packin' Mama" (1943) and "Once Upon a Horse" (1958). He also appeared in plays and television shows. His last role was in "Blazing Stewardesses" (1975), a Western spoof.

Mr. Livingston is survived by a son, Addison Randall of Tarzana.

JOCK MAHONEY; Stuntman Made a Career of Action

From Associated Press, Saturday, December 16, 1989

BREMERTON, Wash. — Jock Mahoney, one of Hollywood's most famous stuntmen-turned-actor and the stepfather of Sally Field, has died of an apparent stroke. He was 70.

Mahoney, a resident of Poulsbo, Wash., died Thursday at Harrison Memorial Hospital where he had been taken after an automobile accident two days earlier.

Kitsap County's chief deputy coroner, Jane Jermy, said an autopsy will be done to verify the cause of death.

Born Jacques Mahoney in Chicago, he was a tall, rugged youth whose film career began in 1945 after he served as a fighter pilot in World War II.

He did stunt work for Errol Flynn, Gregory Peck, Gene Autry and others. Autry signed him to a contract and cast him in "The Ranger Rider," an action-packed television series in the 1950s.

Mahoney socked and tumbled his way through appearances on "The Loretta Young Show," "Rawhide," "Laramie" and other programs until his career began to fade in the 1960s.

He appeared in several "Tarzan" movies during that decade, one of which led to a major bout with illness. While filming in India, Mahoney came down with dengue fever, dysentery and pneumonia.

"I refused to take my own advice: Know your limitations and fight the urge to do the stunt just one more time," he later said.

After more than two years of recovery, Mahoney's star began to rise again in the late 1960s when he appeared on numerous television shows.

On the set of "Kung Fu" in 1973 he suffered a severe stroke

and he made only occasional appearances thereafter. He was seen in several 1981 episodes of "B.J. and the Bear."

He is survived by his wife Autumn (Patricia) Mahoney. A complete list of survivors and funeral arrangements were not available.

KEN MAYNARD
of Westerns Dies

HOLLYWOOD, March 24 (UPI) — Ken Maynard, the white-hatted cowboy hero of some 300 Western movies, died yesterday at the age of 77.

Bashful and Wholesome

Sporting a broad-brimmed white hat and spangled boots, Ken Maynard played the bashful cowboy hero in scores of Hollywood Westerns in the nineteen-twenties and thirties. He never smoked or drank on screen, he strummed his guitar and sang soft ballads, he handled his horse, Tarzan, expertly, he tangled with bandits and Indians and, doing all these things, he flourished as one of the era's most popular movie stars.

Like Tom Mix, another leading Western screen idol, Mr. Maynard did all his own riding tricks on screen. They were tricks he had learned growing up in Texas and performing with circuses and Wild West shows, including those of the Ringling Brothers and Buffalo Bill Cody.

Square-jawed and dark-haired with a rangy build, Mr. Maynard achieved success with such movies as "The Red Raiders," "Songs of the Saddle," "Parade of the West," "Branded Men," "$50,000 Reward," "King of the Arena," "Fiddlin' Buckaroo" and "Strawberry Roan."

By his own estimate not long ago, there were roughly 300 films in all — mostly for First National Pictures and Universal Studios. At his peak, he was making up to $1,000 a week, helping to finance his own pictures, flying and sailing for recreation and living in a mansion in Los Angeles.

Later, the cowboy star went back to rodeo-circus shows that toured the country, giving demonstrations of the expert riding that had first landed him a job in motion pictures.

Ken Maynard was born July 21, 1895, in Mission, Tex., the son of William H. Maynard, a building contractor whose work kept him on the move. When the youngster was 8 years old, his family was living near the Matador Ranch in Texas, and there Ken learned his first riding tricks.

His real education in trick riding and roping came with his first attempts to join the circus. When he was 12, he ran away with a cheap wagon show and remained for three weeks before his father came and took him home.

Several more times, Ken ran away. Finally, his father enrolled him in the Virginia Military Institute, where he learned feats of horsemanship. He eventually graduated as an engineer. In 1914, he joined the Kit Carson show and then went to the Haggenback and Wallace Show, working there until enlisting in the Army in 1918.

After World War I, Mr. Maynard roped and rode as the star performer in Ringling shows and with Buffalo Bill. He recalled being with the Cody show when it was foreclosed in Denver.

In 1923, he drifted to Hollywood and was introduced to the movies by his friends Buck Jones and Tom Mix. His first role was as a horseman of another era, Paul Revere, in "Janice Meredith," a movie starring Marion Davies.

A review of one of his early movies in The New York Times praised him as a "good-looking" hero who "rides so well that he makes extraordinary feats of horsemanship look comparatively simple."

"I never drank nor smoked in a picture," Mr. Maynard said in retrospect. "I never made an issue of it either. In a saloon scene I just ignored it. I never objected. I did it because of all the kids who came to my pictures. I didn't think it was right for them to see drinking and smoking on the screen."

In his later years, Mr. Maynard toured with rodeos and also appeared at parades and was an oc-casional guest on television talk shows. He had a small role in "Bigfoot" in 1969, playing a retired movie star turned general store owner.

For the last few years, Mr. Maynard lived alone in a trailer at a trailer court in the San Fernando Valley.

KERMIT MAYNARD

Kermit Maynard, 73, brother of cowboy star Ken Maynard and a Western star in his own right, died Jan. 16, 1970, in his North Hollywood home of a heart attack.

Maynard, world's rodeo champion in trick and fancy riding in 1933 and an All Western Conference halfback at Indiana Univ. in the 20's, later frequently doubled for stars, including his brother, Victor McLaglen and George O'Brien.

Among his acting credits were "Song of the Trail," "Phantom Patrol," and "The Fighting Texan" in 1936. He served on the Board of Directors of both the Screen Actors Guild and the Screen Extras Guild.

Surviving are his wife, Edith, son William and brother.

COL. TIM McCOY, 86; Cowboy Movie Star

Real Life Indian Expert, Cowhand And Soldier Appeared in More Than 80 Films in 45 Years

by A.H. Weiler

Col. Tim McCoy, one of the dwindling company of colorful cowboy movie stars that included William S. Hart, Tom Mix, Hoot Gibson, Buck Jones, Ken Maynard and William Boyd, died Sunday at the age of 86 in Raymond W. Bliss Army Hospital in Nogales, Ariz., where he had been living for the last 20 years.

Colonel McCoy, on a visit to Los Angeles last month to promote "Tim McCoy Remembers the West," the book published by Doubleday that he wrote with his son Ronald, still looked, according to a reporter, "as if he could outdraw any varmint who dared challenge his gun."

His looks were part of a distinctly colorful personality that combined an arrow collar profile, sparkling blue eyes and a trim, 6-foot figure topped by a white 10-gallon hat.

But, unlike many of his contemporaries in silent and talking westerns, he was an authentic colonel and an authentic Westerner, who had ridden the range as a cowhand and cavalryman and as an expert on Indians, whom he had known from his youth in Wyoming.

Off to Adventure in Wyoming

For Timothy John Fitzgerald McCoy, the transition from Saginaw, Mich., where he was born April 10, 1891, to cowhand, soldier, movie star, circus and Wild West show luminary and television talk-show host, was equally unusual.

The lure of traveling Wild West shows had its effect on the St. Ignatius College student, who left that Chicago campus at 18 to seek adventure and fortune in Wyoming, where he not only worked the range, but also was exposed to rustlers, bank robbers and bounty hunters. He learned the ceremonies of the Indians and sign language, was adopted into their tribes, and became a protégé of Gen. Hugh L. Scott, the Indian authority.

After service in the cavalry in World War I—he also saw service in World War II teaching sign language to intelligence troops—he returned to Wyoming to become state adjutant general.

While in that office in Cheyenne in 1922, he was approached by a Famous Players-Lasky representative to help in hiring 500 Indians to appear in "The Covered Wagon," an $800,000 epic directed by James Cruze; it was to become a landmark Western.

80 Features in 45 Years

Tim McCoy, the Indian's supervisor and translator, became Tim McCoy, the actor, in "The Thundering Herd," a major Western that was released in 1924. It was followed over the next 45 years by more than 80 features, many of them Westerns with such obvious titles as "War Paint," "Below the Border," "Ghost Town Law" and "West of the Law." His performances were straightforwardly handled in the accepted image of a good Western movie hero.

He said this about horses, "I ride for work, but not for pleasure," he said. "I've never been sentimental about my horse. The horse doesn't give a damn about you. If you want to know the truth—horses are dumb."

With Caravan 13 Years

While in recent years he played bits in a variety of films such as "Around the World in Eighty Days" (1956), "Run of the Arrow" (1957), and "Requiem for a Gunfighter" (1965), he worked largely with Tommy Scott and His Country Caravan. "I stayed with it," he said last year, "for 13 years, traveling all over the country in one-night stands. I continued until four years ago when my wife died. That took the life out of me."

Colonel McCoy's first marriage to Agnes Miller, daughter of Henry Miller, the actor, ended in divorce in 1931. They had two sons, D'Arcy and Gerry. In 1946,

he married the Danish journalist Inga Arvad while she was working in Washington. Their two sons, Ronald and Terrence, who frequently toured with their father in his Wild West Show, survive.

A funeral service is to be held today in Nogales.

TOM MIX
Killed in
Highway Mishap
Movie, Circus Star

Sunday Morning, October 13, 1940

FLORENCE, Ariz., Oct. 12 (AP) — Tom Mix, hard-riding star of the silent films and noted circus performer, was killed as his automobile went out of control and overturned 18 miles south of here today.

Mix, traveling alone, was en route to Tucson, Ariz.

The accident occurred on a detour skirting a road construction job. Mix was pinned under his automobile. He was dead when two highway employees, John Adams of Oracle, Ariz., and E. A. Arrmenta of Casa Grande, Ariz., discovered the overturned vehicle. The body was brought here.

As the colorful star of scores of silent Western thrillers, Mix was the idol of millions of young Americans. In recent years, he has been the featured performer in circus-riding exhibitions.

Coroner E. O. Devine said Mix apparently was killed instantly. There will be no inquest.

Local investigators said Mix, who left Tucson at 1 p.m. was serving as advance agent for a circus scheduled to show in Phoenix shortly. The cowboy star was carrying $6,000 in cash, $1,500 in travelers' checks and several valuable jewels.

Mix was a native of El Paso County, Texas. He worked as a cowboy in Texas, Arizona, Wyoming and Montana and won national riding and roping contests at Prescott, Ariz., and Canon City, Colo., in 1909 and 1910.

During the years when he was identified with pictures, Mix always was cast as a hard-riding, gun-toting hero out to thwart unlawful acts in the days of the wild west.

In recent years, he has appeared in wild west circus shows and for a time operated his own circus, the Tom Mix Wild West Show. He also made frequent vaudeville tours and in 1938 and 1939 made personal appearances in Europe.

Mix served with the United States Army in the Philippine Islands, in the Spanish-American War and during the boxer rebellion in China, winning a medal and citation. He was with the British Army at the siege of Ladysmith during the Boer War in South Africa.

As a law enforcement officer, Mix was sheriff of Montgomery County, Kansas, and Washington County, Oklahoma, and later saw service as a deputy U.S. Marshal in the eastern Oklahoma district and with the Texas rangers.

He was livestock foreman of the Miller Brothers "101" Ranch, Bliss, Okla., from 1906 to 1909.

With the advent of talking pictures, Mix turned to circus and vaudeville work exclusively.

MONTIE MONTANA

Legendary Montie Montana, 87, the cowboy roping star who rode in 60 consecutive Rose Parades, died on May 20 at a Newhall, California, hospital after a series of strokes. Montana starred in one B-Western, CIRCLE OF DEATH (Kent, 1935). He also appeared in supporting roles in other Westerns. In 1993 he wrote his autobiography, *Montie Montana—Not Without My Horse*. (1998).

WAYNE MORRIS

Film actor Wayne Morris dropped dead of a heart attack on September 14. The actor was visiting his uncle and Air Squadron 15 leader Captain David McCambell aboard a Navy carrier off Monterey, California when he collapsed on the bridge while watching maneuvers. He was born Bert DeWayne Morris on February 17, 1914, in Los Angeles and gained attention as a star running back at Los Angeles City College. Warners signed him out of the Pasadena Playhouse in 1936. He was a busy actor and played various roles until he entered the Navy in World War II. Ensign Morris joined Air Squadron 15 in the Pacific where he flew 57 combat missions. By the war's end, Lt. Commander Morris was a flying ace and holder of four Distinguished Flying Crosses. He was off screen for some six years and his movie career never picked up steam after the war. He finally joined Allied Artists for a series of cowboy flicks. Morris' will left everything to his second wife, Patricia O'Rouke, and only a dollar to his son.

JAMES NEWILL

Western film actor James Newill died July 31. Born in Pittsburgh, Pennsylvania on August 12, 1911, Newill moved to Gardena, California at an early age. He attended the University of California in the 1930s and then joined the Los Angeles Opera company. He later sang on the *Burns and Allen Show* and with Eddy Duchin, Gus Arnheim, and Abe Lyman. He was also a regular on the show *Say it with Music.* Newill was offered a film contract with Grand National in 1937 where he played the lead in the Renfrew of the Mounties series. When the series ended, he teamed with Dave O'Brien in a western series called the Texas Rangers. Newill later worked in Broadway musicals. He also made thirteen episodes of Renfrew for television. Retired from acting, he and Dave O'Brien went into partnership in a Woodland Hills Ranch which they later sold to cowboy actor Jack Ingram who turned it into a western film location. (1975)

DAVE O'BRIEN

Dave O'Brien 57, chief writer on the Red Skelton TV show and well known for his acting in westerns, serials, and Pete Smith Specialties, died unexpectedly Saturday, November, 8, 1969, aboard his 60-foot racing sloop, "The White Cloud," anchored in Avalon Harbor on Catalina Island. He had used the boat a few hours earlier in competition with other Hollywood personalities in an informal channel regatta. He won the race but suffered a heart attack. A Coast Guard helicopter flew him to Harbor General Hospital in Florence, where he died. Following cremation, his ashes were scattered upon the sea that was his passion.

GEORGE O'BRIEN, Movie Actor

The New York Times,
Friday, September 6, 1985

BROKEN ARROW, Okla., Sept. 5 (AP) — George O'Brien, who acted in 75 films, including the Westerns "Fort Apache" and John Ford's "Iron Horse," died in a convalescent home Wednesday. He was 86 years old.

Mr. O'Brien, whose Hollywood career spanned more than 40 years, had lived in the nursing home since a stroke in 1979.

He began his film career in the early 20's, when a friend introduced him to Tom Mix, a star of Westerns.

Mr. Mix hired Mr. O'Brien as an assistant cameraman at $15 a week. Eventually Mr. O'Brien moved into jobs as a stuntman and extra, including one that called for him to be knocked by Rudolph Valentino from the rigging of ship into the sea.

In 1924, Mr. O'Brien was chosen for his first starring role in "The Iron Horse." One of his most acclaimed roles was in the silent film "Sunrise," which also starred Janet Gaynor.

During the 1920's and 30's, he worked with some of the biggest names in Hollywood, including Mary Astor, Wallace Beery, Douglas Fairbanks Jr., William Powell and Myrna Loy.

After World War II, he appeared in a number of Western epics, including "Fort Apache," with John Wayne, Henry Fonda and Shirley Temple, and "She Wore a Yellow Ribbon," also with Mr. Wayne.

His last film was Mr. Ford's "Cheyenne Autumn," in 1964.

He is survived by a son, Darcy of Tulsa; a daughter, Orin, and a granddaughter, Molly both of New York.

LEE BERRIAN POWELL

Lee Berrian Powell, 35, the original "Lone Ranger" of films, was killed in action in the South Pacific according to word received by his family.

Trained at Pasadena Playhouse. Powell starred in Westerns and serials at various Hollywood studios. He joined the Marines two years ago and was sergeant at the time of his death, having been overseas 22 months.

Survived by daughter, mother and father.

(1944)

JACK RANDALL, Killed Filming a Western

Jack Randall, Husband of Barbara Bennett, Falls From Horse

HOLLYWOOD, July 16 (AP)—Addison (Jack) Randall, age 38, husband of Barbara Bennett, was killed today when he fell from his horse while making a Western thriller at Canoga Park. He had started work on the picture this morning.

While he was riding a horse at break-neck speed past the cameras, the actor's hat blew off and, in attempting to grab it, he lost his balance and fell, striking a tree.

Barbara Bennett was divorced by Morton Downey in 1941. Soon afterward she married Randall at Ensenada, Mexico. They remarried in Beverly Hills in February, 1942. Randall was divorced from Louise Stanley, whom he also had married twice.

DUNCAN RENALDO, TV's 'Cisco Kid' Succumbs at 76

GOLETA, Calif. (AP) — Duncan Renaldo, who became the idol of millions of children in the 1950s as the "Cisco Kid," has died at the age of 76.

He had been suffering from lung cancer and succumbed to heart failure yesterday in Goleta Valley community Hospital.

Renaldo, best known to America's first television generation for his part in 159 episodes of "The Cisco Kid" from 1949-56, also had 164 movies to his credit, including "The Bridge of San Luis Rey," "For Whom the Bell Tolls" and "Zorro Rides Again."

Born Renault Renaldo Duncan, he was stranded in America in 1922 as a merchant marine when his ship burned at dockside in Baltimore. Renaldo went to New York and worked his way up from janitor to scene designer, producer and writer at the old Tec Art movie studio.

He went to Hollywood in 1926. His first leading role was in "Trader Horn," but his life, was disrupted just before the movie's premiere in 1931 when he was arrested by immigration authorities for entering the country illegally.

After a sensational trial, he was found guilty of perjury for claiming he'd been born in New Jersey. Renaldo, who thought he'd been born in Spain, served 18 months in prison.

President Franklin D. Roosevelt granted him an unconditional pardon the day before he was to be released. Renaldo later called that episode "the most interesting and tragic time of my life."

By 1940, he was starring in Westerns, and won the lead role in "The Cisco Kid" movies and TV series in 1944.

He and his sidekick Pancho, played by the late Leo Carrillo, portrayed cowboys who used their wits instead of their guns to bring justice to the Old West.

"'The Cisco Kid' was a cheerful show," he once said. "Pancho and I never killed anyone. The kids that watched our show went to sleep smiling and not with nightmares."

Renaldo always credited "the kids" for his success and said the prayers of 17,000 young fans who sent him get-well cards were responsible for his speedy recovery from a broken neck he received in 1953 during filming of the series.

"It may sound strange to some people," he said then. "But I am convinced that it is the young children who have helped me make a miraculous recovery. There is no other explanation."

Renaldo is survived by his wife, Audrey, daughter Stephanie, and three sons, Richard, Jeremy and Edwin Renaldo.

A funeral Mass will be held tomorrow night at Santa Barbara's Old Mission, with private burial on Saturday.

TEX RITTER, 67, Singing Cowboy of Screen and Records, Is Dead

Country Western Star Sang 'Jingle, Jangle, Jingle' Ran for Senate Seat

NASHVILLE. Jan. 2 (AP) — Tex Ritter, the country music star, died of a heart attack here tonight. The 67-year-old singer, guitar player, actor and politician was visiting a friend at the county jail when he was stricken.

The police administered oxygen and rushed him to the Baptist Hospital, where he died.

Only three weeks ago, the Country and Western entertainer went to Washington to present a special recording to President Nixon. It was an album composed of speeches by the President with narration by Mr. Ritter. There were only two copies of the album. The second was given to the Country Music Hall of Fame here.

Mr. Ritter is survived by his widow, Dorothy, and two sons, Thomas and Johnathan.

Even Tried Politics

Tex Ritter — his real name was Woodward Maurice Ritter, but few, if any, called him anything but "Tex"—tried politics running for the Senate, but the bid failed.

His credits as a performer and

as a writer covered virtually every major phase of Western lore from cowboy songs to "The Lone Ranger."

He made some 78 Western films, playing more or less the same character, the singing cowboy. The songs that bear his stamp included "I've Got Spurs that Jingle, Jangle, Jingle," recorded in 1942 on his own label. Another was the title theme from the Western "High Noon" ("Do Not Forsake Me, Oh My Darling") of 10 years later.

There were also "Rounded Up in Glory," "Blood on the Saddle," "I Dreamed of a Hillbilly Heaven" and dozens of others, all recently packaged in a Capitol Records three album set, "An American Legend."

About this album, a reviewer in The New York Times remarked just a week ago, "It makes the listener realize just how distinctive a performer—in voice and mannerism—Mr. Ritter is."

Nevertheless, Mr. Ritter's movies regularly earned critical disapproval. Most of them were ignored or given a brush-off.

In his bid for the Senate in Tennessee, he was defeated by a margin of better than 3 to 1 in a primary election by Representative William E. Block 3d of Chattanooga.

Mr. Ritter built lucrative careers with his music and his movies, although he had wanted to be a country lawyer. He studied law at the University of Texas, where he developed an interest in folk-

lore and Western music. He took up studying law once more, at Northwestern University. But he had to turn back to music. His reason was, he said, "Money! I ran out of dishes to wash."

Happy Trails, ROY ROGERS

Singing Cowboy, Hollywood Good Guy, Dies

by Michael Fleeman
Associated Press Entertainment Writer

LOS ANGELES — Roy Rogers, the singing cowboy and one of the last of the white hats from the golden era of Hollywood Westerns, died Monday. He was 86.

Rogers died in his sleep of congestive heart failure at his Apple Valley home, in the high desert 90 miles from Los Angeles.

"What a blessing to have

shared my life together with him for almost 51 years," said Dale Evans, Rogers' wife and singing partner.

Rogers was a star of television, radio and movies, turning out country music songs, 87 Westerns — 26 of them with Evans — and a 1950s TV series that continues in reruns. For 12 years, from 1943 to 1954, he was the No. 1 Western star at the box office in a magazine poll of theater operators.

With his trusty horse Trigger, Rogers played the straight-shooting good guy who always fought fair — instead of killing the bad guys, he would shoot the guns out of their hands—and always lived to sing about it.

Rogers' theme song was "Happy Trails to You," sung over a clippity-clop beat and bum-bah-dee-dah bass line. It was co-written by his wife.

His movies included "King of the Cowboys," "Song of Texas," "The Cowboy and the Senorita," "Don't Fence Me In" and "My Pal Trigger." In the movies, his sidekick was whiskered Gabby Hayes; on television, it was Pat Brady.

Rogers and Gene Autry were the most popular cowboy crooners in Hollywood history.

"This is a terrible loss for me," Autry, 90, said in a statement. "I had tremendous respect for Roy and considered him a great humanitarian and an outstanding American. He was, and will always be, a true Western hero."

Clayton Moore, the 83-year-old actor who played the Lone Ranger said: "He certainly was a role model for people all over the world. Just a good, straightforward man. He always treated people with kindness."

A shrewd businessman, Rogers became a millionaire many times over through real estate, Roy Rogers restaurants and television productions.

He opened a museum near his Apple Valley home in 1967. When Trigger died in 1965, Rogers had the golden palomino stuffed and placed on display in the museum, to Evans' chagrin.

"I was so angry, I said, 'All right, but when you go, I'm going to have you stuffed and placed on top of Trigger,' " she said in 1984.

Rogers responded: "I told her just make sure I'm smiling."

Born Leonard Slye in Cincinnati on Nov. 5, 1911 (some reference books give his last name as Sly, and list a different date of birth), Rogers grew up in rural Portsmouth and Duck Run, Ohio. By the time he was a teenager, he had made a name for himself locally as a square-dance caller and yodeler.

During the Depression, his family moved West and Rogers worked as a truck driver, peach picker and singer and guitarist in hillbilly musical groups. He helped found the Pioneer Trio, soon renamed Sons of the Pioneers. It had such hits as "Tumbling Tumbleweeds" and "Cool Water."

Rogers' first screen appearances were with the Sons in movies such as "Rhythm on the Range." But he left the group in the late '30s. He heard they were looking for singing cowboys at Republic Studios, and the only way he could get in was by waiting until the workers began returning from lunch and sneaking in with them, he later recalled.

Rogers replaced Autry as Republic's top cowboy when Autry left to serve in World War II.

Rogers was first teamed with Evans, a radio singer and sometime actress, in "The Cowboy and the Senorita," 1944, and they married in 1947, 14 months after his first wife, Arlene died.

In addition to Evans, he is survived by a son, three daughters, 15 grandchildren and 33 great-grand-children.

A memorial service was planned for Saturday at the Church of the Valley in Apple Valley, followed by a procession around the Roy Rogers-Dale Evans Museum in Victorville.

GILBERT ROLAND

Gilbert Roland, a dashing leading man whose movie career began in the silent era and who became the Mexican Robin Hood figure "Cisco Kid" died May 15 in Los Angeles of cancer. He was 88.

Roland's most famous role in the silent era was as Armand in 1927's "Camille," co-starring Norma Talmadge, and he got some of his best reviews in 1951 for "The Bullfighter and the Lady."

But he earned a place in the pantheon of enduring pop culture figures with his performance as the genial bandit, "Cisco," in 11 B-picture outings, films that ran as second-feature entertainment on a double bill.

"My Cisco Kid might have been a bandit, but he fought for the poor and was a civilized man in the true sense of the word," Roland once said.

One of his last major films was John Ford's final Western, "Cheyenne Autumn" in 1964. But he continued to work in later years, appearing in 1977's "Islands in the Stream."

CESAR ROMERO

Cesar Romero, the urbane "Latin from Manhattan" who charmed audiences in smooth character parts in 1940s musicals and later starred as the Joker on TV's "Batman," died Jan. 1. He was 86.

Romero died at 9:10 p.m. at St. John's Hospital & Health Center in Los Angeles, spokesman Gary Miereanu said. Romero died of complications related to a blood clot after being hospitalized with severe bronchitis and pneumonia.

His swarthy Cuban looks were leavened by a self-mocking smile, which made Romero the perfect romantic foil in scores of motion pictures such as "Weekend in Havana," "The Devil is a Woman," "The Beautiful Blonde From Bashful Bend" and "That Lady in Ermine."

"When I started in motion pictures in 1934, they said I was going to be the next Valentino," he recalled in 1984. "I was never a leading man, and very seldom did I do a picture where I got the girl. But I was saddled with the label because I had a Latin name. My background is Cuban, but I'm from New York City. I'm a Latin from Manhattan."

Romero was born in Manhattan on Feb. 15, 1907, to Cuban immigrants. His mother had a career as a concert singer under the name Maria Mantilla. "My grandfather, Jose Marti, was the liberator of Cuba," Romero said in 1984. "The Cuban war of independence was planned in my grandfather's house."

Romero's initial career was that of dancer, although he had never formally studied dance. He was discovered in the Montmartre nightclub in Manhattan by producer Brock Pemberton, who was looking for a replacement for the hit stage comedy "Strictly Dishonorable." He segued into starring roles in such plays as "Stella Brady," "All Points West," "Social Register" and "Dinner at Eight."

A screen test for MGM landed him a role in "The Thin Man," which eventually led to a three-year contract with Universal, who loaned him out for such films as "The Good Fairy" with Margaret Sullavan and "Love Before Breakfast" opposite Carole Lombard.

His portrayal of Koda-Khan in the Shirley Temple film "Wee Willie Winkie" led to a 14-year contract at 20th Century Fox. His tenure there was interrupted only by World War II; he enlisted in the U.S. Coast Guard and served in the Pacific theater of war.

Fox gave him a starring role in the successful Cisco Kid Western serial, as well as "The Little Princess" with Temple and "Tales of Manhattan" with Ginger Rogers. Romero also appeared in many musicals, including "Weekend in Havana," "Springtime in the Rockies" and "Coney Island."

But he is perhaps best known as the Joker in the "Batman" TV series starring Adam West.

Romero never married. He explained in 1984: "How could I, when I had so many responsibilities? Could I tell a girl: 'Let's get married and you can come and live with my father, my mother, two sisters, a niece and a nephew'? I have no regrets."

Romero is survived by a brother, three nieces, a nephew and three great-nephews.

In lieu of flowers, donations may be made to the Arthritis Foundation.

—Richard Natale

FRED SCOTT

The oldest living B-Western star, FRED SCOTT, died suddenly Dec. 16 of natural causes. He was 89. A product of the San Francisco Opera, Scott starred in 13 singing Westerns for Spectrum (and one PRC mistake — "Rodeo Rhythm") from 1936-1942. The best seven of these co-starred sidekick Al "Fuzzy" St. John. Scott often singled out "Songs and Bullets" and "Two Gun Troubadour" as his favorites. Fred rode a gorgeous silver stallion, White King. They made a striking pair, what with Fred's usual black clothing. Often billed as the "Silvery Voiced Buckaroo," Scott also had feature parts in "Last Outlaw" with Harry Carey and "Thundering Hoofs" with Tim Holt. After making the Westerns, Scott sang for the Florentine Gardens Revue and worked in the MGM sound department before striking gold in the real estate business.

RANDOLPH SCOTT, Hero of Western Films, Dies

Tuesday, March 3, 1987
by Bart Barnes
Washington Post Staff Writer

Randolph Scott, 89, the soft-spoken hero of dozens of Western movies during the 1930s, 1940s and 1950s who was slow to anger but quick on the draw, died yesterday at his home in Los Angeles. He had heart and lung ailments.

Mr. Scott made more than 100 films in a 33-year career that ended with his retirement in 1962 and from 1950 to 1955 he was among the top 10 draws in the motion picture industry.

His pictures included 39 "big budget" Westerns, including "Fort Worth," "Man Behind the Gun," "Ride Lonesome," "Comanche Station," "Gunfighters," "Coroners Creek," "Belle Starr," "Virginia City" and "Santa Fe."

His last movie was "Ride the High Country," a 1962 film in which he played an aging gunfighter opposite another longtime Western favorite, Joel McCrea, under the direction of Sam Peckinpah.

The lanky, 6-foot-2 Mr. Scott was among the last of a generation of Western actors who were generally cast as straight shooters who sat tall in the saddle. He had a long, lean jaw and a rugged outdoors image, and he came across as the type of man to whom beleaguered frontier officials might turn when looking for someone to "clean up the town," which they often did.

Western movies, Mr. Scott once said, "have been the mainstay of the industry ever since its beginning. And they have been good to me. Westerns are the type of picture which everybody can see and enjoy."

Ten years after his retirement, his cinematic endeavors were recalled by the Statler Brothers in a popular cowboy ballad, "Whatever Happened to Randolph Scott, Riding the Trail Alone," which suggested a yearning for the simplicity of the Western movies of an earlier era when it was easy to tell the good guys from the bad, and the good guys invariably won.

Born in Orange County, Va., Mr. Scott was educated in private schools and attended Georgia Tech and the University of North Carolina. After leaving college, he traveled in Europe for a year, then returned to Virginia, where he worked as an engineer for his father before heading West to try his hand at acting.

He began his film career with a bit role in "The Far Call" in 1929.

During the 1930s, he appeared in such movies as "The Last Roundup," "Home on the Range," "The Texans," "Jesse James and "Frontier Marshal."

During World War II, he deviated from the standard Westerns to play military heroes in such films as "Corvette K-225," "Bombardier," "Gung-Ho!" and "China Sky."

Mr. Scott was usually as laconic off the screen as he was in his movies. "Frankly, I don't like publicity," he said in 1961, quoting stage producer David Belasco's dictum, "Never let yourself be seen in public unless they pay for it."

"To me that makes sense," Mr. Scott said. "The most glamorous, the most fascinating star our business ever had was Garbo. Why? Because she kept herself from the public. Each member of the audience had his own idea of what she was really like....But take the stars of today. There is no mystery about them. The public knows what kind of toothpaste they use, whether they sleep in men's pajamas and every intimate fact of their lives."

Two of Mr. Scott's movies, "Sugarfoot" and "Colt .45," became television series. He did play an outlaw once, in "The Doolins of Oklahoma," and he appeared in such musicals as "Roberta" and "Follow the Fleet," with Fred Astaire and Ginger Rogers, and in a comedy, "My Favorite Wife" with Irene Dunne and Cary Grant.

Mr. Scott's marriage to the former Marion duPont Somerville ended in divorce. She was once owner of Montpelier, the Orange County estate that once belonged to James Madison and which she made into one of the most successful horse breeding farms in Virginia.

Mr. Scott is survived by his wife of 43 years, Patricia Stillman Scott; two children by his, second marriage, Christopher Scott and Sandra Scott Tyler, and three grandchildren.

CAL SHRUM

CAL SHRUM (March 11, 1996, age 85, heart attack): popular music performer who joined his brother Walt's group The Colorado Hillbillies and worked in two Gene Autry films. Cal then formed his Rhythm Rangers, which at one time included Spade Cooley and Tex Williams. Cal and his group were in many Westerns with such stars as Charles Starrett, Tex Ritter and James Newill. He went on to star in two independent B-Westerns in 1944, which Astor got around to releasing in 1949.

Actor CHARLES STARRETT, 82, Starred as the Durango Kid

The Associated Press

BORREGO SPRINGS, Calif. — Charles Starrett, who starred as the Durango Kid in scores of low-budget Westerns in the 1930s and '40s, has died at age 82.

Mr. Starrett died Saturday in this city 50 miles northwest of San Diego.

He once described his career as "The West That Wasn't." He wore a white hat, abstained from alcohol, and always triumphed over the bad guys.

At 6 feet, 2 inches and 180 pounds, Mr. Starrett was one of Hollywood's most physically imposing cowboys, if not the best known. His first film was "Fast and Loose" in 1930 and the last was "Rough Tough West" in 1952, when he retired.

Mr. Starrett had been a football star at Dartmouth University in the early 1920s and began his acting career as an extra in the movie "The Quarterback."

BOB STEELE; Prolific Star of Dozens of Western Films

Los Angeles Times,
Friday, December 23, 1988
by Burt A. Folkart, Times Staff Writer

Bob Steele, the prolific star of dozens of Western films that could most charitably be described as economical and who became famous to millions of children through a screen persona that was worthy of his name, died Wednesday.

The star, character actor and bit player seen in nearly 400 movies and television shows was 82 and died at St. Joseph Medical Center in Burbank.

Known in the 1960s as Trooper Duffy in the military TV farce "F Troop," Steele had been one of "The Three Mesquiteers," a group of cowboy stars featured in about three dozen pictures between 1935 and 1943. Others who alternated in making up the three heroes in such films as "Powdersmoke Range," "Riders of the Whistling Range" and "Call of the Mesquiteers" included John Wayne, Bob Livingston, Duncan Reynaldo and Jimmy Dodd.

Because those and other Steele features were made inexpensively, even for Depression times, they were easily affordable to local TV stations who first ventured on the air in the late 1940s. Thus such local late night features as "TripleHeader Movies" on Channel 7 would have announcers intoning several times a week: "And now stay tuned for another action-packed thriller, a Bob Steele Western."

Born Robert North Bradbury Jr. in Pendleton, Ore., the future Bob Steele was the son of Robert Bradbury Sr., a director of silent films. The younger Steele appeared on stage at 2 and in films at 14 with his twin brother, Bill, in "The Adventures of Bob and Bill," a series of nature shorts directed by their father.

He continued in films in juvenile parts and by 1927, despite his small stature, was a full-blown cowboy star.

Steele possessed an icy stare with which he froze the bad guys in the black hats and his stern countenance often proved sufficient to run them out of town without the necessity of gunplay.

Although Steele deprecated his acting talents, telling a 1966 interviewer that "I never went for all this hoop-de-do about being an actor and demanding high salaries," he possessed a talent normally suppressed by the material dealt him.

One exception was the role of Curly in the motion picture production of John Steinbeck's classic "Of Mice and Men" in 1939. In it he is a sadistic bully who torments a simple-minded giant (Lennie played by Lon Chaney Jr.). Critics called his portrayal powerful; many were astounded that an actor of his limited background could give depth to such a dark and profound role.

He played several other villains in later films, most notably Canino in "The Big Sleep" in 1946. He made his last picture, "Something Big," in 1971.

Films, no matter how inconsequential, had been good to him.

"When a lot of 'em [actors] were starving, I was content to do bit parts just to be active...," he said in 1966. "Why disintegrate because of pride?"

FRED C. THOMSON, Screen Actor, Dies

Rival of Tom Mix in Westerns

Roles Was a Minister—Star Athlete While at Princeton

LOS ANGELES, Dec. 26 (AP) — Fred C. Thomson, screen actor, featured in Western roles, died here shortly before midnight last night. He failed to rally from an operation for gallstones, performed three weeks ago.

Mr. Thomson, in his will filed for probate today, left his widow only "my love and affection."

"I do this at her own request and in the belief that she is already provided with sufficient means for her care," he wrote.

Mr. Thomson's will provides that his estate shall be shared equally by his mother, Mrs. Clara F. Thomson, and his 3-year-old son, Fred Jr.

Funeral arrangements for Mr. Thomson awaited the arrival from Princeton, N.J. of his mother and a brother Harrison Thomson, a professor at Princeton University.

Fred C. Thomson, who despite his short career in motion pictures had come to be ranked with Tom Mix as an exponent of Western roles, was also a distinguished athlete and an ordained minister who served overseas as a chaplain during the World War.

He was born in California in 1891, the son of a Presbyterian minister. He attended first Occidental College, then the Princeton Theological Seminary, winning fame as an athlete at both schools. While at Princeton he won the national all-around athletic championship in 1910, 1911 and 1918.

Entering the army as a chaplain, he went overseas in the field artillery, but because of his interest in technical artillery problems he was subsequently appointed ordnance officer of his battalion. At the close of the war he took part in the inter-allied games in Paris, winning the decathlon event in 1919. It was in Paris that he met and married Frances Marian, reputed one of the highest paid scenario writers.

Returning to California with his wife, who continued her motion picture work, he became minister of Hope Church, Eagle Rock Valley, in Southern California. He made his own screen debut by "doubling" for stars in scenes in which unusual athletic skill was required, later deciding to become a full-fledged player in clean and wholesome films.

Death Lifts
TOM TYLER
From Detroit
Obscurity

The Detroit News—Tuesday, May 4, 1954
by Harry Salsinger

Young and old of Detroit paid tribute today to Tom Tyler, a Hamtramck factory worker who became one of Hollywood's first cowboy stars. Living here virtually unknown, Tyler died Sunday after a heart attack.

Although age and illness long ago dragged him from the top ranks of the screen's western heroes, television has made a new hero of Tyler for a younger generation. Youngsters are now seeing the pictures that made his name famous to their parents.

At the Wysocki Funeral Home, 5227 McNichols East, a legion of youngsters file past his casket during the noon recess and after the final school bell this week.

Tyler, who was born Vincent Markowski in Witherbee, N.Y., was brought here by his factory worker father when he was 15 years old.

Young Vincent, already a strapping, handsome boy, went to work in a factory, too–but not for long. His family recalls that he always wanted to be an actor and, after six months in a shop, he ran away from home at 16 and worked his way west.

Stardom wasn't waiting for Tyler when he arrived. He spent seven years waiting for his big chance. Fame came in a rush in 1927 when he was picked to star in "Let's Go Gallagher" for FBO Pictures.

From that time on, Tyler was high in the Hollywood parade.

Aging and periodically crippled by arthritis, Tyler gradually dropped out of his starring roles. He was most recently seen as a trooper in "She Wore a Yellow Ribbon."

Television proved a boon for Tyler, who played, not as a star but as a heavy, in filmed TV shows.

Ill health finally forced him to retire, and in November, 1952, he came here to live with his sister, Mrs. Katherine Slepski, at 13158 Moenart. Mrs. Slepski said he had planned to return to Hollywood next fall.

Services will be at 9:30 a.m. tomorrow at St. Augustine Church, 13504 Justine. Burial will be in Mt. Olivet Cemetery.

JIMMY WAKELY Dies in California

The Indianapolis News,
September 25, 1982

LOS ANGELES (AP) — Jimmy Wakely, 68, known as the "Singing Cowboy," who made 71 Westerns and performed on TV, stage and radio, has died of heart failure, his son said yesterday.

Wakely died Thursday night in Holy Cross Hospital where he had been admitted Aug. 14, just a few days after finishing his last album, said John Wakely, who sang with his father and sister Linda Lee Olsen for the past 20 years.

Wakely lived in Sylmar and had worked for the past several years with his own Shasta record company.

"He was ill for four years. He had asthma. He had been in and out of the hospital" even while still recording music, the younger Wakely said. "Last night his heart just gave up," he said.

Born Feb. 16, 1914, in Mineola Ark., Wakely grew up in Oklahoma on a cattle and hog ranch.

He learned to play guitar at the age of 7, and in 1937 was featured on Oklahoma City radio station WKY as part of the Wakely Trio with Johnny Bond and Dick Reinhart. Through the program, the trio met Gene Autry, who brought them to Hollywood.

Wakely is best remembered for his hit recordings "Slipping Around" and "Silver Bells." He also had hits with "Tennessee Waltz," "Beautiful Brown Eyes," "One Has My Name" with Mary Ford, and "Wide Open Spaces."

In the 1940s, Wakely was ranked just below Autry and Roy Rogers as the favorite singing cowboy, and in the early 1950s he was voted top male vocalist of the year, his son said.

"He was a very, very loved man," the younger Wakely said, noting his father had toured with Bob Hope to entertain U.S. troops, and had performed for a time on the Lawrence Welk TV show.

Another Article from a Different Source

JIMMY WAKELY

Jimmy Wakely, 68, country-western singer and actor, died Sept. 23 of heart failure at a Missions Hills, Calif., hospital, after a lengthy bout with asthma. He had been hospitalized since August, shortly after he finished recording an album.

Born in Mineola, Ark., he moved to Oklahoma with his family when he was four and, at age seven, took his first guitar lesson. In his early 20s, he sang as part of the Wakely Trio on an Oklahoma City radio station. The group was signed by Gene Autry for the cowboy star's "Melody Ranch Show" in Hollywood, remaining for two years.

During the 1940s Wakely was a top c-w singer with such hits as "One Has My Name," "I Love You So Much It Hurts" and "Slipping Around." By 1962 he had sold more than 15,000,000 records but his career ebbed during the 1950s when he played several Nevada casinos. In the 1960s he was signed by KTTV for a weekly vidmusical show.

He appeared in about 30 films including "The Tulsa Kid," "Deep in the Heart of Texas," "Moon Over Montana," and others.

Survivors include his wife, son and three daughters.

JOHN WAYNE Dies at 72

LOS ANGELES (UPI) — John Wayne, who so embodied the American hero in a half century of movies that he became an internationally known symbol of the strong, patriotic American, died of cancer Monday. He was 72.

Wayne's death was announced by Bernard Strohm, administrator of the UCLA Medical Center, where Wayne had been hospitalized since May 1 in the latest of a series of recurring bouts with cancer.

Wayne died at 5:35 p.m. PDT, "with all his children at his side," Strohm said. The seven Wayne children left the hospital before the death was announced three hours

John Wayne

later.

Wayne fought for life until the end. "He had been in considerable pain since Saturday," Strohm said, but "he would not take much medication. He wanted to be awake when he died. He would tolerate the pain just to be near his family."

However he lapsed in and out of a coma Monday.

"Sometimes his vital signs would stabilize and he would look over and call, often in a loud voice, for his children. When they would appear, he would lapse back into the coma."

He was unconscious when he died.

As it became clear death was approaching for the rugged, rumbling-voiced "Duke," he was given many honors. Congress and President Carter authorized a special gold medal — of the kind given to such national figures as the Wright Brothers — and he made his final public appearance at the Academy

Award ceremony in April, drawing an emotional standing ovation from his peers when he strode out to present the Oscar for best picture.

John Wayne rollicked, brawled and shot his way through more than 200 movies but though his role might be Marine, pilot, cowboy, sea captain, prize fighter or cavalryman, he was always the hero and he was always John Wayne.

His pictures made him one of the great box-office draws of all time and of his critics' complaints of the lack of versatility in his performances Wayne was fond of saying: "Nobody likes my acting but the public."

Wayne made his first movie in 1931 and while he starred in such epic films as "Stagecoach," "Back to Bataan," "Red River," "The Quiet Man" and "The Green Berets," he won his first Academy Award playing Rooster Cogburn in "True Grit."

JAY WILSEY
(Buffalo Bill Jr.)

WILSEY, Jay (October 25, 1961, age 61, carcinomatosis, probable broncitogenia peimary): Born in Missouri (Not Wyoming, as many sources say), he reached stardom during the 1920s as Buffalo Bill Jr. in a series of fast moving Westerns produced by Lester Scott's Action Pictures releasing through Artclass, Associated Exhibitors and Pathe Exchanges. With the coming of sound he continued to star in independent Westerns and supporting roles to other stars and to work as a stuntman. He doubled Charles Starrett occasionally at Columbia. He had leads in two serials for Universal in 1929 co-starring with juvenile Western star Newton House in A FINAL RECKONING and PIRATE OF PANAMA. At the time of his death he was self-employed as owner of a trailer park in Los Angeles.

ROSCOE ATES, 67, Comedian, Dies

Veteran of Movies Played Stuttering Cowboy Roles

Special to The *New York Times*

ENCINO, Calif., March 1 — Roscoe Ates, the comedian, died here today of lung cancer at West Valley Community Hospital. He was 67 years old.

Cured His Stammer

The rubber-faced comedian literally stuttered his way to stardom, even though he had cured himself of stammering at the age of 18.

Mr. Ates' best-known role was that of a ranch roustabout in West-ern pictures, and his trademark was the mobile face and the long, drawn-out stutter.

He was born near Hattiesburg, Miss. Intending to make a career as a concert violinist, he graduated from a conservatory in Warren, Ohio.

One of the classes at the conservatory was group singing, and Mr. Ates discovered that he had no stutter when he sang. He later said that he rid himself of his speech defect by reciting song lyrics, then practicing tongue-twister word in front of a mirror.

He gave up his violin career to tour the vaudeville and repertory circuit as a comedian, and eventually wound up in Hollywood in 1930.

In the role as a dying old man in a film called "Billy the Kid," the comedian attracted the attention of film director Wesley Ruggles, who gave him a role in the movie "Cimmaron."

He later appeared in a number of successful pictures with Marie Dressler, Wallace Beery and Polly Moran.

During World War II Mr. Ates spent two years as a major in the Army Air Forces. He was placed on inactive duty in 1944, but finished the war as a United Service Organizations entertainer.

At the height of his career, he was known as a scene-stealer, whose impersonations of "Casper Milquetoast" character had a wide audience appeal.

PAT BRADY, Film Cowboy, Dies;

Roy Rogers' Sidekick Was 57

COLORADO SPRINGS, Colo., Feb. 28 1972 (UPI)—Pat Brady, musician, singer and comic sidekick of Roy Rogers, the movie cowboy, died yesterday while visiting friends in nearby Green Mountain Falls. He was 57 years old.

Mr. Brady appeared in nearly 80 motion pictures, usually as the genial Western character he made so popular. He was a familiar figure to millions of Americans because of the movies and a TV series he did with Mr. Rogers. He made his jeep "Nellie Bell" a household word with his catch phrase while trying to stop the vehicle—"Whooaa, Nellie Bell."

Mr. Brady was born in Toledo, Ohio, Dec. 31, 1914, the son of John Edward Brady and the former Lucille Brewer. Both parents were in show business, and Mr. Brady made his theatrical debut at the age of 4 with his parents in a stage production called "Mrs. Wiggs of the Cabbage Patch."

While in high school Mr. Brady moved to California and began playing with his father at a nightclub in Sunset Beach. He played bass guitar in the group and was spotted by Leonard Sly.

Mr. Sly, who became famous as Roy Rogers, was at that time with the Sons of the Pioneers singing group. When he went into movies he helped Mr. Brady join the group as his replacement.

Mr. Brady stayed with the group until 1942, when he entered the Army. A tour in France with General Patton's Third Army won him citations for valor and two Purple Hearts. He returned to the Sons in 1945 and left again in 1955. He still appeared occasionally with the group until moving to Colorado two years ago.

He had been working with the Pine Cone Ranch near Colorado Springs and a local automotive agency. The authorities said death came from natural causes.

Mr. Brady was separated from his wife.

SMILEY BURNETTE Of 'Autry' Fame Succumbs At 55

ENCINO, Calif. (AP) —A musical saw and an accordion boosted Smiley Burnette to success as a comic with Gene Autry and other Western film stars during a career in which he had made 171 pictures up until his death Thursday night.

Smiley, whose checkered shirt and tattered cowboy hat were familiar to thousands of theatergoers, succumbed to leukemia, friends said. He was 55 and had

Smiley Burnette

been under hospital treatment since Feb. 8.

During the heyday of Westerns, Burnette was one of the top money-making performers, appearing in the 1930s and 1940s with Autry, Roy Rogers and others.

In recent years he appeared in television, most recently as the railroad engineer in "Petticoat Junction." He was fond of recalling how he met Autry, who gave him his first big chance in radio.

Thirty-eight years ago Burnette was performing with saw and squeeze-box for a radio station in Tuscola, Ill., shortly after finishing high school. One day he got a phone call.

"This is Gene Autry," a voice said. "Sure, and I'm Gen. Grant," Smiley replied.

Finally convinced, he heard Autry ask, "How much are you making at that radio station?"

"I'm gettin' $18 a week and gettin' it regular."

"I can pay you $35," said Autry, "Think it over and let me know."

"I've thunk it over," said Smiley, "and I'll take it."

After a long series of radio and personal appearances with Autry, Burnette made 81 movies with the star.

When television's impact impeded Western films, Burnette retired temporarily then emerged for personal appearances. He wrote 353 Western tunes during his career and made innumerable appearances from refreshment stand roofs to drive-in theaters and in shopping centers. At last he too joined the television clan.

PAT BUTTRAM; Gene Autry's Sidekick, TV Actor, Comic

by Burt A. Folkart
Times Staff Writer

Pat Buttram, the bulbous-nosed raconteur who rode Melody Ranch with Gene Autry, portrayed a shrewd landowner amid the verdant scenery of "Green Acres," and more recently had been an irreverent presence over the airwaves of Los Angeles, died Saturday, January 8, 1994.

Buttram died of kidney failure after a week's hospitalization at UCLA Medical Center, said long-

Pat Buttram

time friend Bill Ward, general manager of radio stations KMPC and KLITE.

He was in his 80s, Ward said.

Buttram, who rode more daises than he did horses, was an omni-present master of ceremonies for many Los Angeles organizations.

He probably was at his best when shredding his peers, particularly at the bimonthly luncheons of Pacific Pioneer Broadcasters, and organization of radio veterans.

His gentle sarcasm and slightly ribald tales were a fixture at Sportsmen's Lodge in Studio City and at other watering holes across the Southland.

He also was the annual emcee for the Motion Picture and Television Fund's annual Golden Boot awards, where millions have been raised for the charity, and at political rallies for old friends.

He rode in parades, helped install stars on the Hollywood Walk of Fame (including his own in 1988), and had been a regular fixture on Robert W. Morgan's morning KMPC radio program until recently.

Buttram said on taking the job in 1989 that he had gotten "tired of all the deejays in the morning quoting my jokes.... I decided to start getting paid."

Born Maxwell E. Buttram in Alabama, in a year he refused to divulge, he was the son of a circuit-riding minister and studied theology at Birmingham Southern College. He got into show business when a radio station hired him after the management saw him in a college play.

His big break came when he went to the Chicago World's Fair in 1933 and was interviewed in the audience at "National Barn Dance." Everything he said in that voice—compared to a jackass with a sore throat—got laughs and he was signed as a comic.

He and Autry first met more than 50 years ago in Chicago when both were appearing on the "National Barn Dance," the nation's first hillbilly radio show.

They remained close friends over the years, meeting each other for lunch at Lakeside Country Club and other spots several times a week.

"He was never at a loss for a good story or a good one-liner," Autry said Saturday. "I'm going to miss him a lot."

Buttram appeared in more than 40 films, mostly as Autry's constantly amazed partner, and had done hundreds of TV appearances.

From 1965 to 1971, Buttram played the annoying Mr. Haney on CBS' "Green Acres." It was Haney who sold a tumbledown farm to Oliver Wendell Douglas (Eddie Albert) and Lisa Douglas (Eva Gabor).

Buttram played himself on "The Gene Autry Show" from 1950 to 1956 on CBS, calling the boss "Mister Artery" while helping the singing cowboy keep the peace in the Southwest. Years earlier, from 1940-56, he also had been heard as Autry's sidekick on radio's Gene Autry's Melody Ranch."

Buttram also appeared repeatedly on "The Ed Sullivan Show," Arthur Godfrey's programs, and in episodes of such programs as "Alfred Hitchcock Presents."

Buttram is survived by a daughter, Kerry Galgano. A private funeral is pending in Alabama.

LEO CARRILLO, 81, Dies Of Cancer

SANTA MONICA, Calif.,— Leo Carrillo, a movie star for three decades who made his biggest hit as the lovable Pancho of television's Cisco Kid series, died Sunday of cancer. He was 81.

The end came at the Mexican-style ranch house where Carrillo

Leo Carrillo

had lived with his daughter, Antoinette. His wife, Edith, died in 1953 after 40 years of marriage.

Born in Los Angeles, Carrillo was a newspaper cartoonist before turning actor in his early 20s. He played in vaudeville, toured with stock companies and appeared on Broadway before he turned to Hollywood and movie roles.

In early years he specialized in Spanish and Italian roles, but finally became typed as a hard-riding Spaniard of the border days. His trademarks were a flat-brimmed sombrero and carefully waxed mustache.

Carrillo appeared in hundreds of silent movies, short subjects and talkies. He made more than 150 of the Cisco Kid TV films co-starring as Pancho, the Western Robin Hood's fat funny sidekick from 1949 to 1955.

ANDY CLYDE, Long a Film Actor, Dies

The *New York Times*,
Friday, May 19, 1967

LOS ANGELES, May 18, 1967 (UPI) — Andy Clyde, star of numerous two-reel silent comedies and William Boyd's partner in the early Hopalong Cassidy movies, died in his sleep in his home here today. His age was 75.

Mr. Clyde, husband of Elsie Maud Tarron, a Mack Sennett bathing beauty, had featured roles in such television series as "The Real McCoys," "Lassie" and "No Time for Sergeants."

His last appearance was in a "Lassie" feature.

His widow is his only survivor. His sister-in-law is Fay Holden, actress widow of Mr. Clyde's brother, David.

A funeral service will be held Saturday afternoon in Santa Monica, Calif.

Played the Old Geezer

When Andy Clyde appeared in "McFadden's Flats," a 1935 Paramount film, the critic for The New York Times observed that he had been around "a long time and he knows that the audience expects him to squeeze the nickel until the buffalo howls."

Thirty years ago, of course, a nickel could be squeezed a lot harder than it can be today. The old-time buffalo nickel has become something of a rarity but there are still many people who remember it and who also can recall Andy Clyde—although they may get him confused in their mind's eye with Chester Conklin or Ben Turpin.

In his movie character, Mr. Clyde usually was the bewhiskered old geezer, homely, rather pathetic but still lovable and something of a philosopher.

Strangers meeting Mr. Clyde off the screen at the height of his career were likely to be astonished to find him smooth shaven, dapper and rather handsome in contrast to the bespectacled, whiskery and grizzled character he played on the screen.

Mr. Clyde, a native of Blairgowrie, Scotland, and the son of a theatrical producer and manager, performed in vaudeville in the late nineteen-twenties, went to Hollywood as that decade was nearing its end and got his start in the movies as an extra with Mr. Sennett, the impresario of bathing beauties and the pie-in-the-face.

Mr. Clyde appeared in a hundred movies, beginning in 1929 with "Blindfold" and "Clancy at the Bat" and continuing on through such films as "Yellow Dust," "Bad Lands," "Annie Oakley," "Abe Lincoln in Illinois" and "This Above All." He was perhaps best remembered for his appearances in the Hopalong Cassidy series.

ANDY DEVINE, Squeaky-Voiced TV and Film Star, Dies

ORANGE, Calif., Feb. 19 (AP)—Andy Devine, the squeaky-voiced deputy of television's "Wild Bill Hickok" series, died yesterday in a local hospital, a family spokesman said.

Mr. Devine, who was 71 years old, had suffered from leukemia and periodically required hospital treatment.

Football Saved His Career

by Robert Hanley

Hollywood's transition from silent films to talkies in the late 1920's almost ended Andy Devine's movie career.

He had some success in the silents, but with the film industry's transition, his high-pitched, crackly voice—his ultimate trademark—made casting directors cringe.

But his background as a college football player saved him. One day in late 1930, he went to a Universal studio during casting for "The Spirit of Notre Dame," a football story dedicated to Knute Rockne, the coach at Notre Dame.

Mr. Devine pointed out that he had once been a college football star. That won him a part. His raspy-voiced, comic-tinged performance drew critical acclaim, and he won a long-term contract in 1931.

300 Movies in 25 Years

He was always cast in the same secondary roles—the bulky (300-pound), bumbling sidekick of fast-shooting, flashy cowboys; the misery-loving tramp; the slow-witted jolly man providing comic relief with a squeaky giggle, and a sad-eyed soft touch for con artists.

Film makers' demand for Mr. Devine seemed unsatiated. Each year in the late 1930's and early '40's, he appeared in at least six films, and sometimes as many as nine. By 1950, he once said, he had made about 300 movies in 25 years.

But with all that screen work, he believed that he gained his widest exposure and popularity playing Jingles, the merry buddy of actor Guy Madison, in the "Wild

Bill Hickok" western series on television in the 1950's. Millions of children tuned in weekly to chuckle at Jingles, as their parents had at Mr. Devine's screen characters a generation earlier.

Though his roles were limited, Mr. Devine, always good-humored and content, told interviewers that he "loved every minute" of his career.

He never had an acting lesson. His ability, he said, was traceable to a "lot of Arizona hayseed."

Andrew Devine was born in Flagstaff, Ariz., on Oct. 7, 1905. His father, Tom, ran a hotel there. His mother, Amy, was the daughter of Adm. James Harmon Ward, who was instrumental in founding the United States Naval Academy at Annapolis.

He wasn't born with his distinct voice. It resulted from a childhood mishap when he fell while he had a stick in his mouth. The roof of his mouth and his vocal cords were injured.

On Oct. 28, 1933, his career firmly established, Mr. Devine and Dorothy Irene House, whom he had met on a movie set, were married in Las Vegas. In November 1934, they had a son, Timothy. In January 1939, their other son, Dennis, was born.

The Devines settled in a house in Van Nuys, Calif., started accumulating real estate, and avoided the hectic, highlife of Hollywood, concentrating on raising their sons.

Devoted to His Family

Mr. Devine seemed a devoted father. "I made a deal with my boys years ago," he said in 1957. "If they'd do nothing to embarrass me, I'd do nothing to embarrass them. It's worked out fine."

He seldom ventured away from home for any extended period. Probably the longest period was in the summer of 1957 when—his wealth established from residuals of the Hickok western—he came to the Jones Beach, L.I., Marine Theater to play "Cap'n Andy" in Guy Lombardo's production of the Hammerstein-Kern musical, "Show Boat."

"This is the first time I've ever acted in a play," he said then, "and I'm loving every minute of it."

Surviving are his wife, Dorothy, and sons, Timothy and Dennis.

CLIFF EDWARDS

Cliff (Ukulele Ike) Edwards, 76, singer-actor best remembered for his voice portrayal of Jiminy Cricket in Disney's 1940 animated "Pinocchio," in which he sang "When You Wish Upon A Star," died July 17, 1971 in Los Angeles after a long retirement. To an older generation he was known as Ukulele Ike and was possibly the best-known player of the stringed instrument.

A native of Missouri, he started his show business career in St. Louis saloons, using his trick voice and talent on the ukulele to become a vaudeville headliner. Teamed with pianist Bobby Carleton, who wrote "Ja-Da," Edwards' recording became a smash hit. In George White's "Scandals" in 1936, he replaced Rudy Vallee when the latter had a fight with the producer.

Edwards was also on Broadway in "Lady Be Good," "Sunny" and "Ziegfeld Follies," before going to Hollywood. He introduced "Singin' In The Rain" in the "Hollywood Revue of 1929," his first major film and before his retirement, played in more than 100 films. He was also reprised as the voice of Jiminy Cricket in Disney's moppet tele-series, "The Mickey Mouse Club" and recorded an album, "Ukulele Ike Sings Again" for Disneyland Records.

He was twice married and divorced, to singer Irene Wiley and actress Nancy Dover. Although he had a small income from Disney, which continued paying him for years after he had left their employ, Edwards was almost destitute at the time of death and his burial was paid for by the Actors Fund.

RAYMOND HATTON, Actor, Dead; In First Hollywood Feature Film

'Squaw Man' of '12 Followed by Wallace Beery Movies —Also in Vaudeville

Special to The New York Times

PALMDALE, Calif., Oct. 22—Raymond Hatton, a vaudeville performer and silent-screen actor who appeared in "The Squaw Man," the first feature made in Hollywood, was found dead last evening, apparently of a heart attack. He was 84 years old.

500 Film Appearances

An actor for almost 65 years, Raymond Hatton's long and busy career spanned vaudeville, the legitimate stage, films—close to 500 in all—and television.

Mr. Hatton became stage-struck at the age of 10, when he appeared in a school play in his hometown of Red Oak, Iowa. His father, a Quaker physician, had started him out to study medicine, but the boy liked the limelight so much that he ran away from home to go on the stage.

He appeared in many stage, vaudeville and repertory productions and in 1912 joined the infant film industry in Hollywood, where "The Squaw Man," based on the stage play first performed at The Lambs in New York, was going before the camera of Cecil B. de Mille. Mr. Hatton's last film, completed just before he retired, was based on Truman Capote's fact-based novel "In Cold Blood."

Among the other features Mr. Hatton appeared in were the silent version of "The Hunchback of Notre Dame," starring Lon Chaney, "A Bell of Penance," "Three Wise Fools," "The Top of the World," "The Devil's Cargo," starring Wallace Beery, and "The Big Cage," based on the Clyde Beatty book.

Other films included "Polly of the Circus," in which Marion Davies and Clark Gable played the leads; "Honeymoon Lane," in support of Eddie Dowling; and "Trent's Last Case," in which he was seen as a vicar.

Several films with Wallace Beery made the two actors a team, and later, Mr. Hatton, who was one of the stage-trained performers who made an easy transition to talking pictures, repeated the characterization of the comic sidekick in several films with Hoot Gibson, Harry Carey, Ken Maynard and Tom Mix.

Reviewing a 1928 film, "Partners in Crime," Mordaunt Hall, motion-picture critic of The New York Times, called it "the latest picture with those friendly enemies, Wallace Beery and Raymond Hatton." Mr. Hatton, playing a dual role, drew special commendation for playing "a cocksure, eager reporter and also the dreaded "Knife' Reagan."

Mr. Hatton's appearance in support of Clyde Beatty in "The Big Cage," the story of the animal trainer's life, was one of the few occasions when the veteran actor used a double, in this case Mr. Beatty himself.

The action called for Mr. Hatton, as an old and inebriated trainer, to enter an arena where a tiger leaped upon him. Advance discussion indicated the result might have been disastrous, so Mr. Beatty, made up to resemble Mr. Hatton, staggered into the cage.

The animal recognized him and, as directed, pounced in gently as the cameras whirred.

Film Star 'GABBY' HAYES Dies

HOLLYWOOD (UPI)— George "Gabby" Hayes, the grizzled, cantankerous sidekick of dozens of western movie heroes, died Sunday at the age of 83.

The comic cowboy actor succumbed at St. Joseph Hospital in Burbank at 9:40 a.m. He was admitted to the hospital a week ago for treatment of heart ailment.

Sporting a beard of mousey hue and long hair, Hayes supplied the "durn tootin'" comedy relief in 174 Western motion pictures, including many of the Hopalong Cassidy films and later the Roy Rogers series of musical westerns.

Born a tenderfoot in Wellesville, N.Y., on May 7, 1885, Hayes began appearing in amateur theatrical productions at the age of eight. During his high school summer vacations he played semi-pro baseball with teams in New York and Ohio.

At age 17, Hayes ran away from home to join a stock company and for the next 27 years sang and danced in a burlesque troupe and later on the old Keith and Orpheum vaudeville circuits.

He made his first movie, "Rainbow Man," in which he played a trapeze artist, in 1929. He became an instant success and a year later he grew the beard that was to become his trademark. He once explained to an interviewer how it all began:

"A movie studio owner named Trem Carr saw me in my false beard in my theater act and asked me to grow a real one for the six-day movies he was making with John Wayne and Bob Steele.

"I shaved it only once since then—in 1939, when I had four months off. But my housekeeper saw me without my beard and was scared to death. I looked in the mirror, and it sure scared me too. I never shaved it again."

Harry Sherman, producer of the Hopalong Cassidy movies, signed Hayes to create the role of "Windy Halliday," and subsequently he alternated these roles with similar characterizations in "Smiling Irish Eyes," "Winner Takes All" and later "Mr. Deeds Goes to Town" and "The Plainsman."

Semi-retired since his network television show went off the air in 1953, Hayes lived alone in a 10-unit apartment building which he owned in suburban North Hollywood. His wife, Dorothy, died in 1958 after 43 years of marriage.

STERLING HOLLOWAY, Actor, Voice of Pooh

The Associated Press
Los Angeles

Actor Sterling Holloway, who gave the voice to the cartoon Winnie the Pooh and the snake in "The Jungle Book," has died, his agent said Monday.

Holloway, 87, died Sunday morning at Good Samaritan Hospital, agent Kingsley Colton said.

His acting career began in the silent era with a series of short comedies.

With his distinctive red hair and raspy voice, he prospered with the coming of sound. In the 1930s and '40s playing comic roles in such films as "Gold Diggers of 1933" and "The Beautiful Blonde from Bashful Bend." He often played country bumpkins or delivery boys.

Walt Disney put the voice to good use in a number of cartoons, including "Alice in Wonderland," (as the Cheshire Cat); "Dumbo," (as the stork); "Winnie the Pooh"; "The Aristocats"; and "The Jungle Book."

For the honey-grubbing bear Pooh, Holloway created a sweet and innocent, sing-song voice for several short films.

ARTHUR HUNNICUTT

Arthur Hunnicutt, 68, veteran character actor, died Sept. 27 of cancer at the Motion Picture Country House, in Woodland Hills, California. He had been a resident of the home for the past year.

Most frequently appearing in westerns, Hunnicutt was nominated for a best supporting actor Academy Award in 1952 for Howard Hawks' "The Big Sky." He was also memorable in such pictures as "Broken Arrow," "The Red Badge Of Courage," "Cat Ballou" and "El Dorado."

FUZZY KNIGHT

Fuzzy Knight, 74, western comedian who played the sidekick to many oater stars, died in his sleep Feb. 23, 1976 at Motion Picture Country House, Hollywood, where he and his wife, Patricia, had lived since last June. He had been retired since 1953, after a career which included vaudeville, musicals, revues, stints with name bands and nitery stands.

Born in Fairmont, W. Va., his particular style of delivery and bent for comedy led to his entering showbiz shortly after leaving U. of West Virginia, first heading his own band. After a thorough grounding in vaude and revues, he played the drums for such bandleaders as Irving Aaronson and George Olsen before turning to the screen for a series of shorts for both MGM and Paramount from 1928 to '31.

Paramount rewarded his comicking with his first feature appearance with Mae West in "She Done Him Wrong," in 1932. Thereafter, he was in great demand for both regular features and westerns, and for years he was under contract at such studios as Republic, Universal, RKO, and Grand National.

While occasionally playing a straight dramatic role, Knight was best known for his costarring appearances with such western names as Johnny Mack Brown — with whom he made more than 25 films — Russ Hayden, Tex Ritter and Bob Baker. He always played an awkward, stuttering bumpkin who usually drew a bigger hand with audiences than the top-billed star. In 1940, he was voted one of the top money-making western stars of the year.

In addition to his thesping, he also was a composer and had several songs published.

His wife survives.

PINKY LEE — 85

Pinky Lee, the vaudeville comic who delighted kids with his television shows in the 1950s and '60s, died April 3 in Mission Viejo, CA, of a heart attack.

Though he is best known for "The Pinky Lee Show," telecast from Los Angeles on NBC starting in 1954, Lee's first TV series was a primetime variety show telecast in 1950. A year later with Vivian Blaine and Martha Stewart, he co-hosted "Those Two," a 15 minute musical variety series that ran for a 1 1/2 years.

"The Pinky Lee Show" ran for two years, and was broadcast immediately after "Howdy Doody." On the half-hour show, Lee, in hat and checkered coat, sang, danced and told stories. In 1957 he hosted another children's program, NBC's "Gumby Show," but left the program and NBC several months later having accused the network of losing interest in children's programming.

Born Pincus Leff, Lee was a native of St. Paul, Minn. He began his career in burlesque in the '30s and his comic manner and distinctive lisp brought him recognition in the industry. In 1947, he asked Lloyd's of Long to insure his speech impediment for $50,000.

He is survived by his wife, Bebe; a son, Morgan; and a daughter, Patricia.

(April 3, 1993)

RICHARD ("CHITO") MARTIN

RICHARD ("CHITO") MARTIN, 75, died Sept. 4 of complications from leukemia in Newport Beach, CA. Martin met his wife, gracious leading lady Elaine Riley, when they were both contract players at RKO. From 1947-1952 Dick co-starred with Tim Holt in 29 above average B-westerns as Chito Jose Gonzales Bustamonte Rafferty ('My mother, she is Spanish, my father, he was Irish.'). Before Tim Holt returned from WWII, Dick essayed the Chito character in two westerns with Robert Mitchum ("Nevada," "West of the Pecos") and one with James Warren ("Wanderer of the Wasteland").

FRANK MITCHELL

Frank Mitchell, of the vaudeville team of Mitchell & Durant, died Jan. 21, 1991, in North Hollywood of cardiac arrest.

He headlined with his partner Jack Durant at the London Palladium in 1929 and appeared in two Broadway productions: George White's series of comedy sketches "Scandals" and Earl Carroll's "Vanities."

Following his success in vaudeville, Mitchell appeared in numerous films, beginning in 1934 — some with and some without Durant.

He was in Shirley Temple's first pic, "Stand Up And Cheer," and later co-starred in "She Learned About Sailors," starring Lew Ayres and Alice Faye.

Other credits include "365 Nights In Hollywood," "Music Is Magic," "The Singing Kid," "Sons Of Guns," "Neptune's Daughter," "Anchors Aweigh," "Scaramouche," "Advance To The Rear," "Which Way To The Front" and "Papa's Delicate Condition."

During the 1960s, he had a recurring role in the "Wagon Train" TV series and appeared in many Westerns. For his performances in those films, he received an honorary plaque at the 1990 Golden Boot Awards.

Survived by two daughters, a sister, two grandchildren and three great-grandchildren.

SLIM PICKENS, Cowboy in the Movies, Dies

Associated Press

MODESTO, Calif. — Slim Pickens, the gravel-voiced cowboy actor who rode a nuclear bomb from the belly of a B-52 bomber in the movie "Dr. Strangelove," has died at the age of 64.

Maggie Pickens said Friday that her husband died Thursday night at Evergreen Convalescent Hospital in Modesto, where he had been since Oct. 11.

In August 1982, neurosurgeons removed a brain tumor from him at the University of California at San Francisco.

The former rodeo rider's movie career soared after his role as the drawling, cowboy-style pilot Maj. King Kong in Stanley Kubrick's "Dr. Strangelove" in 1964. In the closing scene of the film, a whooping, hollering Pickens rides an atomic bomb like a horse as it falls to its target.

"After 'Dr. Strangelove,' my salary jumped five times," he said in 1981. "And assistant directors started saying, 'Hey, Slim,' instead of 'Hey, you.'"

"I thought he was terrific," another cowboy, Roy Rogers, said Friday. "I would have been proud to have had him as a sidekick. He was funny and also a good cowboy. He was a heck of a cowboy."

"The movies, God bless 'em, has been real good to me," Pickens once said in an interview. "I'm happier than hell right now, and I only wished I'd given up rodeoing sooner."

"As far as I'm concerned, acting is like a license to steal," he said. "I know of no occupation where with less money invested you can make so much money. Hell, an actor will tell you how hard he's working, but you just go and ask him when was the last time he dug ditches or post holes."

Pickens, who was born Louis Bert Lindley, Jr., in Kingsburg, on June 29, 1919, was a rodeo performer in the 1930s and began his screen career in the 1940s. He chose his stage name during his rodeo riding days when a promoter suggested Slim Pickens, saying, "That's all you'll get in this rodeo."

When directors wanted a stagecoach driven, an outlaw plugged or a cast beefed up, the call often went out to Pickens.

Pickens' movie career started in 1945 when he was paid $25 to appear in the film "Smoky."

Pickens continued his rodeo career after "Smoky" but became an actor full time in 1950, when director William Keighley hired him for an Errol Flynn western, "Rocky Mountain."

"I know I'll never be an actor, but let them find that out for themselves," he said.

Pickens' other film credits include "Pat Garrett and Billy the Kid," "Blazing Saddles," "Rancho Deluxe," "White Line Fever," "Beyond the Poseidon Adventure" and "The Apple Dumpling Gang."

His television credits include "Bonanza," "Gunsmoke," "Ironside," "Mannix," "Name of the Game" and "Alias Smith and Jones."

A funeral was planned for Tuesday.

Jay Silverheels

JAY SILVERHEELS
Film and Television Actor

Born: Six Nations Indian Reservation, Ontario, Canada, ca. 1919
Died: Woodland Hills, California, U.S.A., March 5th, 1980
Birth name: Harold J. Smith

Jay Silverheels, a Mohawk Indian of the Iroquois Nation, and an accomplished sportsman, portrayed American Indians to cinema and television audiences in an acting career that spanned 35 years.

Silverheels was born on the Six Nations Indian Reservation in Ontario, Canada, and was brought up in the traditions of his tribe. He first came to Hollywood in 1933 as a member of a touring professional lacrosse team and later achieved a reputation as a professional boxer, meantime securing occasional bit parts in movies. He appeared with Tyrone Power in Captain from Castille in 1947. During the 1950s, he made a specialty of playing the Bendonkohe Apache Indian chief Geronimo, whom he portrayed in Broken Arrow, Battle at Apache Pass, and Walk the Proud Land.

Silverheels became best known for his television role as Tonto, the faithful Indian sidekick of the Lone Ranger. Both characters were invented by Fran Striker for a radio show of the 1930s. Silverheels played Tonto in all 221 episodes of the television series, which ran from 1949 to 1957 and is still in syndicated reruns. He and Clayton Moore, as the masked man who fired silver bullets, also appeared in two feature films that grew out of the series. Silverheel's other film credits included roles in True Grit, Key Largo, The Will Rogers Story, and The Man Who Loved Cat Dancing.

Marriage to an Italian did nothing to weaken Silverheels' ties to his Indian background. He described his four children as "Indalian." All were raised in the strict Mohawk traditions of honesty, respect for elders, and respect for the natural environment as the universal provider. When his children complained about the inaccurate, often malicious representation of American Indians in films and television, Silverheels responded with his own philosophy: "Let me remind you that the people who write these things don't know the truth. But don't be angry. Remember our Indian proverb: 'Let me never condemn my brother until I have walked sun-up to sun-down in his moccasins.' Be slow to judge; respect the traditions and practices of others. Never be afraid to tell the truth; obey the laws wherever you live; show courtesy to all fellow human beings and tenderness to animals. What has endured is good and will be made better as we move, generation after generation towards

perfection."

In the early 1960s, Silverheels founded the Indian Actors Workshop, in Hollywood. as a means of helping aspiring Indian actors into the profession. In August 1979, he became the first American Indian to have a star set for him in Hollywood's Walk of Fame along Hollywood Boulevard.

After his retirement from the screen, Silverheels continued as an enthusiastic sportsman. In 1974 he obtained a harness racing license and became a familiar figure at tracks across the United States. His death at the Motion Picture and Television Country House in California was caused by complications arising from pneumonia.

AL ST. JOHN, Comic of Westerns, Dies

LYONS, Ga. (AP) — A trouper till the last, Al St. John, the comical Fuzzy Q. Jones of Western movies, died of a heart attack

Monday in the arms of his wife, Flo-Bell Moore.

The 70-year-old St. John was stricken at his motel, as he awaited a personal appearance with his wife, Monday night in nearby Vidalia.

Despite his years, St. John and his wife had made the rounds of U.S. air bases near London in Britain's ice and snow last winter. They also did television appearances from time to time. He made his first movie in 1911.

The St. Johns made their home at their Double F Ranch at Homosassa Springs, Fla.

DUB TAYLOR;
Character Actor

By Myrna Oliver
Times Staff Writer

Dub Taylor, the grizzled character actor who appeared in about 500 Westerns and other films over six decades, including this summer's "Maverick," has died. He was 87.

The veteran actor died Monday night at Westlake Convalescent Hospital, his family said.

The Georgia-born Walter Clarence Taylor II began his career in vaudeville.

He made his film debut in the legendary Frank Capra's 1938 classic "You Can't Take It With You" and never looked back.

"I have just been lucky and I like people," Taylor mused in a 1992 Times interview. "I had one of the greatest directors start me off in the business...I just loved him."

Taylor clearly enjoyed his work but never took himself or the film industry too seriously. "Acting," he once said, "is the most embarrassing business in the world. You never know when you're going to eat."

Although he was an avid hunter who frequently traveled to Mexico, Taylor often said he would never retire. "I can't retire," he said at age 84. "I got too many damn bills."

Often seen as a heavyset cowboy or hillbilly, Taylor portrayed Cannonball, the lovable sidekick of Western hero Bill Elliott in several feature films of the 1940s.

Some of his other memorable roles were Andy Griffith's father in "No Time for Sergeants" in 1968, the father of a gang member in "Bonnie and Clyde" in 1967 and the crotchety 80-year-old grandfather of John Cougar Mellencamp in "Falling From Grace" in 1992.

Taylor was described as "the glorious Dub Taylor" in a Times review of the recent "Maverick," starring Mel Gibson and James Garner and including a gallery of Western character actors.

A widower who lived in Woodland Hills, Taylor is survived by his son, actor Buck Taylor; daughter, Faydean Tharp, and several grandchildren.

CHIEF THUNDERCLOUD, 56

Cherokee Had Acted in Many Movies— Was First Tonto

VENTURA, Calif., Dec. 2, 1955 (UP) — Victor Daniel, a Cherokee Indian who, under the stage name of Chief Thundercloud, was the original Tonto of the "Lone Ranger" radio and film series, died yesterday in Ventura County Hospital at the age of 56.

As Chief Thundercloud he had appeared in more than 100 motion pictures. For the last few years he had been in retirement because of a heart ailment.

Chief Thundercloud appeared in the films "Typhoon" (1940), "Northwest Mounted Police" (1940), "Traveling Saleswoman," "Colt .45," "Davy Crockett, Indian Scout" and "Ambush" (all in 1950).

He toured this city on several occasions in tribal regalia to publicize flights for Transcontinental and Western Airways.

GUY WILKERSON

Guy Wilkerson, 70, vet western character thespian, died of cancer in Hollywood July 15, 1971.

Following a short career on Broadway, Wilkerson came to Hollywood in the early 1920's to play in silents and talkies. His credits numbered over 200 for roles in features and TV since then.

Wife, daughter survive.

Movie Actor CHILL WILLS Dies at 76

ENCINO, Calif. (AP) — Chill Wills, who appeared in hundreds of western movies as the forlorn and loyal sidekick to dashing cowboy heroes, died shortly after returning home from a hospital, a spokeswoman said Saturday. He was 76.

Wills' wife, Novadeen, reported the death Friday night to the Motion Picture and Television Hospital, where he had been receiving treatment for an undisclosed ailment.

Ruth Gray, a hospital spokeswoman, said Wills had been in the hospital for only a few days.

His last performance was for a television special, "Stubby Pringle's Christmas," taped earlier this year and scheduled for airing today on NBC.

Wills appeared in more than 300 movies during a career that spanned more than a half-century and was perhaps best known for his role as Beekeeper, a Tennessee volunteer, in the 1960 movie "The Alamo." He was one of the first stars signed up by John Wayne for the epic $12 million United Artists production.

Wills' famous gravelly voice also was used for the talking mule in the "Francis" movie series.

Chill Theodore Wills was born July 18, 1902 in Seagoville, Texas, son of Robert and Fanny Wills. He was named after a Dr. Childress, the attending physician.

In 1935, Wills tried out during a "talent night" at a nightclub in Hollywood. He sang and told jokes. He signed a six-month contract with RKO.

Wills' other movies included "Boom Town," "Best Foot Forward," "The Harvey Girls," "Raw Deal," "High Lonesome," "Bronco Buster," "City That Never Sleeps," "Timberjack," "Giant," "The Deadly Companions" and "The Cardinal."

He had two television series to his credit, "Frontier Circus" and "The Rounders," as well as a television movie entitled "The Over the Hill Gang Rides Again."

Died on December 15, 1978.

HANK WORDEN, Actor

The Associated Press, Los Angeles

Character actor Hank Worden, whose half-century career included appearances in more than 100 films and in such TV shows as "The Lone Ranger" and "Twin Peaks," has died. He was 91.

Mr. Worden died in his sleep Sunday at his home here.

Mr. Worden began his career in Cecil B. De Mille's "The Plainsman" in 1936 and appeared in Paul Hogan's "Almost An Angel" in 1990.

Perhaps his best-known film role was Mose Harper, the spectral fool in John Ford's classic film, "The Searchers."

He appeared in 15 John Wayne films including "Red River" and "Big Jake." He also acted with Clint Eastwood in "Every Which Way But Loose" and "Bronco Billy."

He made guest appearances on such TV series as "The Lone Ranger" and "Bonanza." He played the decrepit waiter in the quirky TV show "Twin Peaks." His last performance was in the final episode of the short-lived series, "Cop Rock."

Born Norton Earl Worden in Rolfe, Iowa, Mr. Worden grew up on a ranch in Montana.

He attended Stanford University and the University of Nevada, and was a bronco rider.

Mr. Worden was cast frequently as sidekick to Tex Ritter in Westerns.

Services are scheduled for today.

JUDITH ALLEN

B-Western leading lady, JUDITH ALLEN, 85, died October 5, of congestive heart failure in Yucca Valley, Ca. For her last 23 years Allen was active in a religious community near Joshua Tree, CA. The New York born actress was on screen from 1933, co-starring with Bing Crosby, W. C. Fields, Shirley Temple, Richard Arlen and others. Her first B-Western was Zane Grey's "The Thundering Herd" w/Randolph Scott. She appeared in two with Gene Autry, "Boots and Saddles" and "Git Along, Little Dogies" as well as "It Happened Out West" w/ Paul Kelly and "Texas Trail" w/ William Boyd. Off screen for ten years ('40-'50), she returned to do two at Lippert w/Don Barry, "Train To Tombstone" and "I Shot Billy The Kid".

LINA BASQUETTE; Star of Silent Movies

Wednesday, October 5, 1994

Lina Basquette, the raven-haired dancer and actress best remembered as the leading lady in Cecil B. DeMille's final silent film "The Godless Girl," has died. She was 87.

She died Friday at her home in Wheeling, W.V., from lymphoma, her grandson, Michael Hiatt, said Tuesday in Los Angeles.

After "The Godless Girl" in 1929, Miss Basquette's on-screen popularity waned. She appeared in several Buck Jones and Hoot Gibson Westerns in the 1930s. Her only recent performance was as a grandmother in a 1991 independent film, "Paradise Park."

MADGE BELLAMY

MADGE BELLAMY/Margaret Philpott died January 29, 1990, age was variously reported between 89 and 96. She was a leading silent screen actress who worked for some of the leading directors of the era and continued on in the sound period until her retirement in 1935. Her final public appearance was November 1989 at Gene Autry's Western Heritage Museum where she spoke in conjunction with a screening of THE IRON HORSE. She appeared with Jack Holt in THE CALL OF THE NORTH (1921), THE IRON HORSE, with George O'Brien (1924) and with Buck Jones in LAZYBONES (1925). IN 1933, she again appeared with Buck Jones, in the Universal serial, GORDON OF GHOST CITY.

ing Pioneer" w/Jack Holt, "Local Badman" w/ Hoot Gibson, "Heritage of the Desert" and "Wild Horse Mesa" w/Randolph Scott, and "Fighting Mad" w/James Newill. Sister Polly Ann Young died earlier this year.

LUCILE BROWNE

Lucile Browne Flavin, 69, film actress who played in serials during the 1930s, died May 10, in Los Angeles. Her husband, also deceased, was the actor, James Flavin. A son survives.

SALLY BLANE

Sally Blane, 87, the older sister of Loretta Young, who appeared in nearly 80 films from 1917-1955, died August 27 in Palm Springs, CA. The Salida, CO, born actress made her screen debut with a small bit in Jack Mulhall's "Sirens of the Sea" ('17). She soon had roles in several of the Collegians shorts at Universal, billed as Betty Jean Young. Moving into features in 1927 she was billed as Sally Blane. Around 1937 she married director Norman Foster, curtailing her screen career by '39 but coming out of retirement in '55 to appear in "A Bullet For Joey." Her westerns are: "Shootin' Irons" w/Jack Luden, "A Horseman of the Plains," "King Cowboy" and "Outlawed" w/Tom Mix, "Vanish-

RENO BROWNE
(Josephine Ruth Clarke)

Reno native Josephine Ruth Clarke, 67, died Wednesday at Physicians Hospital for Extended Care

She was born April 20, 1924, to John Robb and Moss M. Edwards Clarke.

Reno's first rodeo queen in 1945, Mrs. Clarke was known in Hollywood as "Reno Browne" in the late 1940s when she was cast in Western movies with stars such as Johnny Mack Brown, Smiley Burnette, William Boyd, Sunset Carson, Roy Rogers, Dale Evans, and Alfred "Lash" LaRue, King of the Bullwhip, whom she later mar-

Mrs. Clarke was featured in Western Screen magazines as the "Golden Girl," on her champion palomino stallion, Major, when she traveled throughout the country on behalf of Monogram Studios and owned a hotel and restaurant.

After the death of her mother, she retired from Hollywood and returned to Reno. She continued to travel throughout the World and was presented to the king and queen of England in 1949 and was blessed by Pope John Paul II in Rome in 1984. She appeared on the Johnny Carson Show and also had a comic book series written about her.

She was a member of Daughters of the American Revolution, Screen Actors Guild, Actors Equity Association and Renown Toastmistress of Region 8.

Her father was a longtime Reno lawyer and served as a lieutenant colonel on the staffs of three Nevada governors, James G. Scrugham, Fred B. Balzar and Morey Griswold.

Surviving is a stepsister, Clair G. Egan of Grosse Pointe, Mich.

A memorial service is scheduled for 10 a.m. Monday at Mountain View Cemetery Chapel, with interment in the family plot at the cemetery.

A memorial is being established with the Cancer Research Institute, 77 Pringle Way, Reno 89502.

CAROLINA COTTON

Pretty and peppy Carolina Cotton died of cancer on June 10, 1997. She attended many film conventions around the country and was a big favorite with the fans. She had a quick wit, pleasing personality and enjoyed joking and talking to the fans, and demonstrating her remarkable yodeling skills. She developed a personal relationship with many of the fans and often sent them post cards from her travels abroad.

An interesting thing happened to Carolina on one of these trips. She stopped in one city (I think she told me the country was Switzerland), where the locals were holding a yodeling contest. Carolina promptly entered the contest...and she won! She said she did not think it fair to deprive a local from winning and relinquished her trophy to the runner-up.

Carolina Cotton was born Helen Hagstrom in Cash, Arkansas, on October 20, 1933 {Although Carolina claimed she was born in 1933, it must be obvious to anyone who has seen her in the 1945 Charles Starrett film, "Outlaws of the Prairie," that she was certainly more than 12 years old (She looked 18-20). Carolina was so secretive about her age that even her own daughter did not know how old she was. I would guess she was born in 1925-27.}.

Her family later relocated to California where young Helen took dancing and singing lessons. When she went to work for singer/bandleader Dude Martin, he decided the name Helen Hagstrom was not right for his new yodeling teenager and changed her name to Carolina.

Her first film was 1944 and titled "Sing, Neighbor, Sing" for Republic Pictures and featured several other singers including Roy Acuff. Carolina only had a brief yodeling song in the picture. Her next role was for Universal in "Singing Sheriff" with Bob Crosby and Spade Cooley, and again she only yodeled one song. She then jumped over to PRC and made "I'm From Arkansas" starring Slim Summerfield.

In 1945 Carolina signed a contract with Columbia and the rest of her films were with that studio, with the exception of two features. She appeared in three pictures with Charles Starrett, three with Ken Curtis, two with Gene Autry, two with Eddy Arnold and one with Roy Acuff. Her two non-Columbia pictures were a Warner Brothers short with Spade Cooley and a Ken Curtis films for Astor.

During her movie career she continued to sing, record and make personal appearances. She toured with some of the biggest names in the music industry including the Sons of the Pioneers, Eddy Arnold, and Bob Wills and the Texas Play Boys. She later became one of the first female disc jockeys and her program was broadcast over the Armed Forces Radio Network making her very popular with the GI's. Carolina even authored a regular column in a Country and Western publication for a while.

After working in the entertainment field for several years, Carolina decided to become a teacher and went on to receive a master's degree in education and taught fourth grade for many years in Bakersfield, California.

GAIL DAVIS; Starred as 'Annie Oakley' on TV

From Staff and Wire Reports

Actress Gail Davis, best known for her role as a gun-toting, pigtailed rancher in the popular 1950s television series "Annie Oakley," has died of cancer. She was 71.

Davis died Saturday at St. Joseph Medical Center in Burbank. Her daughter, Terrie Manning, was with her at her death.

A skilled rider and a crack shot, Davis appeared in several Gene Autry westerns and did most of her own stunt work. Autry created the syndicated "Annie Oakley" TV series for Davis in 1953, a children's western set in the town of Diablo. The show, the first western to star a woman, ran for four years and continued on into the '60s in reruns.

Davis stayed with Autry's personal appearance tours for many years before retiring. In 1994 she received a "Golden Boot" award for her work in westerns.

Born in McGhee, Ark., Davis at age 2 was named most beautiful baby in Arkansas. She later attended the University of Texas at Austin, where she studied drama and dance and married fellow student Bob Davis. They were divorced in 1952, six months after the birth of their daughter.

Davis later married auto dealer Carl Guerriero, who died in 1982. She is survived by her daughter, Terrie, of Irving, Texas.

Funeral arrangements at Forest Lawn Hollywood Hills were pending.

SHIRLEY DEANE

Shirley Deane (26 April 1983): She was in PRAIRIE MOON, with Gene Autry.

Penny Edwards

Pretty Penny Edwards, 70, died of lung cancer August 26 at her daughter's home in Friendswood, Texas. Born Millicent Edwards on August 24, 1928, in Jackson Heights, New York, Penny worked on Broadway at age 15 in the Ziegfield Follies. Edwards appeared in B-Westerns with Roy Rogers, Rex Allen and Allan Lane. (1998)

CAROL FORMAN

'The Queen of Serial Villainesses', CAROL FORMAN, 78 died July 9 at a Burbank, CA, hospital of natural causes. Forman, born in Epps, AL, signed with RKO in '46 and appeared in features, shorts and three westerns: "Code of the West" w/James Warren, "Under the Tonto Rim" and "Brothers In the Saddle" w/Tim Holt. She forever became "The Black Widow" at Republic in '47 and made three other serials at Columbia... "Brick Bradford," "Superman" (as the Spider Lady) and "Blackhawk" and another for Republic, "Federal Agents VS Underworld Inc." Also has a small role in "Oh, Susanna" w/Rod Cameron and was in 3 "Cisco Kid" TVers. Forman said at the '84 Memphis Film Fest, "I liked being the heavy. Not everyone can be as convincing as I am. I'd think of all the mean and ugly things I could when I was Sombra or the Spider Lady."

JANE FRAZEE

JANE FRAZEE/Mary Jane Frehse (6th Sepember 1985, age 67) Known as the Queen of the B Musicals, she began with her sister as the singing-dancing Frazee Sisters, appearing in clubs, theatres, on radio in musical shorts. Going it alone, she built a career in low-budget musicals for Columbia, Universal and Republic. At Columbia, during 1944 she worked with Charles Starrett in COWBOY CANTEEN and with "Red River Dave" McEnery in SWING IN THE SADDLE. At Republic, she certainly was the most talented of the Roy Rogers heroines, appearing with him in SPRINGTIME IN THE SIERRAS, ON THE OLD SPANISH TRAIL, THE GAY RANCHERO, UNDER CALIFORNIA STARS and GRAND CANYON TRAIL. Her last Western was LAST OF THE WILD HORSES (Screen Guild, 1948) with James Ellison. During 1954/55 she portrayed the wife of George O'Hanlon in the successful Joe McDoakes 2-reel comedies made by Warner Bros. Active in early television, she appeared in DEATH VALLEY DAYS and other shows before leaving the screen to become a successful real estate agent.

JUNE GALE

Hoot Gibson's leading lady in three mid '30s pictures, JUNE GALE, 78, died of pneumonia Nov. 13 in an L.A. hospital. One of the four singing Gale sisters (actually two sets of twins), June was married to Oscar Levant from 1939 until his death in '72. She supported Hoot in "Swifty," "Rainbow's End" and "Riding Avenger" as well as Ken Maynard in "Heroes of the Range."

FRANCES GIFFORD

FRANCES GIFFORD, 72, Republic serial's "Jungle Girl," died Jan. 22 of emphysema. Born Mary Frances Gifford in Long Beach, CA, she broke into films right after high school in 1937. In 1948 she was seriously hurt in a traffic accident and appeared in only two more movies. "Jungle Girl" director William Witney told me, "Everybody loved her. She could do everything...run, jump, ride, fight. She did it all beautifully." Gifford was also in "Border Vigilantes" with William Boyd, "American Empire" with Richard Dix and "Tarzan Triumphs."

FRANCES GRANT

FRANCES GRANT (22 Feb. 1982): She made RED RIVER VALLEY and OH, SUSANNA! with Gene Autry, and THUNDER MOUNTAIN, with George O'Brien.

JULIE HAYDON

Julie Haydon, 84, who achieved long lasting fame on Broadway in the role of the crippled Laura in Tennessee Williams' "The Glass Menagerie" ('45), died December 24 in La Crosse, WI, of abdominal cancer.

Haydon began her career in MGM's "Great Meadow" ('31) w/ Johnny Mack Brown. She was in three early RKO Tom Keene B's, "Come On Danger," "Son of the Border" and "Scarlet River" (as herself—a guest star in this behind the movie scenes western). Also

in "The Conquerors" with Richard Dix. It's not widely known, but Haydon supplied Fay Wray's horrifying scream in "King Kong."

LINDA HAYES

LINDA HAYES (12/19/95, age 73, pneumonia): Appeared with Roy Rogers in three Westerns. Mother of actress Cathy Lee Crosby.

RUTH HILL

Ruth Hill, 65, daughter of late cowboy star Tom Mix, died Sept. 21, 1977 in Corpus Christi, Texas.

JENNIFER HOLT

Jennifer Holt, 76, popular, gorgeous, talented Western heroine of 38 '40s B-Westerns died Sept. 21 of lung cancer at her home in Sherbourne, Dorset, England. Jennifer built her own special place for over seven years in B-Westerns, never trading on the fame of her famous father, Jack, or brother, Tim. Leading lady Elaine Riley told us, "I met her through her brother. From what I know of her, she was a beautiful, charming, sophisticated woman and certainly loved Tim. She was very nice to

Jennifer Holt

Dick (Elaine's late husband, Richard Martin). Dick was very impressed with her." Born Nov. 10, 1920, Jennifer was sent off to Belgium at seven to be raised by a nanny when her parents were undergoing rough times in their marriage, which eventually led to a divorce. She returned to California in 1930, but her young years continued to be unhappy ones as she lived at times with one parent or another and was put in various schools in the U.S. and Chile. Graduating from a girls school in 1939 (at 19), she enrolled in drama classes under Maria Ouspenskaya and appeared in several plays in New Hampshire and New York. A meeting with Jerry Colonna's agent led to her first film role, "Stick To Your Guns" (41') with Hopalong Cassidy where she was billed as Jacqueline Holt, always a source of irritation to Jennifer. A screen test led to a two year contract at Universal, where she made

her best Westerns opposite Johnny Mack Brown and Tex Ritter as well as a serial, "Adventures of the Flying Cadets." She made another serial in 1946 for Columbia, "Hop Harrigan," opposite one of her husbands, William Bakewell. Leaving Universal, she freelanced at Monogram, PRC, Columbia and even Universal until 1948. During this time she was often heard as a singer on CBS' "Hollywood Barn Dance." In the late '40s Jennifer went to Chicago and found lucrative employment in industrial films being lensed there. She also starred in the children's TV series, "Adventures of Uncle Mistletoe and Count Judy" for Marshall Field in Chicago and then "Panhandle Pete and Jennifer" for ABC, then NBC. In 1962 Jennifer originated "Championship Debate" on NBC, altho she did not appear on the show. In the '70s, she became an interior designer and also one of the most popular guests at Western film festivals. Jennifer's love life was never as successful as her careers, she was in her 9th marriage at the time of her death.

CAROL HUGHES

CAROL HUGHES (August 8, 1996, age 75): One-time leading lady to James Newill, Gene Autry, Roy Rogers, and Tim Holt. Was in two serials: FLASH GORDON CONQUERS THE UNIVERSE, wherein replacing the original Jean Rogers as Dale Arden, and JUNGLE RAIDERS.

KAY HUGHES

B-Western and serial leading lady Kay Hughes, 84, died April 4 in Palm Springs, California. She had suffered with heart problems for some time. Hughes worked in three serials and appeared in Westerns with Gene Autry, Charles Starrett, Buster Crabbe, The Three Mesquiteers, and The Texas Rangers. (1998)

Mary Beth Hughes

MARY BETH HUGHES

Mary Beth Hughes, 75, died August 17 in L.A. After a career at MGM and Fox she became the epitome of the blonde babe B-movie actress. When Mary Beth's film career ended in the late '50s, she developed a night club act, playing electric bass and singing. Mary Beth's westerns are: "Lucky Cisco Kid," "Ride On Vaquero," "Cowboy and The Blonde," "Ox Bow Incident," "Timber Queen," "Return Of Wildfire," "Last Of The Wild Horses," "Rimfire," "El Paso," "Riders In The Sky," "Square Dance Jubilee," "Rockin' In The Rockies," "Passage West" and "Gun Battle at Monterey." Also in Charlie Chan, Joe Palooka, Bowery Boys, Michael Shayne and Ritz Brothers films. On TV: "Frontier Doctor," "Deputy," "Colt .45," "Buckskin," "Rin Tin Tin," "Wanted Dead or Alive" and "Rawhide."

ELEANOR HUNT

Eleanor Hunt (12 June 1981, age 71): Played leads in a number of independent programmers of the thirties, and once married to Western star Rex Lease.

MARY LEE

Mary Lee, 71, Republic's only

Mary Lee

CARYL LINCOLN

Caryl Lincoln (20 Feb. 1983, age 74): She appeared opposite Tom Mix in HELLO, CHEYENNE, Bob Steele in THE LAND OF MISSING MEN and Tom Tyler in THE MAN FROM NEW MEXICO. Married to the brother of Barbara Stanwyck, Lincoln later became a character actress.

BETTY MACK / Idalene Thurber

teen star, died June 6 in the Agoura Hills, CA, area. The Illinois born talent had been a band singer with Ted Weems orchestra and was only 15 in 1939 when she began her co-starring duties with Gene Autry. Usually known as Patsy on screen, she was in nine Autry westerns, "South of the Border," "Carolina Moon," "Gaucho Serenade," "Melody Ranch," "Rancho Grande," "Ride Tenderfoot Ride," "Back in the Saddle," "Ridin' On a Rainbow," and "The Singing Hill." She then co-starred w/Roy Rogers in two "Cowboy and the Senorita" and "Song of Nevada," as well as the '41 short, "Meet Roy Rogers," before leaving show business. For many years she worked with the S. California Good Sam Club.

BETTY MACK / Idalene Thurber (November 5, 1980; age 79): Entered films after some years in musical comedy. She was a popular leading lady in minor Westerns but is perhaps best remembered as Charley Chase's leading lady in many of his Hal Roach/MGM two-reel comedies, which gave her an opportunity to sing on screen. Some of her Westerns: PARTNERS OF THE TRAIL, GOD'S COUNTRY AND THE MAN and GALLOPING THRU (all Tom Tyler); LAW OF THE RIO GRANDE and HEADIN' FOR TROUBLE (both Bob Custer); THE RECKLESS BUCKAROO (Bill Cody); OUTLAW RULE (Reb Russell); and TOLL OF THE DESERT (Fred Kohler, Jr.).

PATRICIA "PATTI" McCARTHY

PATRICIA "Patti" McCAR-THY (July 7, 1985; age 64): A minor leading lady in Westerns, she worked with Buster Crabbe, James Newill and Charles Starrett. Prior to her brief screen career, she had been a dancer/singer in clubs and theatres.

CHRISTINE McINTYRE

Christine McIntyre (July 8, 1984): A minor leading lady in 40s Westerns, she appeared with Johnny Mack Brown and Buck Jones, amongst others. Possibly her best work was done in Columbia 2-reel comedies where she often worked with The Three Stooges.

WANDA McKAY

Wanda McKay, 80, co-star of several early 40's B-westerns, died April 11, in L.A. of cancer. The Fort Worth, TX, native (born Dorothy Quack-enbush) won the title of "Miss American Aviation" in 1938, which sent her off to Holly-wood and a one year Paramount contract. Undistinguished in several roles there, she began appearing in Westerns.

GERTRUDE MESSINGER

GERTRUDE MESSINGER (November 8, 1995; age 84): Former child actress, later in Westerns with Bob Steele, Lane Chandler, Gene Autry, Bill Cody, and Harry Carey.

PATSY MONTANA

She was born Ruby Blevins on October 30, 1914 in Hot Springs, AR and became the first woman in country music to have a million-selling record when "I Want To Be A Cowboy's Sweetheart" was released in 1935. Her wonderful yodeling added tremendously to the song. Patsy wrote most of her own material, including "Sweet-heart"—because women were rare in country music then, and men wrote most of the songs for men.

Patsy began her early career with silent film cowboy star Monte Montana (no relation), and later appeared on the National Barn Dance radio show (1934-52). She recorded for ARC, Decca and RCA for many years before leaving them and Chicago for the west coast in 1952. Patsy continued to record and perform whenever possible almost until her death—she died with bookings in Texas and Arizona—and had made more than 8,000 personal appearances. She received the Pioneer Award from the Academy of Country Music.

Patsy's irrepressible attitude, unrivaled spunk and spirit have influenced many female artists who came after her. Patsy said that when she started, there were no girls in country music. One of the important things Patsy did for women in country music was insisting on being treated equal. When her employer wanted to pay her half as much as he was paying the boys, she insisted on equal pay and got it!

At one point in her career, Patsy and her two daughters toured as the Patsy Montana Trio.

Patsy died knowing she had been nominated for the Country Music Hall of Fame, and it's sad that she was never able to take her place there during her lifetime. It was the one jewel that was missing from her cowboy hat!

At the private memorial service, her husband of 61 years, Paul, said "even though she was not a superstar by today's standards, these so-called superstars will never reach her magnitude and never have the kind of fans she had." She did many things to open doors for women in country music, many of them unrecognized. Patsy never stopped doing what she loved most—making music.

MARIAN NIXON

MARIAN NIXON (Feb. 18, 1983): She began her long career in silent films and played in Westerns with both Tom Mix and Buck Jones at Fox Films and with Hoot Gibson at Universal.

NELL O'DAY

Nell O'Day, 79, Broadway star and dancer who went on to work in Westerns with Johnny Mack Brown, died Jan. 3 in Los Angeles of cardiac arrest.

She started out as a child dancer, and later teamed with the Tommy Atkins Sextet. She worked in east coast theaters, then went on tour with the "Laces And Graces" revue that opened at Paramount theaters around the country.

She worked in several other revues and appeared in a series of Westerns starring Brown.

Her play, "The Bride of Demark Hill" (co-written with Lawrence Williams) was produced in London, Australia and New Zealand.

SHIRLEY PATTERSON

Shirley Patterson, 72, B-western leading lady to Bill Elliott, Tex Ritter, Eddie Dean, Johnny Mack Brown, Charles Starrett and Russell Hayden, died April 3 of cancer in Ft. Lauderdale, FL.

SALLY PAYNE

The Washington Post
May 15, 1999

Sally Payne Kelly, 85, an actress who appeared in a series of 1940s Westerns with Roy Rogers and Gene Autry before illustrating a series of "Small Star" children's books, including "Neighbors," died May 8 in Los Angeles. The cause of death was not reported.

Originally known as the "Sunshine Girl" of artists' models, Sally Payne came to Hollywood under contract to appear in Republic Studios cowboy films. She made her debut in a bit part as a tourist in the 1934 film "Hollywood Hobbies." By 1940, before moving into a series of westerns, she had

appeared as a maid in "No, No, Nanette" and as Lucy Endover in "La Conga Nights."

LUCILLE POWERS

Lucille Powers (11 Sept. 1981, age 69): A charming leading lady in independent programmers of the thirties, she appeared with Tom Mix in THE TEXAS BAD MAN.

MARJORIE REYNOLDS

MARJORIE REYNOLDS/ Mar-jorie Goodspeed (February 1, 1997, age 79, heart failure): Leading lady in B-Westerns and programmers who became a leading lady for Bing Crosby in HOLIDAY INN and later, on TV, became the

134

wife of William Bendix in the comedy series, LIFE OF RILEY. In Westerns she worked with Bob Baker, George O'Brien, Tex Ritter, Buck Jones, Jack Randall, Roy Rogers, and Tim Holt. On television she guested on TALES OF WELLS FARGO, WHISPERING SMITH and LARAMIE.

OF THE DUANES and RIDERS OF THE PURPLE SAGE (both with George Montgomery), SIOUX CITY SUE and BLAZING SUN (both with Gene Autry). She was in two serials, THE LONE RANGER and DICK TRACY RETURNS. She was active in television until her retirement from the business.

LYNNE ROBERTS
(Theda Mae Roberts)

LYNNE ROBERTS/Theda Mae Roberts (April 4, 1978, age 59): Vivacious leading lady of many Westerns and second features, she died of intra-cranial hemorrhage. As Mary Hart she co-starred with Roy Rogers in six of the excellent frontier period Westerns produced by Republic: COME ON RANGERS, SHINE ON HARVEST MOON, ROUGH RIDERS' ROUNDUP, FRONTIER PONY EXPRESS, SOUTHWARD HO! and IN OLD CALIENTE. Earlier, as Lynne Roberts, she had appeared with Roy in BILLY THE KID RETURNS and later in EYES OF TEXAS with him. Reverting back to Lynne Roberts she continued to appear in Westerns, including HEART OF THE ROCKIES and CALL THE MESQUITEERS (both Three Mesquiteers), ROMANCE OF THE RIO GRANDE and RIDE ON, VAQUERO (both with Cesar Romero), THE LAST

BILLIE SEWARD

Billie Seward (20 March 1983): She was Tim McCoy's favorite leading lady, appearing with him first at Columbia, and later in Excelsior Pictures.

LOUISE STANLEY

Louise Stanley (28 Dec. 1982): She worked with Bob Steele and Johnny Mack Brown and appeared in several films with Jack Randall, to whom she was once wed.

LINDA STIRLING; Star of '40s Adventure Film Serials

by Myrna Oliver
Times **Staff Writer**

Linda Stirling, who was known as "the Serial Queen" for her stardom in the weekly cliffhanger adventure shorts that enticed young moviegoers to theaters in the 1940s and early 1950s, has died. She was 75.

Stirling, known in later years as Linda Nibley, died July 20 of cancer at her home in Studio City, her fan club announced this week.

Born in Long Beach, Stirling started acting in summer stock when she was 15. During her years of drama classes, the auburn beauty with classic features became a photographer's model, appearing in several national magazines.

She was signed by Republic Pictures in 1944 to make such serial fare as "The Tiger Woman" and "Zorro's Black Whip."

Stirling appeared in two dozen westerns and other feature films as well as the serials. Among her credits were "The San Antonio Kid," "The Sheriff of Sundown," "Vigilantes of Dodge City," "The Cherokee Flash," "The Sheriff of Cimarron," "Topeka Terror," "The Mysterious Mr. Valentine" and "The Invisible Informer."

Her favorite work, she recently said in a newsletter to her fans, was "The Tiger Woman" serial.

"Even though I didn't know what I was doing half the time," she said, "the stuntmen were always so helpful and full of fun, they made the long hours and grueling pace go by quickly."

Stirling had small roles on television and acted at the Pasadena Playhouse during the 1950s and '60s, but generally aimed toward a new career in teaching.

After earning bachelor's and master's degrees from UCLA, she taught English and literature at Glendale College for 27 years. In 1990, she earned the Distinguished Faculty Award for outstanding teaching.

In her retirement years, Stirling was active in the Group Repertory Theater in North Hollywood.

Her husband of 44 years, writer and producer A. Sloan Nibley, died in 1990. Stirling is survived by two sons, Christopher and Tim Nibley; her mother, Mary Weiss; and her sister, Alice Ogden.

The family has asked that any memorial donations be made to the Linda Stirling Nibley Memorial Scholarship Fund at Glendale College, 1500 N. Verdugo Road, Glendale, CA 91208.

JUNE STOREY, Gene Autry's Leading Lady, Dies

JUNE STOREY, singing cowboy Gene Autry's leading lady in ten movies, died of cancer December 18, 1991, at Vista, California. Her last public appearance was at the Silver Boot Awards, Knoxville, Tennessee, on April 25-27, 1991.

Born Mary June Storey in Toronto, Ontario, Canada, on April 20, 1918, Storey was a graduate of Laguna Beach High School in June 1936 after her family traveled West in 1930.

Briefly a photographer's model, Storey was signed by Fox in 1936 and appeared in feature roles in Girls Dormitory, In Old Chicago, Island in the Sky and The Snake Pit.

In 1938 she was signed to a long term contract by Republic Pictures, and became Gene Autry's leading lady in ten of his best known movies, South of the Border, Blue Montana Skies, In Old Monterey, Rancho Grande, Home on the Prairie, Colorado Sunset, Carolina Moon, Gaucho Serenade, Mountain Rhythm and Ride Tenderfoot Ride. At the same time she was loaned to Universal for a featured role in the Deanna Durbin smash First Love.

When Gene Autry interrupted his picture work to enlist in World War II, Storey worked at Columbia in various films including musical westerns with the Hoosier Hot Shots and features like The Lone Wolf Takes a Chance.

Widely active in youth work through the Grace Presbyterian Church, Vista, California, Storey in recent years accepted invitations to Western Memorabilia Festivals where thousands of fans crowded around her for autographs.

Storey is survived by her husband, Lincoln Clark of Vista, her sister, Maxine Storey Dougan of San Juan Capistrano, her son Eric and daughter Marina of Florence, Oregon, and three grandchildren.

The June Clark Memorial Fund for youth work at Grace Presbyterian Church continues her activities.

ALINE TOWNE

Aline Towne, 66, Republic's last 'Serial Queen,' died February 2, 1996. The former beauty queen at the Universities of Wisconsin and Iowa (where she graduated with honors) won a CHICAGO DAILY NEWS personality/beauty contest over 1,400 contestants which brought her to the attention of MGM in 1948, essayed bit roles in "Kissing Bandit" and others.

ROSA TURICH

Noted character actress ROSA TURICH, 95, died Nov. 20 in Santa Ana, CA, following two strokes. The Tucson, AZ, born actress moved to California with her family and married Filipe (Felipe) Turich in 1921. Billed as Fillipin y Rosita they had a comedy act for Spanish language audiences in L.A. for years before becoming screen actors in the late '30s. Felipe, also a veteran of many B-Westerns, died in 1992.

JOAN VALERIE

Joan Valerie (30 Jan. 1983): As Helen Valkis, she made Westerns with Gene Autry and Dick Foran.

LOIS WILDE

Lois Wilde, 87, who had a busy two-year period in B-westerns and serials from 1936-'38, died February 16, 1995, in Attleboro, MA. Wilde was a member of the Ziegfeld Follies as a teenager and did stage work in the East as well as modeling.

LOIS WILSON, Actress of Stage, Television and Silent-Film Era

RENO, March 9, 1988 (AP) — Lois Wilson, an actress who appeared in more than 100 early films including the 1923 Western epic "The Covered Wagon," died of pneumonia on March 3 at Riverside Hospital for Skilled Care. She was 93 years old.

Miss Wilson sought fame in Hollywood after winning a 1915 statewide beauty contest in her native Alabama. After her arrival in Hollywood, she landed a small part in "The dumb Girl of Portici," which starred the ballerina Anna Pavlova. She went on to act in more than 100 silent and sound films over the next 33 years.

Her best-known portrayals included Molly Wingate in "The Covered Wagon" and Daisy Buchanan in the 1926 version of "The Great Gatsby." She acted op-

138

posite such leading men as Rudolph Valentino and John Gilbert.

After retiring from motion pictures in 1941 — except for a bit part in the 1949 comedy "The Girl From Jones Beach," starring Ronald Reagan — Miss Wilson turned to the Broadway stage and eventually television.

"The Guilding Light" and "The Edge of Night" were among the network soap operas in which she played featured character roles.

Although she never married, Miss Wilson was once described as cultivating a screen image of "the soft, marrying kind of woman." Selected in 1924 by Paramount to represent the motion-picture industry at the British Empire Exposition, Miss Wilson was termed "a typical example of the American girl in character, culture and beauty."

Miss Wilson was buried Monday at Forest Lawn Memorial Park in Glendale, Calif., after a service at the Church of the Good Shepherd in Beverly Hills.

JOAN WOODBURY

Joan Woodbury, 73, sultry star of dozens of low-budget action films in the 1930s and '40s, died Feb. 22 in Desert Hot Springs, Calif., of respiratory failure.

Joan Woodbury

Woodbury retired from film 25 years ago but soon after founded the Valley Players Guild in Palm Springs. She worked on more than 120 productions there over the years with her husband Ray Mitchell.

Films include "Eagle's Brood" in 1935 and "Anthony Adverse" the following year. She played saloon girls and otherwise hardened women in films such as "Crashing Hollywood," "Algiers," "King Of The Zombies," "Confessions Of Boston Blackie" and "The Arnelo Affair."

In 1945 she had the title role in a 13-part serialization of the "Brenda Starr" comic strip.

She appeared in "The Ten Commandments" in 1956 and "The Time Travelers," her last film, in 1964.

Raised in a convent in San Francisco, Woodbury moved to Los Angeles during the Depression. She danced in Mexican restaurants there and in Tijuana, sometimes with Rita Cansino, who later became Rita Hayworth.

She was married to actor and radio personality Ray Mitchell for 25 years. Previously, she was married to British film star Henry Wilcoxon, with whom she had three children.

Last year, the Desert Theater League presented her with its first lifetime achievement award.

POLLY ANN YOUNG

POLLY ANN YOUNG (January 14, 1997, age 88): Elder sister of Loretta Young she made Westerns with George O'Brien, Kermit

Polly Ann Young

Maynard, John Wayne, and Buck Jones. With Jones, she appeared in THE CRIMSON TRAIL, arguably the best of his Universal films, none of which were outstanding. She retired in 1941.

HEAVIES
AND
HELPERS

ROY ACUFF,
Opry Veteran

The Associated Press,
Nashville, Tenn.

Roy Acuff was a gentleman showman and flamboyant patriarch who earned the title, "The King of Country Music," during 54 years of zesty singing and fiddling on the Grand Ole Opry.

Mr. Acuff, known for such twangy tunes as "Wabash Cannonball" and "The Great Speckled Bird," died at Baptist Hospital early Monday of congestive heart failure. He was 89.

Before Mr. Acuff entered the hospital Oct. 30, he sang on the Opry just about every weekend with full-throated verve.

During commercial breaks, he did yo-yo tricks and balanced his ever-present fiddle upright on the bridge of his nose.

He was a gracious entertainer who always kept his dressing room door open backstage at the Opry where he warmly greeted visitors and swapped jokes.

Country singer George Jones recalled climbing into his mother's bed and asking her to be sure to wake him when it was Mr. Acuff's turn to sing on the Opry broadcast.

"When I came to the Opry for the first time in '56, he was the most kind, gently man I'd ever met."

President-elect Bill Clinton said he listened to Mr. Acuff and his band, the Smoky Mountain Boys, playing on Opry broadcasts every Friday and Saturday night of his youth.

The Opry won't be the same "with the passing of the man who just 'rared back and sang it,' "Clinton said.

President Bush, a country music fan, said Mr. Acuff leaves behind "a touch of the American dream."

In one of Mr. Acuff's final public appearances, the ailing star was helped to a Nashville stage Sept. 29 for a campaign rally for Bush.

The once robust star welcomed the audience in a weak voice, but left the singing to other performers while he relished his role as industry ambassador and father figure.

In a 1983 interview, he recalled that his singing style in the 1930s was new to country music: "I reared back and sang it. I did it like I was going for the cows in Union County."

In the 1970s and 1980s, Mr. Acuff was a regular on the TV show "Hee Haw." A street on Nashville's Music Row and a theater at Opryland are named in his honor.

He was natty, engaging and witty. About 15 years ago, when a group of political figures gathered in his dressing room, Mr. Acuff cracked: "We're not running for anything but the county line."

Country veteran Little Jimmy Dickens recalled that Mr. Acuff once gave him this advice:

"He said when you go on stage, don't think about 'fans.' He said those people out there are your friends and they're there to help you.

"He also said don't ever walk away from a man or a woman or a child who has come up to talk to you."

Mr. Acuff, a native of the east Tennessee hills, originally yearned for a baseball career and didn't sing professionally until he was almost 30.

The son of a Baptist minister, he became a regular Opry cast member in 1938 after getting his start singing and fiddling in a medicine show in the mountains of Virginia and Tennessee.

Over the years, Mr. Acuff sold more than 25 million records with hits like "Wreck on the Highway," "Fireball Mail," "Night Train to Memphis," "Low and Lonely" and "Pins and Needles."

Although Mr. Acuff liked to sing about trains, his "Wabash Cannonball" had a twist in the last verse when the lyrics refer to a train by that name carrying people "home to victory" after "the earthly race is over."

RICHARD ALEXANDER

Richard Alexander, 86, character actor who debuted in films with "Leopard Lady" in 1924, died Aug. 9, 1989, in Woodland Hills, Calif., of pulmonary edema.

The Dallas native played a prisoner in "Modern Times" with Charlie Chaplin and appeared with Buster Crabbe in two Flash Gordon serials released in 1936 and 1938.

He also appeared in "The Sin Sisters," "All Quiet On The Western Front," "See America Thirst," "The Viking," "The Big Broadcast Of 1936," "Mars Attacks The World" and "Outcast."

He retired in 1969. No survivors.

KIRK ALYN, Movies' First Superman, Dead at 88

HOUSTON (CNN) — Actor Kirk Alyn, the first man to play Superman in the movies, has died after a long illness, his family said Monday. He was 88.

Alyn was a dancer who followed friend Red Skelton to Hollywood before donning the cape and tights of the Man of Steel in 1948. He died Sunday in a hospital near his home in The Woodlands, Texas, just north of Houston.

Alyn's real name was John Feggo Jr. The Oxford, New Jersey native appeared in vaudeville acts and chorus lines in New York before going into films. He was 37 when he appeared in the first Superman film serial, titled simply "Superman." He went on to play the part again in 1950's "Atom Man vs. Superman."

"I didn't think you could ever put Superman on film," Alyn told The Associated Press in 1987, the superhero's 50th Anniversary. "They brought the people from D.C. Comics over and they said, 'Hey, he looks just like Clark Kent.' "

Alyn later complained that his role as Superman had typecast him, as it would his successor in the part, George Reeves. But he returned to the superhero's story in 1978, appearing unbilled as young Lois Lane's father while Christopher Reeve played Superman.

HOLLY BANE

Holly Bane/Mike Ragan, 77, died August 25 of emphysema at a Los Angeles hospital where he had been for the last five months. Alternating throughout his Western badman career between the two monikers, he first appeared in WAKE ISLAND (1942). It wasn't until after WWII that he restarted his career, moving primarily into the Western field. He also worked in scores of TV Westerns. (1995)

BUZZ BARTON (William Andrew Lamoreaux)

BORN
September 3, 1913
Gallatin, Missouri

PASSED AWAY
November 20, 1980
Reseda, California

SERVICES
Chapel Of The Oaks
Eternal Valley Memorial Park
Monday November 24, 1980
2:00 P.M.

OFFICIANT
Rev. Robert Bingham
First Presbyterian Church

INTERMENT
Garden of Memory
Eternal Valley Memorial Park
Newhall, California

NOAH BEERY, JR.

Character actor Noah Beery, Jr., 81 died Nov. 1 at his ranch outside Tehachapi, California. Beery had been in ill health in recent years following a stroke in the mid 80s. His last public appearance was to receive a Golden Boot Award in 1990. Beery was born into a family of great Hollywood actors, his father was Noah Beery, Sr. and his uncle was Wallace Beery. He made his first western in 1933 with Tom Mix. Although he enjoyed a long career in movies, he is best known for his role as James Garner's father, Rocky, in the TV series *The Rockford Files.* Beery was once married to Buck Jones' daughter, Maxine. They had a son named Bucklind.

NOAH BEERY, SR., 62, Film Veteran Dies

Villain on Screen for Many Years, Star of Todd Stage Show, Succumbs on Coast

HOLLYWOOD, Calif., April 1 (AP)—Noah Beery, Sr., veteran film actor, died here today in the arms of his brother Wallace Beery. He was at Wallace's home on a leave from his engagement in a New York stage play, "Up in Central Park." His death occurred on Wallace's birthday. He was 62 years old.

The two brothers, with Wallace's daughter, Carol Ann, were scheduled to appear on a radio show tonight. Wallace and Carol Ann went on as planned.

In New York, Morton Nathanson, press representative for Michael Todd Productions, said Mr. Beery had been scheduled to return next Sunday to his role of Boss Tweed in "Up in Central Park." Mr. Beery left the show on March 21 for a two-week vacation after playing the role since the premiére on Jan. 27, 1945.

Disliked Parts He Played

During his long career in professional villainy, Noah Beery's repertoire of malevolence ranged from a child beater in "The Godless Girl" to hard-boiled army sergeant in "Beau Geste."

Mr. Beery took his cinematic misdeeds seriously and once confessed that the man who plays the role of villain continuously suffers. "If he puts his heart into his work he can't throw off his characterizations promptly and at will," he said, adding that "they linger hours, sometimes days, in his mind." He always regretted playing the fiendish guard who beat and tortured the helpless children of the reformatory in "The Godless Girl."

Mr. Beery was born on a farm in Western Missouri. He led the life of a farm boy until his fourteenth birthday, when he left home to hawk newspapers in Kansas City. Subsequently he ran errands and sold peanuts and candy at circuses and in theatres.

His turn to the stage as a professional was due chiefly to a business in lemon drops that took him nightly to the old Gillis Theatre in Kansas City. He paid $10 a week for the privilege of selling his drops there and he made the deal pay by strolling up and down the aisles between acts, shouting the merits of "Noah's Delicious Lemon Drops."

Booming Voice Gained Attention

One night his booming voice penetrated backstage to the dressing room of Ned Risley, actor, who came out to see the man who could make so much noise. Risley called young Beery to his room and told him the voice was not only loud but worthy of cultivation for singing on the stage. The boy took a few singing lessons and started his stage career. He sang for a season at Electric Park in Kansas City and had a week at Hammerstein's Roof in this city, but drifted into melodrama under William A. Brady.

He had achieved only a moderate success after an earnest apprenticeship on the stage when in 1912 his young son, Noah, Jr., emerged from a serious illness with an $8,000 bill. In an effort to wipe out this debt Mr. Beery decided to try his luck with the movies. He arrived in Los Angeles broke and had to sell his extra suit to buy food. Making the rounds of the studios he landed a day's work in a suit of armor with Cecil B. De Mille's "Joan of Arc."

A second role in Mae Murray's "The Mormon" gave him another opportunity and it led to a contract with Paramount. Thereafter, he was sought constantly by directors for the most important villain roles. Money was no longer a problem to the Missouri farm boy.

MONTE BLUE
Dies; Film Star Was 73

Turned to Western Roles After Advent of Talkies

Associated Press
Tuesday, February 19, 1963

MILWAUKEE, Feb. 18 (AP)—Monte Blue, a star of the silent films who specialized in Western roles after the advent of talking pictures, died today. He was 73 years old.

Mr. Blue in recent years had been an advance man for the Hamid-Morton Circus, which is playing here. He collapsed at a hotel Thursday and died of a coronary attack, complicated by influenza.

His wife, Betty, had been called from their home at Beverly Hills, Calif., and was resting in a nearby room when he died.

Mr. Blue, who was part Cherokee Indian, was born in Indianapolis. He worked as a reporter, miner, seaman, cowhand and circus bareback rider before going to

146

California for a job as a movie studio laborer. He worked five years as a stunt man for D. W. Griffith, noted director, before he tried acting.

After appearances in "Intolerance" and "Birth of a Nation," he became a star at Warner Brothers in the 1920's. Perhaps his best role was in "White Shadows in the South Seas."

He retired in 1931 after the advent of the talkies and went on a world cruise. When he returned he found that the savings he had invested were gone.

"I looked in the mirror and saw I was no Little Lord Fauntleroy," he once told a reporter. "I decided to build my new career on rock instead of sand. So I started out at the bottom as an extra. I was in the awkward stage between stardom and character parts."

He rose through bit parts to become a top character actor, with most of his roles in Westerns. Among his films were "Geronimo," "Cheyenne," "Warpath," and "Apache."

Starred With Clara Bow
Special to *The New York Times*

NEW YORK—Gerald Montgomery Blue, the son of a Civil War veteran, was brought up in the Soldiers and Sailors Orphan Home in Knightston, Ind., after his father's death. He was a shipping clerk in Chicago before going to Hollywood.

One of his early successes was in "Orphans of the Storm." He acted under direction of Ernest Lubitsch in "So This Is Paris" and in "Kiss Me Again," in which he was starred with Marie Prevost and Clara Bow.

JOHNNY BOND

BURBANK. Calif. June 13 (UPI) — Johnny Bond, the country entertainer whose early hits "Divorce Me C.O.D." "Smoke! Smoke! Smoke!" and "Tennessee Saturday Night" became country-western standards, died here yesterday. He was 63 years old.

The singer, guitarist and songwriter, died at St. Joseph's Medical Center in Burbank, where he had lived for 32 years.

In 1940, he joined Gene Autry, remaining with Mr. Autry's Melody Ranch Show for 14 years.

Mr. Bond was one of the principal country stars at Columbia Records in the early '40's. He was a prolific writer, turning out more than 400 songs by the mid-'60's. He had a big hit in 1965 with "10 Little Bottles."

He is survived by his wife, Dorothy, three daughters, two sisters, two brothers and four grandchildren.

(1978)

WARD BOND,
Movie And TV Star, 55, Dies Of Heart Attack

DALLAS, Tex. (AP) — Ward Bond, 55, movie and television star who captured the hearts of millions of TV watchers as the rugged boss of "Wagon Train," died of a heart attack Saturday in a motel.

Bond was to make a personal appearance today at halftime ceremonies in the Cotton Bowl during the Dallas Cowboys and the Los Angeles Rams National League football contest.

His wife, Mary Lou, made the trip here with him. The National Broadcasting Co., which carried his hour-long television program, said she was his only survivor. They were married five years ago.

Bond was married previously to Dorris Sellers. They were divorced in 1944.

For years Bond played in the shadow of his friend John Wayne, a fellow cowboy actor. The two remained great friends.

Bond recalled that "for years, people would look at me and say "There's something familiar about your face; don't I know you from somewhere?" I'd say they'd probably seen me in pictures and they'd say, "Oh yeah, you're the fella who's always in those John Wayne movies."

With the success of "Wagon Train" on television, Bond said, "I finally became known on my own."

Wayne, contacted by telephone at his home in Encino, Calif., spoke softly and in a hesitating voice of the death of his friend.

"I feel that I've lost a very dear friend. And I think that he has many," Wayne said.

"I think we lost a man who has dedicated a great deal more of his time than his physical setup would allow in thinking of his country, the United States of America.

"I'm going to miss him terribly."

Bond entered the movie world in 1928 while still attending the University of Southern California.

Some of his major movies were "Fort Apache," "Unconquered," "Quiet Man," "Hondo," "Searchers," "Johnny Guitar," "It Happened One Night," "My Darling Clementine," and "Fugitive."

Bond and Wayne, both big, rugged, lusty looking men, had strong ideas about the American way of life. Together they helped found the Motion Picture Alliance, which fought what it believed to be an unwholesome left-wing element in the movie industry.

Bond's movie career flourished, but he was never the big star Wayne was until he landed the role as Major Adams in the TV series. For the past few seasons Bond has been one of television's top-rated stars.

Bond played football at Southern California under Coach Howard Jones and one of his teammates there was Wayne. Ward appeared in all the Wayne movies directed by John Ford.

WALTER BRENNAN
Dead at 80; Winner of 3 Academy Awards

Character Actor in Over 100 Films — Appeared on TV in 'The Real McCoys'

OXNARD, Calif., Sept. 21 (AP)—The veteran actor Walter Brennan, who won three Academy Awards, died Saturday night after a long battle with emphysema. He was 80 years old.

Mr. Brennan died at St. John's Hospital here, a hospital spokesman said. He had been under treatment since July 25 for respiratory problems.

His wife, Ruth, and three children were with him when he died.

STEVE BRODIE, 72

Steve Brodie was a rugged Academy Award nominee who acted in more than 200 westerns and other action films.

He had been nominated for an Oscar for best supporting actor in the 1949 film, "Home of the Brave."

His last film was "Mugsy's Girls," directed by his son in 1986. Brodie had remained active by doing voice-overs for commercials.

Brodie was a familiar character actor in films of the 1940s, 50s, and 60s. Among them were "Thirty Seconds Over Tokyo," "This Man's Navy," "Code of the West," "Arizona Ranger," "Rose of the Yukon," and "Winchester '73."

His films also included "Only The Valiant," "Lady in the Iron Mask," "The Charge at Feather River," "The Far Country," "Roustabout," and "The Wild World of Batwoman."

(January 9, 1992)

RALPH BYRD

TARZANA, Calif., Aug. 18 (AP)—Ralph Byrd, veteran movie character, died today of a heart attack at the age of 43.

Born in Dayton, Ohio, he had been in films for eighteen years. He played in Alexander Korda's "Jungle Book" and recently completed a series of Dick Tracy films for television.

His widow, Virginia Carroll, former actress, and a daughter, Carol, survive.

Mr. Byrd, who created the part of Dick Tracy on the screen, was seen in supporting roles in "Moontide," "Stallion Road," "Canon City," "The Son of Monte Cristo," "The Penalty," "The Golden Fleecing," "Dark Streets of Cairo," "S. O. S. Tidal Wave" and "Mickey, the Kid." (1952)

Yakima Canutt

YAKIMA CANUTT Dies; Stunt Man in Movies

New York Times, Tuesday, May 27, 1986

LOS ANGELES May 26 (AP) — Yakima Canutt, an Oscar-winning stunt man who doubled for John Wayne and other stars in dozens of movies, died Saturday at the North Hollywood Medical Center. He was 89 years old.

Mr. Canutt, who began his film career in the 1920's, was awarded a special Oscar in 1966 for helping to create the stunt man's profession and for developing safety devices used by stunt men everywhere.

Among his movie credits was the choreography of the chariot race in the 1959 epic "Ben Hur." For the race, Mr. Canutt started work in Italy two years before regular production began, training 80 horses to pull chariots.

Enos Edward Canutt was born Nov. 29, 1896, in Colfax, Wash., and took his nickname from Washington's Yakima Valley. After a stint as a prize-winning rodeo rider, he moved on to Hollywood in the early 1920's, working first as an actor in silent westerns.

He turned to full-time stunt work after the advent of the talkies, substituting for a long list of stars including Mr. Wayne, Errol Flynn, Tyrone Power, Clark Gable, Henry Fonda, Roy Rogers, Randolph Scott and Tex Ritter.

Mr. Canutt also directed several westerns, including "Sheriff of Cimarron" in 1945 and "Oklahoma Badlands" in 1948.

He is survived by his wife, a son, a brother and a sister.

KEN CARSON, Singing Cowboy, Dies at 79

BOCA RATON, Fla. — The thing that made him famous was the fact that he made 22 movies with Roy Rogers during the 1940s.

But one of the things that made Ken Carson a little different from most men, at least in his wife's eyes, was the fact that he rode across the country on horseback at the age of 19.

Carson died Thursday at the age of 79, after a career in radio, television and film that spanned nearly 60 years. He and his wife, Gretchen, 72, moved to Delray Beach, Fla., in 1979.

"He was some kind of man," said Gretchen Carson, poring over dozens of photos of her husband in their modest Sherwood Park home. "He could do anything."

In one picture, Ken Carson is smiling broadly with a young Johnny Carson. In another, he's posing with Audrey Meadows at a charity telethon. Another, taken at the Roy Rogers Museum in California, shows the spurs Ken Carson wore as one of the Sons of the Pioneers, the singing cowboys

in Roy Rogers' films.

Carson wore those same spurs on his trek from California to New York City, done as a publicity stunt with the Ranch Boys trio, a country-western group he performed with in the '30s.

Movie fans will remember Ken Carson as the guitar-playing man who sings "The Man on the Flying Trapeze" when Clark Gable and Claudette Colbert first meet in the 1934 film, "It Happened One Night."

He recorded dozens of songs, including "Cool Water" and "Tumbling Tumbleweeds." His talent also got him invited to sing at the weddings of two Nixon daughters, Julie and Tricia.

(4/11/94)

BILL CODY JR.

BILL CODY JR. (August 11, 1989, age 64): He entered films in the mid-1930s, appearing with his father, Bill Cody, in a series of Westerns produced by Ray Kirkwood Productions and released by Spectrum Pictures. He later worked with Johnny Mack Brown, Tom Keene and, in THE GIRL OF THE GOLDEN WEST (MGM, 1938), with Nelson Eddy, probably his best screen role. He made three Universal serials: SCOUTS TO THE RESCUE, THE OREGON TRAIL and SKY RAIDERS. During WWII, he served with the US Navy and saw action in the South Pacific. He never returned to the movie business.

Indian actor, IRON EYES CODY dies

The Knoxville News-Sentinel,
Tuesday, January 5, 1999
by The Associated Press

LOS ANGELES — Iron Eyes Cody, the "Crying Indian" whose tearful face in 1970s television commercials became a powerful symbol of the anti-littering campaign, died Monday. He was in his 80s or early 90s.

Cody died of natural causes at 1:30 p.m. in his home in the Los Feliz section of Los Angeles, police spokesman Ed Funes said.

Cody, whose acting credits date back to silent movies and include dozens of films and television shows, was best known for the ads from the group Keep America Beautiful that showed him shedding a single tear as he watched people litter.

He was born in Oklahoma, but the exact date of birth wasn't known. Reference books give various dates, from 1904 to 1915. Based on his credits, his most likely date of birth was 1907.

Cody followed his Cherokee Indian father, Thomas Long Plume, as a performer in circuses and Wild West shows and made his first film appearance as an extra in the 1919 silent "Back to God's Country."

Cody went on to appear in more than 80 films in Indian roles; often his character was listed as simply "Indian," "Indian Chief," or "Indian Joe."

His other credits included "Sitting Bull" in 1954, "The Great Sioux Massacre" in 1965, "Nevada Smith" in 1966, "A Man Called Horse" in 1970 and "Ernest Goes to Camp" in 1987.

In television, he had guest appearances on "Bonanza," "Gunsmoke" and "Rawhide."

Another article from a different source

IRON EYES CODY Not Indian But Italian

IRON EYES CODY, 94, whose career stretched back to 1919, died

January 4 of natural causes at his home in Los Feliz, CA. Although truly Italian, Iron Eyes was probably more Indian than many Native Americans because he truly loved it and lived it. Iron Eyes' historic 1971 Crying Indian public service spot for Keep America Beautiful made him more recognizable than hundreds of Western films were able to do. A 1996 article in THE NEW ORLEANS TIMES-PICAYUNE, republished in INDIAN COUNTRY TODAY, the nation's leading Indian newspaper, traced his family history and found Cody born Espera De Corti, April 3, 1904, in Gueydan, LA. He went by the name Oscar. His father was an Italian immigrant, his mother was from Sicily. They lived in Gueydan where they owned a small grocery. First Americans in the Arts, Hollywood's leading Native American advocacy group, gave Cody its prestigious Trustee Award four years ago. However, during the presentation, they made it quite clear the award was being presented to Cody as a "non-native". But, Cody's movie legend may long outlive the facts. In 1936, Cody wed Bertha Parker, a Native American archeologist. They adopted two Indian sons. His "life" was told in two bios, IRON EYES—MY LIFE AS A HOLLYWOOD INDIAN ('82) and IRON EYES CODY—THE PROUD AMERICAN ('88).

TRISTRAM COFFIN

Appearing in hundreds of low budget westerns, movie serials, and TV shows, Tris Coffin was a character actor and occasional leading man.

His best known role was Capt. Tom Rynning in 26 Men. The series ran 78 episodes from 1957-59.

Born in Mammoth, Utah, he studied acting there. He went on to become a radio newscaster in Boston where he was noticed by Universal Studios.

Some of his nearly 400 films included Queen of the Yukon, Lady In The Dark, Flamingo Road, The Fountainhead, The Eddie Cantor Story, Prairie Gunsmoke, and Last Stagecoach West.

His film serials included Jungle Girl and Jesse James Rides Again.

He died in Santa Monica, California, and is survived by his wife.
(March 26, 1990)

SPADE COOLEY, Musician, Dies; Jailed for Murdering His Wife

Special to The New York Times

OAKLAND, Calif., Nov. 24, 1969—Donnell (Spade) Cooley, the country fiddler once known as

Spade Cooley

the "King of Western Swing," died here yesterday during an intermission in his first public performance in over a decade. He was 59 years old.

Cooley had been granted a 72-hour furlough from the California State Medical Facility at Vacaville, the minimum security state prison where he had been since his 1961 conviction for the murder of his wife, Ella Mae, at their ranch in Kern County. He was scheduled for parole Feb. 22, 1970.

Despite the fortune he amassed as an entertainer, friends said Cooley died as penniless as the day he was born in a storm cellar under a shack near Saddle Paddle Creek, Okla., Dec. 17, 1910.

The son of an itinerant baseball pitcher and fiddler who was half-Cherokee Indian, he was discovered for show business at the gate of Republic Studios Hollywood by Roy Rogers, the cowboy star, who said he had "sensed something unusual about him." Mr. Rogers found a movie stand-in job for Cooley.

Around that time, according to Cooley, he acquired the nickname "Spade" in a poker game after filling successive spade flushes.

His work in the movies led to offers to perform as a musician, and he got several bookings as a fiddler. On the advice of a promoter who told him, "If you're good enough to play for all those bands, you're good enough to have your own," Cooley formed a band during the peak days of radio. He subsequently wrote the best-selling song "Shame, Shame on You."

When his popularity faded, he went into the real-estate business.

Survivors include a son, Donnell Jr., and a daughter, Melody.

JAMES CRAIG, Actor, 74, Dies; Once Called Gable Successor

TUSTIN, Calif., July 9 (AP) — James Craig, the actor once promoted as a successor to Clark Gable, died of lung cancer June 27 at Western Medical Center here. He was 74 years old.

Mr. Craig began his film career in the 1930's and found himself stepping into Gable-style roles when the movie idol went into the armed services in World War II. Among Mr. Craig's movies during this period were "The Devil and Daniel Webster," "Lost Angel," "Marriage Is a Private Affair," "The Human Comedy" and "Heavenly Body."

Mr. Craig, whose real name was James Henry Meador, was born in Nashville, Tenn. He went to Hollywood to study acting in 1934 and landed his first leading role in the 1937 film "Arizona Ames," in which he took the name James Mead. Later, when he was cast in a planned film titled "Craig's Wife," he became James Craig.

In the 1970's, Mr. Craig had some TV roles but retired from show business and became a real-estate agent.

He is survived by three children: James, Jr., Diane and Michael, and four grandchildren.

FRANKIE DARRO

Frankie Darro, 59, onetime child actor who bridged the gap into adult roles, died suddenly Dec. 25, 1977, of a heart attack, while visiting friends in Huntington Beach, Calif. His wife, Dorothy, was with him at the time.

Darro, best known in recent years as the "Old Lady" on the Red Skelton Show, launched his long career at the age of four and a half and for years was one of the best-known boy actors, specializing in hardboiled characters. As a juvenile, he was with FBO in many westerns.

Among his best-known films were "The Rainbow Man," "The Mayor of Hell," "Three Kids and a Queen," "Juvenile Court."

In the Navy during World War II, he returned to acting when mustered out of service and was active until several years ago.

DENVER DIXON

Denver Dixon, 82, pioneer producer, director, actor and indie distributor (real name, Victor Adamson) who specialized in westerns and action films, died of a heart attack in Hollywood Nov. 9, 1972.

Born in Kansas City, he later became a vaudeville performer. In 1910 in New Zealand, where his family had taken him as a child, he produced the first western film in that country. He later returned to the U.S. and appeared in a score of films, including "Birth of a Nation" and "The Squaw Man." Later he produced and directed more than 150 western and adventure films. In 1927 his "Compassion" won England's equivalent to the Oscar.

He built three indie studios in the 1917 period, and during the early 1920s was best known for a series starring Art Mix. He also was credited with having given Jean Arthur one of her first film breaks.

Surviving is a son, Al

Adamson, producer-director, another son and three daughters.

JOHN DOUCETTE

JOHN DOUCETTE, who could play nasty villains as easily as likable heavies, died August 16 of cancer at his home in Cabazon, CA. He was 73.

GENE EVANS, 75

Actor who played film tough guys

Los Angeles Times

Gene Evans, a character actor known as the quintessential tough guy in films such as "The Steel Helmet" has died. He was 75.

Mr. Evans, often cast as a soldier, lawman, or heavy in more

than 30 films, died Wednesday in Jackson, Tenn., where he had retired to a farm.

His other films included the 1959 comedy "Operation Petticoat," starring Cary Grant, "The War Wagon," "Support Your Local Sheriff," and "Pat Garrett and Billy the Kid."

On television, he was Montana rancher Rob McLaughlin, who owned the horse Flicka, in "My Friend Flicka" in 1956-58, and Sergeant Hanrahan to Anthony Franciosa's detective in "Matt Helm" in 1975-76.

WILLIAM FARNUM, Actor, 76, Is Dead

Star of Silent Screen Earned $10,000 a Week in Heyday — Famed for 'Spoilers'

HOLLYWOOD, Calif., June 5, 1953 (UP)—William Farnum, veteran character actor who once was the highest-paid matinee idol in film history, died today of cancer at the age of 76. He entered Cedars of Lebanon Hospital on May 27 for an emergency operation, his third in a year.

His wife, Mrs. Isabelle Farnum, was at his side when death came.

William Farnum

Performer for Six Decades

A professional actor for more than sixty years, William Farnum made his debut at the age of 10 in a play with Edwin Booth. Joining a stock company in New Orleans at 16, he later became a member of the Boston Amusement Stock Company and appeared with Helen Modjeska, Margaret Mather and Mme. Janauschek.

Mr. Farnum's parents, Adela Le Gros and G. D. Farnum, were actors who trained their sons, William, Dustin and Marshall, for the stage.

After touring for five years in "Ben Hur," Mr. Farnum formed his own repertory company and co-starred with his brother, Dustin, in "The Little Rebel."

His first motion picture was "The Spoilers," which brought a profit of several million dollars to Col. William Selig, the producer. It also put Mr. Farnum on the path to fame and fortune.

One of the handsomest actors of the silent screen, he also became the highest paid star of that era. He was under contract to William Fox for $10,000 a week and for four years, earned $520,000 annually. Mr. Farnum was said to have lost $2,000,000 in the stock market crash of 1929.

He returned to the stage in 1925, as Sir Ralph Morgan in "The Buccaneer." The next year he played Marc Antony in a Hollywood Bowl spectacle of "Julius Caesar." Two years later, Broadway saw him again as Banquo in "Macbeth."

Tried Screen Comeback

Having made famous the part of François Villon in the original film version of "If I Were King" in 1920, he sought to make a screen comeback in 1931 as King Louis XV in "Du Barry." Mr. Farnum starred in "Ten Nights in a Barroom" the same year.

His fame seemed to have fled with his fortune after these pictures, and he was forced to play bit parts for $25 a day. In 1933, the actor filed a petition in bankruptcy, listing assets of $500 in clothing.

When "The Spoilers" was first filmed, Mr. Farnum was its leading man. In 1942, when the story was remade, he played a minor role. He performed some of his old-time antics in "The Perils of Pauline" in 1947. Three years later, he was signed to portray himself in "Hollywood Story," a studio murder mystery set in a film studio.

The motion pictures in which Mr. Farnum appeared include "Are We Civilized," "The Silver Streak," "Return of Hannibal," "Painted Desert," "Frontier Badmen," "Mr. Robinson Crusoe," "Bride of Vengeance," "Samson and Delilah," "Jack and the Beanstalk" and "Lone Star," the last having been released in 1952.

He was honored by The Lambs on Sept. 23, 1950, the sixty-fourth anniversary of his stage debut.

Mr. Farnum married Olive Ann White in Sag Harbor, L.I., in 1906. They were divorced in 1931.

The next year, he married Mrs. Isabelle Major.

FRANK FERGUSON

Frank Ferguson, 69, Hollywood character actor for over 40 years who appeared, among other films, in many westerns, died Sept. 12, 1978, of cancer in Los Angeles.

In addition to a career in motion pictures that saw him in over 100 films, Ferguson worked also in TV. Pictures include "The Great Sioux Massacre," "The Marksman," "Wagons West," "Miracle of The Bells," "Sunrise At Campobello," "Pocketful of Miracles," "The Eternal Sea," "Battle Cry" and "Johnny Guitar."

Among his TV credits were "Peyton Place," "Perry Mason" and the role of grandpa in "How The West Was Won."

Ferguson had served as the Pasadena Playhouse's original director.

DOUGLAS FOWLEY, Character Actor in Westerns, 86

Los Angeles Times 5/28/98

Douglas Fowley, character actor who appeared in more than 200 films and television shows, but is probably best remembered as Doc Holliday in the long-running 1950s series "The Life and Legend of Wyatt Earp," has died. He was 86.

Mr. Fowley died May 21 at the Motion Picture & Television Hospital in Los Angeles.

Most frequently a villain or gangster in films from the 1930s through the 1970s, Mr. Fowley was also memorable as the 1920s-era motion picture director in the Gene Kelly musical "Singin' in the Rain" released in 1952.

During his long and varied career, the handsome Mr. Fowley appeared in many westerns and could change his appearance and persona like a chameleon. He was the dapper, alcoholic and tuberculin Doc in the Wyatt Earp series, which starred Hugh O'Brien from 1955 through 1961. Gray-bearded and squinting behind wire-rimmed glasses, he was also the sharp-shooting patriarch Grandpa Hanks in the shorter series "Pistols 'n' Petticoats," starring Ann Sheridan in 1966-67.

Also on the small screen, Mr. Fowley appeared in the popular series "The Streets of San Francisco," "CHIPs," "The Rockford Files" and "Perry Mason."

Born Daniel Vincent Fowley in New York City, he began acting on stage and appeared in several off-Broadway shows before moving to Los Angeles. He served in the Navy during World War II.

Mr. Fowley made his screen debut in "The Mad Game" starring Spencer Tracy in 1933.

ROBERT W. FRAZER

Robert W. Frazer, 50, stage and screen actor, died Aug. 17, 1944, in Los Angeles, after a lingering illness.

On the Broadway stage he played in such productions as "Ben Hur," "The Wanderer" and "The Mirage" before moving to Hollywood where he appeared in a long list of character roles during his 16-year film career.

Surviving is his widow, Mildred Bright, actress.

TERRY FROST

TERRY FROST (March 1, 1993, age 86, heart attack): Second-string character actor who started in vaudeville. His credits are countless and include work with most of the Western stars and in most of the TV Westerns. A popular guest at many B-Western conventions over the last 20 years.

FRED GRAHAM

Fred Graham, 61, veteran actor, stunt coordinator and former chief of motion picture development in Arizona, died Oct. 10, 1979, in Scottsdale, Ariz.

A charter member of the Screen Actors Guild, Graham appeared in the 1935 production of "Mutiny On The Bounty" and went on to double and coordinate stunts for John Wayne, Errol Flynn and Ward Bond in pictures. He appeared in 26 films with Wayne, four of which were for John Ford.

After working in the MGM sound department, Graham moved to Arizona in 1963. From 1972-76 he headed up the Arizona Governor's Office for Motion Picture Development and was also v.p. and g.m. of CineLogistics, subsidiary of Southwest Research and Development, operators of the Graham Studios in Carefree, Ariz.

He is survived by his wife, Dink, son and daughter.

REED HADLEY, 63, TV Series Star

LOS ANGELES, Dec. 12, 1974 (UPI)—Actor Reed Hadley, television star of the Racket Squad and Public Defender series during the 1950s, died Wednesday of a heart attack at the age of 63.

Mr. Hadley broke into acting as a radio performer in the 1940s, as the voice of Red Ryder.

Mr. Hadley was perhaps best known in the role of Capt. John Braddock in Racket Squad. His last feature was "St. Valentine's Day Massacre."

He is survived by his wife, Helen, and son, Dale, 32, of Las Vegas, Nev.

Gospel-country singer STUART HAMBLEN dies

by The Associated Press

SANTA MONICA, Calif. — Gospel-country singer Stuart Hamblen, who wrote inspirational songs and once ran for president as a Prohibition Party candidate after swearing off booze and horse racing, died today. He was 80.

Hamblen, who lapsed into a coma after surgery Feb. 28 to remove a malignant brain tumor, died at 3 a.m., said Armen Markarian, spokesman for St. John's Hospital and Health Center.

Hamblen also had been suffering from inoperable lung cancer, said another hospital spokesman, Garth Hintz.

Hamblen was host of "The Cowboy Church" radio show in Los Angeles, which is still heard in reruns around the country.

He was best known for his 1950s spiritual tunes, "It Is No Secret What God Can Do" and "This Old House." He also recorded "Open Up your Heart (And Let the Sun Shine In)," "Remember Me, I'm the One Who Loves You" and "Texas Plains."

The former hard drinker and hillbilly singer led a colorful life that started in Kellysville, Texas, where his father was a Methodist preacher.

After winning an amateur contest, he left Texas and signed recording contracts. He also appeared on television and performed nationwide.

He loved horse racing and owned one of the leading race horse stables in the West, and admitted he was an alcoholic who once ran up a $250 bar tab in Hollywood in the 1950s.

His life changed one night when he visited a tent revival conducted by evangelist Billy Graham. His conversion was immediate and Hamblen gave up drinking and race horses.

In 1952, ex-alcoholic Hamblen became the Prohibition Party's nominee for president in an election won by Dwight D. Eisenhower.

In recent years, the retired Hamblen and his wife of 51 years, Suzy, raised rare Peruvian Paso horses at their ranch in Canyon Country.

During his illness, Hamblen received calls from Mr. Graham, former President Reagan, and country stars Roy Rogers, Dale Evans and Gene Autry and fans nationwide.

Hamblen is survived by his wife and three daughters.

AL HOXIE

Al Hoxie, 80, silent screen Western actor, died April 6 in Redlands.

A native of Idaho, Hoxie moved to Hollywood in 1919 to join his brother Jack, who had been appearing in films for several years. Shortly thereafter, he got a job as a bit player in "Kentucky Colonel" and then was co-starred in "Thunderbolt Jack," one of his brother's serials for National Film Corp.

The two worked together steadily until 1925, with Al doubling for Jack and acting in other pictures as well.

In 1925, Al signed with Anchor Film Distributors to star in eight westerns directed by J. P. McGowen. In 1926-27 he made a series of eight films for Bud Barsky and the following year made eight more for William M. Pizor.

Among his credits were "Unseen Enemies," "Buried Gold," "Road Agent," "The Lost Trail," "Red Blood" and "The Ace Of Clubs."

Hoxie retired from films with the advent of sound. He later worked as a street car conductor, with the California State Forestry Service, the Anaheim Police Dept. and as chief security officer at Patton State Hospital in San Bernardino County.

I. STANFORD JOLLEY

I. Stanford Jolley, 78, the black-hearted, black-hatted heavy in 475 features, film serials and TV westerns, died Dec. 7 in the Motion Picture & TV Hospital, Woodland Hills, Calif.

Starting with "Silver Spurs" in 1940, Jolley was a bad guy in scores of motion pictures, almost always in western attire. He was the villain in "Arizona," with William Holden and Jean Arthur. Some other titles were "Midnight Limited," "Rolling Home To Texas," "A Gentleman From Dixie" and "West Of Dodge City."

Some of his pictures were not westerns. Jolley was in the World War II film, "Corregidor." Those, however, were exceptions. More characteristic was the serial, "Danger Of The Canadian Mounted," one of 13 in which he appeared as the evil gunslinger. He figured in most of Hopalong Cassidy features, with Bill Boyd, and turned up often in Gene Autry and Roy Rogers films.

In TV, naturally enough, his wicked acting ways cast him in similar roles. Jolley was in a spate of "Gunsmoke" segments, among many others. He was seen most recently in the Purina Pet Food commercials.

JACK O. WATT (Brad King), Hopalong Cassidy sidekick

LODI, Calif. — A graveside funeral for Battle Mountain native Jack O. Watt, 72, who died November 1, 1991, at his residence, was held Thursday at Cherokee Memorial Park.

Watt's stage name was Brad King in the Hopalong Cassidy films. He played the character Johnny Nelson in the Westerns released by Paramount in the late 1930s and early 1940s. He entered the movie business after winning the Western States Rodeo Championship and being Nevada State Rodeo Champion.

A native of Valley of the Moon Ranch near Battle Mountain, he was born Nov. 23, 1918, and was raised on the family ranch, where he developed riding and roping skills that eventually led him to a movie career and parts in 17 Hopalong pictures.

During World War II, he served in the Army, working his way from a private who broke Army horses to a captain piloting P-38 airplanes in the Army Air Corps. After being shot down over North Africa, he was placed into special service making war movies. During this time, he co-starred in "Thirty Seconds Over Tokyo," and "Wing and a Prayer." In later years, he appeared in 25 other movies, including "Big Town."

Watt moved to the Lodi area in 1949 to go into ranching. He formed the BK Cattle Co., with ranches in Lodi, Stockton, San Jose, Battle Mountain and later British Columbia. He also founded the King Nelson Meat Co., serving the Lodi-Stockton area for 17 years.

A country-western singer and composer, Watt sang in films, on stage, radio and television where he performed in the series "Life on King's Dude Ranch." He wrote Western songs such as "Twilight on the Trail," "Tag Along," "Funny Old Hills," and "Blue Moon on the Silver Sage." He founded Crystal Records, which later became the country-western division of Capitol Records.

Watt was a trustee for the old Morada-Davis School District in Stockton, a member of the Veterans of Foreign Wars, the Screen Actors Guild and Academy of Motion Picture Arts and Sciences.

Surviving are his widow Doris of Lodi; sons Jack and Jeff, both of Reno, Jim of Colorado and Bill of Lodi; brothers Jim and Bill, both of British Columbia, and Russ of Texas and two grandchildren.

Arrangements were under the direction of Gierhart, Wells and Donahue Funeral Home.

Charles King

CHARLES KING

NAME: Charles Lafayette King, Jr.
PLACE OF DEATH: John Wesley County Hospital, Los Angeles.
DATE OF DEATH: May 7, 1957.
HOUR: 7:45 p.m.
DATE OF BIRTH: February 21, 1895.
SPECIFY MARRIAGE OR: Divorced.
USUAL OCCUPATION: Actor.
KIND OF BUSINESS OF INDUSTRY: Motion Picture Studio.
NAME AND BIRTHPLACE OF FATHER: Charles Lafayette King, Sr., Kentucky.
MAIDEN NAME AND BIRTHPLACE OF MOTHER: Unknown.
BIRTHPLACE: Texas.
SOCIAL SECURITY NUMBER: 561-01-4156.
INFORMANT: Mr. Charles S. King.
ARMED FORCES? Yes, WW II.
LAST USUAL RESIDENCE: 4914 Bellaire Avenue, North Hollywood.
CAUSE OF DEATH: Hepatic coma.
ANTECEDANT CAUSES: Cirrhosis and chronic alcoholism.
BURIAL: Cremation.

FRED KOHLER, JR.

FRED KOHLER JR. (January 7, 1993, Scottsdale, Arizona): Son of the noted screen character actor. I first noticed him as Bud Means in THE HOOSIER SCHOOLMASTER (Monogram, 1935) and liked his work enough to follow his career over the years. Producer William Berke signed him for a series of B-Westerns (Commdore Pictures) but only two were made, TOLL OF THE DESERT and THE PECOS KID. Kohler failed to catch the public's fancy as a Western star and he was soon back in his best remembered parts, that of a Western heavy, just like his dad, but without the talent.

Fred Kohler, Sr.

FRED KOHLER, SR., Actor, Dies in His Sleep

Veteran 'Bad Man' of Films Had Played in Many Pictures

Special to *New York Times*

HOLLYWOOD, Oct. 28 — Fred Kohler, motion picture character actor, died in his sleep of a heart attack early today at the age of 49. He was counted as one of the oldest "heavies" on the screen in point of service.

Born in Kansas City, the son of an inventor, Mr. Kohler began his theatrical career as a spear carrier in the Willis Wood Theatre in his home city. From then on he had a varied career, playing in stock, vaudeville, tent shows and one-night stands.

Twenty-seven years ago he was playing in stock in Los Angeles when he heard that Hobart Bosworth was making a picture, "Code of Honor," and that the people who worked in movies could stay in one place and have a home. Mr. Kohler applied for and received a job and remained in Hollywood after that with the exception of several personal appearance tours.

Standing 6 feet 2 inches, Mr. Kohler always played "bad man" roles. One of the busiest actors, his most recent pictures were "The Buccaneer" and "Blockade."

He is survived by his widow, Mrs. Marjorie Kohler, who was vacationing in the high Sierras when he died, and a son, Fred Kohler, Jr., who has been following his father's footsteps in motion pictures.

GEORGE J. LEWIS

Mexican born serial and western hero and heavy, GEORGE J. LEWIS, 91, died of a stroke December 10, two days shy of his 92nd birthday at his home in Rancho Santa Fe, CA.

WALLACE MacDONALD

Wallace MacDonald, 87, who drew on wide experience as an actor and story editor to become a producer of over 100 films for Columbia pictures, died Oct. 30 in his Santa Barbara, Calif. home.

MacDonald retired in 1965. His career started with dramatic roles on the stage, and from there he went into motion pictures, playing character roles in "The Spoilers," "The Sea Hawk," and starring in westerns.

In those early days he worked at the old Vitagraph Studios, and for Goldwyn, Universal, Metro,

First National and others. In 1936 he quit as supervisor of writers for Republic and became a producer at Columbia.

Among his credits are "Sailor's Holiday," "Calling All Stars," "A Guy, A Gal, And A Pal," "My Name Is Julie Ross," "Out Of The Depths," "When A Girl's Beautiful," "Counterspy Meets Scotland Yard," "Harem Girl," "Okinawa," "El Alamein," "Outlaw Stallion," "Apache Ambush," "Cell 2455 Death Row" and "Return To Warbow."

Survivors include his wife.

PIERCE LYDEN

Pierce Lyden, 90, the oldest living B-Western black hat, yet one of the sweetest, most humble, thoughtful human beings you could ever have met, died on October 10 in an Orange County, California, hospice following a brave six-month battle with cancer. Pierce worked in over 125 movie westerns with practically all the cowboy stars since the 1940s. He was also seen in countless TV Westerns. He appeared at many film festivals and was a fan favorite. In the 1980s, Lyden authored five books about his Hollywood experiences. He received several Masonic honors, recognition in his hometown, and was presented with a Golden Boot Award. He had recently returned from a film festival in England. (1998)

PHILO McCULLOUGH

Philo McCullough, 87, veteran character actor, died June 5, 1981, at his home in Burbank, Calif.

A native of San Bernadino, McCullough was an original member of the Burbank Stock Company and played in stock for eight years before beginning his motion picture career in 1912. During silent days he appeared in Fatty Arbuckle comedies and Selig's shorts, as well as the "Rin Tin Tin" series.

After spending four years at Fox and two at First National, he freelanced as an actor for several years before becoming a contract player at Warner Brothers, where he remained for 28 years.

Among his many credits were "Untamed Justice," "The Leatherneck," "Laughing At Life," "Tarzan The Fearless," "Riding Through," "I Hate Women," "The Buccaneer," "That Way With Women," "The Great Race," and "They Shoot Horses, Don't They?"

He is survived by his wife.

CHARLES B. MIDDLETON

LOS ANGELES, April 24, 1949 — Charles B. Middleton, who acted in 230 stage and screen shows and spent fifty-three years in show business, died Friday night in Torrance Memorial Hospital.

A native of Kentucky, he entertained in circuses, carnivals and vaudeville and had owned several stock companies. His last stage appearance was in "January Thaw" on Broadway in 1945.

Mr. Middleton appeared in such films as "Kongo," "Bellamy Trail," "David Harum," "Capt. Fury" and "Grapes of Wrath." He was a member of the Masquers Club and the Comedy Club.

He leaves a daughter, Mrs. William F. Ladd.

PETE MORRISON

George (Pete) Morrison, 82, actor who did more than 200 Westerns during silent film days, died Feb. 5 in Los Angeles. He started as a stunt man in 1910 and doubled for William S. Hart and Wallace

Beery.

Morrison also appeared in films with Tom Mix, John Barrymore, and Ramon Novarro and worked rodeos with Hoot Gibson. His grandfather founded Morrison, Colo. in 1859.

His two sons survive.

HANK NEWMAN

HENRY (HANK) NEWMAN, 73, country and western singer in the 1930s and a recording artist for RCA Victor, died July 25 in Columbus, Ohio. Newman and his brothers formed the Georgia Crackers musical group in 1931 and played for WHKC, Columbus. He played in several Hollywood cowboy films before retiring in 1954. He later operated a restaurant in Columbus. (1978)

BOB NOLAN

Composer Bob Nolan, who wrote the Western song classics "Cool Water" and "Tumbling Tumbleweeds," and sang with the original Sons of the Pioneers for 17 years, has died of an apparent heart attack. He was 72. Nolan had been on a Newport Harbor, California boat outing with a son and a daughter when he became ill while returning to his Los Angeles (Studio City) home. He died before reaching the hospital. His

wife, two sons, and a daughter survive him. In an article appearing in the May 1978 issue of *The Nostalgia Merchant,* Laurence J. Zwisohn wrote of Nolan: "Few people can measure up to the level of Bob's many talents. As a singer Bob was equally adept at solos and in the trio. The beauty and sensitivity in his voice along with its unique tone made it the definitive sound of the Pioneers. As a songwriter he is in a class by himself. The lyrics to his songs are pure poetry, which paint the most beautiful word pictures imaginable."

DENVER PYLE, 77, Best Known For 'Dukes of Hazzard' Role

by David Rohde

The New York Times Obituaries
Sunday, December 28, 1997

Denver Pyle, a television and film actor known for his roles as a wise Southern uncle on "The Dukes of Hazzard" and a melodic mountain man on "The Andy Griffith Show," died Thursday in Providence St. Joseph Medical Center in Burbank, Calif. He was 77.

Mr. Pyle was suffering from lung cancer. Born in a Colorado ranch town of 40 people, Mr. Pyle enjoyed an acting career that spanned four decades by playing

Denver Pyle

character roles in film and television programs primarily set in the South or old West. In the latter stage of his career, Mr. Pyle was best known for his portrayal of Uncle Jesse on the CBS television show "The Dukes of Hazzard" from 1979 to 1985. His trademark was his white hair and a scraggly beard.

After growing up in Bethune, Colo., Mr. Pyle briefly attended Colorado State University. In 1940, he moved to Los Angeles and joined the Navy. He was wounded off Guadalcanal in World War II and received a medical discharge in 1942.

While working at an aircraft plant in Los Angeles, Mr. Pyle had his first role in a play. He went on to study acting and made his film debut in "The Guilt of Janet Ames" in 1947. In television, he appeared in Western series like "The Roy Rogers Show" from 1951 to 1964, "Bonanza" in 1964, and "Gunsmoke" from 1956 to 1964.

From 1960 to 1968, Mr. Pyle played Briscoe Darling, a singing mountain man on "The Andy Griffith Show." He also appeared on "The Dick Van Dyke Show" in 1963 and played Doris Day's father on "The Doris Day Show" from 1968 to 1970. Mr. Pyle, who also directed television programs, played Mad Jack in the NBC series "The Life and Times of Grizzly Adams" in 1977 and 1978. Mr. Pyle appeared in a "Dukes of Hazzard" reunion movie last April.

He also appeared in numerous films, including "The Alamo" in 1960, "The Man Who Shot Liberty Valance" in 1962, "Shenandoah" in 1965, "Bonnie and Clyde" in 1967, and "Bandolero" and "Five Card Stud" in 1968.

He is survived by his wife, Tippy, whom he married in 1983 and two sons, David of Newport Beach, Calif., and Tony of San Clemente, Calif.

Mr. Pyle was awarded a star on the Hollywood Walk of Fame only two weeks ago and attended the ceremony despite his illness. According to The Los Angeles Daily News, he reminisced about his first visit to Hollywood with his brother Willie.

"Willie pointed out the stars to me and said, 'Someday you'll be part of this street,' " Mr. Pyle said. "I didn't know it then, but I guess I am now. I'll see you down the road."

JULIAN RIVERO

Julian Rivero, 85, veteran stage and screen actor, died in Hollywood Feb. 24.

Rivero's career in Hollywood, following work on the Broadway stage, encompassed a period of 62 years, climaxing at the age of 85 with an appearance as Gitano in the Bell Telephone Hour's "The Red Pony." He came to Hollywood in 1915 and appeared with such early oater stars as Tom Mix, later continuing in westerns with Bob Steele, Roy Rogers and Gene Autry.

For a period early in his career he directed comedies for World Film Co. and Canadian Films. He returned to acting and later was with such directors as Josef von Sternberg, Fritz Lang, Howard Hawks, John Farrow. One of his better-known films was "Treasure of the Sierra Madre." TV stints included such early series as "The Cisco Kid" and "The Lone Ranger," and later, "The Bold Ones," "Marcus Welby," "Medical Center," and "Cade's County."

Surviving are a daughter, four brothers and four grandchildren.

DAVID SHARPE

David Sharpe, 70, stuntman, died March 30 of Parkinson's disease in La Vina Hospital, Altadena, Calif.

David Sharpe

Sharpe, who performed swashbuckling stunts with Douglas Fairbanks, Sr. and Jr., first noticed symptoms of his disease while working on "The Life And Times Of Judge Roy Bean," with Paul Newman, in 1972. But he decided to continue working until he felt it was no longer safe.

His last film was with Warren Beatty in 1978 when he did stunts for "Heaven Can Wait."

TOM STEELE

TOM STEELE (November 4, 1990, age 81): One of the finest of the stuntmen and a small parts player, mostly in serials at Columbia, Republic and Universal. He began his career with George O'Brien in THE LONE STAR RANGER (Fox, 1930) and was active into the 1970s.

Cowboy Actor GLENN STRANGE Dies of Cancer

LOS ANGELES, 1973 — Actor Glenn Strange, a bad guy in cowboy films, Frankenstein's monster and Sam the bartender for 11 years on television's "Gunsmoke," is dead at 74. Leathery, drawling, with a face as lined as a dried creek bottom, Strange died Thursday night of cancer at a local hospital.

The 6-foot-4 Strange played Frankenstein's monster in three films after taking over the role from Boris Karloff.

He appeared in more than 500 television shows. On the first "Lone Ranger" he was Butch Cavedish, who wiped out all but one of the Texas Rangers.

Strange made his first "Gunsmoke" television show in 1959 after James Arness ran into him and asked, "When are you going to do a "Gunsmoke? I like to work with big guys."

Surviving are his widow, Nin, and a daughter, Jannie Nix.

Funeral services are pending.

CARL "ALFALFA" SWITZER
Actor Slain, Row Over $50 Debt Blamed

Former Friend Jailed In Death of Switzer, Boy Movie Star

SAN FERNANDO, Calif. (AP) — Actor Carl (Alfalfa) Switzer, 33 — a freckle-faced, wide-eyed movie star as a boy — was shot to death Wednesday night. Police said the shooting had occurred during an argument with another man over money.

Switzer was a favorite of moviegoers a generation ago when he appeared in "Our Gang" and "Regular Fellers" comedies. He became known again with reissue of the films to television under the title "The Little Rascals."

But in recent years his movie parts had been minor, and he worked as a bartender and hunting guide when not acting. He realized nothing from reissue of the old films.

Police said Switzer had gone to the home of a friend, M. M. Stiliz, 38, Wednesday night in an effort to collect a $50 loan.

JOE 'TADPOLE' STRAUCH, JR.

JOE 'Tadpole' STRAUCH, JR. (May 21, 1986, age 56): An easily forgotten juvenile player who teamed up with Smiley Burnette in several of Gene Autry's Republic Westerns.

FLOYD T. ALDERSON (Hal Taliaferro)

Floyd Taliaferro Alderson, 84, former western actor known as Wally Wales from 1925-36 and as Hal Taliaferro from 1936-52, died Feb. 12, 1980, of pneumonia at a nursing home in Sheridan, Wyo.

He had suffered a stroke three years ago.

A native of Montana, Alderson attended the San Francisco World's Fair in 1915 and subsequently continued on to Los Angeles, where he began working as an extra at Universal and in pictures with Tom Mix.

After Army service, he performed bit parts until his first featured role in 1921 in Associated Photoplay's "Western Hearts."

In 1925, Lester F. Scott of Action Pictures signed him to a five-year contract, changed his name to Wally Wales and produced his first starrer, "Tearin' Loose." By the mid-1930s he had appeared in more than 60 westerns.

His starring days on the wane, Alderson changed his name to Hal Taliaferro and for the next 15 years lent support to such actors as Ken Maynard, Gene Autry, The Three Mesquiteers, Roy Rogers, Tex Ritter and Williams Boyd in B Westerns and also appeared in many larger studio productions in small roles.

In 1952 he retired from acting, moving to Alaska and later back to Montana, where he worked for 20 years as a real-life cowboy.

Among his credits were "Saddle Mates," "Hell's Valley," "West Of The Law," "Duel In The Sun," "Ramrod," "San Antonio" and "Blood On The Moon."

'TEX' TERRY Dies; Actor Portrayed Western Villains

Associated Press

COXVILLE, Ind. — Edward Earl "Tex" Terry, who portrayed Western villains opposite such silver screen greats as Roy Rogers, Gene Autry and John Wayne, has died at age 82.

Terry, who died Saturday at Union Hospital in Terre Haute after being stricken with a gasping attack while eating, appeared in more than 300 motion pictures in a career that began in 1922. He had been in poor health in recent years.

He appeared in such movies as "The Badlanders" with Alan Ladd and Ernest Borgnine, "Oregon Trail" with Fred MacMurray and "Stars in My Crown" with Joel McCrea. He also appeared in "Gunsmoke," "Death Valley Days" and other television Westerns.

In 1922, Terry traveled with a vaudeville show to California and became involved in movies, at first as a stunt man. His acting career lasted 50 years.

Terry was born Aug. 22, 1902, in Coxville, a small community in southern Parke County. Neighbors spoke fondly of him.

"He put Coxville on the map," said one neighbor, Kris Staszak, who was among those who tried to revive Terry after he was stricken. "Tex was like everybody's grandpa."

"It's kind of like a mountain falling down. He stood for the right things, always," said another neighbor, Elizabeth Kinsey, after the death.

Terry met motion picture agent Isabelle Draesemer through a friend in 1962. They married in 1964 and returned to Indiana in 1967, relocating in Coxville in 1978.

Terry had lost both kidneys, his wife said. He had returned home April 26 from the last of four hospital stays, she added.

He will be privately buried in Coxville Cemetery on Wednesday.

ANTHONY WARDE

Anthony Warde, 66, former screen actor, died in Hollywood Jan. 8, 1975. In recent years owner

Anthony Warde

of a men's clothing store, he had played mostly heavies in serials and B pix. One of the serials was "Buck Rogers."

Surviving are his wife, Frances, and son, Robert.

ROBERT J. WILKE

ROBERT J. WILKE (March 28, 1989, age 74): One-time stuntman who became a popular heavy in B-Westerns and serials and who developed into a fine character actor in major films and on television. He was in countless Westerns and TV programs. He had a continuing role as Marshall Sam Corbett on THE LEGEND OF JESSE JAMES during the 1965-66 season.

GUINN WILLIAMS, Actor, 63, Dies; Played in Many Western Films

Performer of Comic Roles Was Known as Big Boy—Expert Polo Player

VAN NUYS, Calif., June 6 (UPI) — Guinn Williams, a screen actor who played cowboy roles, died today of uremic poisoning at a hospital here, his manager, Al Kingston, reported. He was 63 years old.

Mr. Williams, who was lean and lanky, carved a career in Westerns as a dull-witted comic relief type. He played in the late Nineteen Twenties with such stars as Tom Mix and Harry Carey and later played supporting roles in several John Wayne Westerns. His last film was "Comancheros" with John Wayne.

Will Rogers, the late humorist, gave him the nickname Big Boy when he met the towering Williams as an extra on the set of "Almost a Husband." The name stuck.

Mr. Williams starred in thirty-four movies in the Twenties. His screen credits included "The Desperadoes," "Badmen of Tombstone," "Stations West" and "Massacre at Moccasin Pass."

Mr. Williams, who was born in Decatur, Tex., also played some non-Western roles, such as in "My Man" with Fannie Brice, and "Private Worlds."

In his comic roles, his trademark was a puzzled squint as he tried to figure out an involved situation.

Mr. Williams spent two years working with Rogers and picked up extra money performing in rodeos. He learned to ride and punch cattle on his father's ranch in Texas.

Later he bought his own 5,500-acre spread near Spofford, Tex. He recently sold the property.

In private life Mr. Williams was a colorful character and loved the athletic, outdoor life. At one time he owned 125 polo ponies and he was an expert player. He was known as the Babe Ruth of polo because he was such a long hitter.

He is survived by his widow, Dorothy; a son, Tyler, and three sisters.

Other Roles

Mr. Williams had also appeared in "Al Jennings of Oklahoma," "Billy the Kid," "Belle of the Yukon," "Virginia City" and "Springfield Rifle."

His non-Western pictures included "Dulcy," "Thirty Seconds Over Tokyo" and "The Glass Key."

He was to have been starred in a television series, "Buttons and Bows," for which he had already made a pilot film.

SOL "TEX" WILLIAMS

SOL "Tex" WILLIAMS (11th October 1985, age 68): After many years as a musician and singer, he joined the Spade Cooley band as a sideman and lead vocalist and, in 1946, formed his own group, The Western Caravan. His recording of "Smoke! Smoke! Smoke! (That Cigarette)" became the first million-seller for Capitol Records. He also recorded for Decca, Monument, Liberty and Granite Records. During the late 40s, Williams starred in a series of Western featurettes for Universal-International. He was a good singing hero and there is little doubt that, had he started earlier, he would have become an important one.

FOY WILLING

Foy Willing, 63, a singer of westerns during the big band era, who appeared most frequently with the Riders of the Purple Sage, was found dead July 24, 1978, in Nashville, apparently of a heart attack.

Willing sang in films and on radio as a soloist in a career that started in 1933 and continued late into the 1950s. He recorded, among others, for Decca, Capitol, Columbia and Majestic.

Among his motion pictures were "Susanna Pass," with Roy Rogers, and "Out California Way," with Monte Hale.

Willing also made live appearances on tours, the last of them in 1959 with Gene Autry.

During the 1940s his voice and guitar were familiar to millions of radio listeners through his warbling on two popular programs: "Hollywood Barn Dance" and "All Stars Western Theatre."

About 1960 he returned to Texas — he was born in Bosque County — and found employment in ventures outside showbiz. About two years ago Willing started to hit the comeback trail, and he was in Nashville to supervise recording sessions.

Survivors include his mother and a sister.

BOB WILLS Dies; Country Singer

Originated Western Swing And Led Texas Playboys

The New York Times,
Wednesday, May 14, 1973

FORT WORTH, May 13 (UPI) — Bob Wills, founder of the Texas Playboys and originator of Western Swing country music, died today of bronchial pneumonia. He was 70 years old.

Mr. Wills, composer of "San Antonio Rose," starred in 26 movies and was a member of the Country Music Hall of Fame. A fiddle player from the Southwest, he developed, over 40 years, a recognizable style, an amalgam of country music, blues, jazz licks and plain sentimentality. He was among the first to make use of drums in country music.

He and the members of Texas Playboys were joined by Merle Haggard for a final recording session in Dallas in 1973. The album, "Bob Wills and His Texas Playboys: For the Last Time," won a Wrangler Award from the National Cowboy Hall of Fame and Western Heritage Center this year.

In 1968 Mr. Wills was named to the Country Music Hall of

Fame. He worked as a barber until 1929, when he joined a medicine show in Fort Worth and became a full-time entertainer. He teamed with Herman Arnspiger and Milton Brown, the group that eventually became the Texas Playboys.

"I would say he probably performed before more people than any entertainer in the business," said Tommy Allsup, a Nashville record producer, "and that includes the Beatles."

A Dallas recording official described Mr. Wills as "a super-giant before there were super-giants, an Elvis Presley of the nineteen-thirties and forties."

Survivors include his widow, the former Betty Anderson; 3 daughters, Caroline Johnson, Dee Ann Arnold and Cindy James; a son, James Robert Wills, 2nd, three brothers and four sisters.

The funeral and burial will be in Tulsa, Okla., but no date was announced.

COWBOYS AND COWGIRLS AT REST

Burial Locations of Western Performers

(C) indicates cremated

NAME	CEMETERY	CITY	STATE
Art Acord	Forest Lawn	Glendale	CA
Rex Allen	(C)		
Don Alvarado	Forest Lawn	Hollywood Hills	CA
Bronco Billy Anderson	Chapel of the Pines (C)	Los Angeles	CA
Stanley Andrews	Glen Haven	San Fernando	CA
Earl Askam	Oakhill	San Jose	CA
Roscoe Ates	Forest Lawn	Glendale	CA
Gene Autry	Forest Lawn	Hollywood Hills	CA
Irving Bacon	Fort Rosecrans	San Diego	CA
Bob Baker	Clearcreek	Camp Verde	AZ
Smith Ballew	Laurel Land	Fort Worth	TX
Holly Bane	(C) ashes scattered in Pacific Ocean		
Jim Bannon	(C)		
Robert Barratt	Valhalla	N. Hollywood	CA
Don Barry	Forest Lawn	Hollywood Hills	CA
Buzz Barton	Eternal Valley	Newhall	CA
Warner Baxter	Forest Lawn	Glendale	CA
Noah Beery, Jr.	Forest Lawn	Hollywood Hills	CA
Noah Beery, Sr.	Forest Lawn	Hollywood Hills	CA
Rex Bell	Forest Lawn	Glendale	CA
Robert Bice	Eternal Valley	Newhall	CA
Buffalo Bill, Jr.	(C)		
Amanda Blake	(C)		
Sally Blane	Holy Cross	Culver City	CA
Monte Blue	Forest Lawn	Glendale	CA
Johnny Bond	buried at sea		
Ward Bond	Forest Lawn (C)	Glendale	CA
Richard Boone	(C) ashes scattered in Hawaii		
William Boyd	Forest Lawn	Glendale	CA
Lane Bradford	(C) Ashes scattered in ocean		
Pat Brady	Evergreen	Colorado Springs	CO
Scott Brady	Holy Cross	Los Angeles	CA
Neville Brand	East Lawn	Sacramento	CA
Henry Brandon	(C)		
Walter Brennan	San Fernando Mission	Mission Hills	CA

NAME	CEMETERY	CITY	STATE
Evelyn Brent	San Fernando Mission	Mission Hills	CA
Steve Brodie	(C)		
Johnny Mack Brown	Forest Lawn (C)	Glendale	CA
Reno Browne	Mountain View	Reno	NV
Edgar Buchanan	Forest Lawn	Hollywood Hills	CA
Smiley Burnette	Forest Lawn	Hollywood Hills	CA
Fred Burns	(C)		
Pat Buttram	Maxwell Chapel	Haleyville	AL
Yakima Canutt	Steptoe Butte (C)	Colfax	WA
Harry Carey, Sr.	Valhalla	North Hollywood	CA
Horace Carpenter	Hollywood Forever	Los Angeles	CA
Leo Carrillo	Woodland	Santa Monica	CA
Sunset Carson	Highland Memorial Park	Jackson	TN
John Cason	Grangeville	Amore	CA
Ed Cassidy	Chapel of the Pines (C)	Los Angeles	CA
Fred Church	(C)		
Steve Clark	Valhalla	N. Hollywood	CA
Andy Clyde	Forest Lawn	Glendale	CA
Ed Cobb	Valhalla	N. Hollywood	CA
Bill Cody, Jr.	Forest Lawn	Hollywood Hills	CA
Iron Eyes Cody	Hollywood Forever (C)	Los Angeles	CA
Lois Collier	Hollywood Forever	Los Angeles	CA
Joyce Compton	Forest Lawn	Hollywood Hills	CA
Buck Connors	(behind a Chinese restaurant)	Quartzite	AZ
Chuck Connors	Mission Hills	Los Angeles	CA
Spade Cooley	(C)		
Gary Cooper	Sacred Heart	Long Island	NY
Tex Cooper	Valhalla	N. Hollywood	CA
Ray Corrigan	Inglewood Park	Inglewood	CA
Buster Crabbe	Green Acres	Scottsdale	AZ
Dick Curtis	Holy Cross	Los Angeles	CA
Ken Curtis	(C) Ashes scattered in Colorado		
Bob Custer	Green Hills	San Pedro	CA
Gail Davis	Forest Lawn	Hollywood Hills	CA
Jim Davis	Forest Lawn	Glendale	CA
Marceline Day	(C)		
Eddie Dean	Valley Oaks	Westlake VIllage	CA
Andy Devine	Pacific View (C)	Newport Beach	CA
Art Dillard	San Mission	Van Nuys	CA
Jimmie Dodd	Forest Lawn	Hollywood Hills	CA
John Doucette	(C)		
Curley Dresden	Holly Cross	Spokane	WA
Douglass Dumbrille	Valhalla	N. Hollywood	CA
Kenne Duncan	(C) Grandview	Glendale	CA
Cliff Edwards	Valhalla	N. Hollywood	CA
John Eldredge	(C)		
Sally Eilers	Forest Lawn	Glendale	CA
Bill Elliott	Palm Mortuary (C)	Las Vegas	NV
Franklyn Farnum	Woodland Hills	N. Hollywood	CA
William Farnum	Forest Lawn	Glendale	CA
Dorothy Faye	Pioneer	Prescott	AZ
Al Ferguson	Forest Lawn	Glendale	CA
Robert Fiske	Forest Lawn	Glendale	CA
Paul Fix	Woodland (C)	Santa Monica	CA
Eric Fleming	University of Peru	Peru	
Henry Fonda	(C)		

NAME	CEMETERY	CITY	STATE
Dick Foran	San Fernando Mission	San Fernando	CA
Douglas Fowley	Laurel	Murrieta	CA
Bud Geary	Forest Lawn	Glendale	CA
Hoot Gibson	Inglewood Park	Inglewood	CA
Kirby Grant	Missoula	Missoula	MT
Lorne Greene	Hillside Memorial	Los Angeles	CA
Karl Hackett	Veterans	Los Angeles	CA
Kenneth Harlan	Hollywood Forever	Los Angeles	CA
Neal Hart	Holy Cross	Culver City	CA
William S. Hart	Greenwood	Brooklyn	NY
Harry Harvey	Valhalla	N. Hollywood	CA
Raymond Hatton	Joshua	Los Angeles	CA
Russell Hayden	Oakwood Park	Chatsworth	CA
Gabby Hayes	Forest Lawn	Hollywood Hills	CA
Rita Hayworth	Holy Cross	Culver City	CA
Bill Henry	Chapel of the Pines (C)	Los Angeles	CA
Buzz Henry	Mission	Los Angeles	CA
Carol Henry	Valhalla	N. Hollywood	CA
Weldon Heyburn	Arlington	Fort Myer	VA
Earle Hodgins	Valhalla	N. Hollywood	CA
Jack Holt	National Cemetery (C)	Westwood	CA
Tim Holt	Memory Lane	Harrah	OK
Reed Howes	Fort Rosecrans	San Diego	CA
Al Hoxie	Hillside Memorial	Redlands	CA
Jack Hoxie	Willowbar	Keyes	OK
Jack Ingram	Oakwood	Woodland Hills	CA
Si Jenks	Forest Lawn	Hollywood Hills	CA
Al Jennings	Oakwood Memorial Park	Los Angeles	CA
I. Stanford Jolley	Forest Lawn	Hollywood Hills	CA
Buck Jones	(C) ashes scattered in Pacific Ocean		
Gordon Jones	Forest Lawn	Glendale	CA
Tom Keene	Forest Lawn	Glendale	CA
Cy Kendall	Mt. View	Los Angeles	CA
Charlie King	(C)		
Jack Kirk	Valhalla	Glendale	CA
Fuzzy Knight	Valhalla	N. Hollywood	CA
Fred Kohler	Inglewood	Inglewood	CA
Bob Kortman	Montecito (C)	Colton	CA
Frank Lackteen	Valhalla	N. Hollywood	CA
Alan Ladd	Forest Lawn	Glendale	CA
Ethan Laidlaw	Forest Lawn	Hollywood Hills	CA
Jack Lambert	(C) ashes scattered in Pacific Ocean		
Michael Landon	Hillside Memorial	Los Angeles	CA
Allan Lane	Inglewood Park	Inglewood	CA
Lash LaRue	Forest Lawn (C)	Glendale	CA
Nan Leslie	Pacific View	Newport Beach	CA
George J. Lewis	(C)		
Bob Livingston	Forest Lawn	Glendale	CA
Arthur Loft	Forest Lawn	Glendale	CA
Tom London	Forest Lawn (C)	Glendale	CA
Pierce Lyden	Fair Haven	Santa Ana	CA
Emmett Lynn	Valhalla	N. Hollywood	CA
Kenneth MacDonald	Forest Lawn	Hollywood Hills	CA
Barton MacLane	Valhalla	North Hollywood	CA
Frank McCarroll	Forest Lawn (C)	Glendale	CA
Doug McClure	Woodlawn	Santa Monica	CA

NAME	CEMETERY	CITY	STATE
Tim McCoy	Mt. Olivet (C)	Saginaw	MI
Francis McDonald	Valhalla	Glendale	CA
Christine McIntyre	Holy Cross	Culver City	CA
Lafe McKee (Lafayette)	Grandview	Glendale	CA
Steve McQueen	(C) ashes scattered in Pacific Ocean		
Guy Madison	Desert Memorial Pk.	Cathedral City	CA
Rory Mallinson	Hollywood	Atlanta	GA
Chris-Pin Martin	Odd Fellows	Fallbrook	CA
LeRoy Mason	Forest Lawn	Glendale	CA
Ken Maynard	Forest Lawn	Cypress	CA
Kermit Maynard	Valhalla Memorial Park (C)	N. Hollywood	CA
Lew Meehan	(C)		
Blanche Mehaffy	Forest Lawn	Glendale	CA
Iris Meredith	Forest Lawn	Glendale	CA
Gertrude Messenger	Forest Lawn	Hollywood Hills	CA
Charles Middleton	Hollywood Forever	Los Angeles	CA
Walter Miller	Calvary	Evanston	IL
Robert Mitchum	(C) ashes scattered in Pacific Ocean		
Art Mix	Forest Lawn	Glendale	CA
Tom Mix	Forest Lawn	Glendale	CA
Monte Montague	(C)		
Montie Montana	Oakwood	Chatsworth	CA
George Montgomery	Palm Springs	Cathedral City	CA
Clayton Moore	Forest Lawn	Glendale	CA
Dennis Moore	Mt. View	Big Bear Lake	CA
Wayne Morris	Arlington	Arlington	VA
Perry Murdock	(C)		
Audie Murphy	Arlington	Arlington	VA
Zon Murray	Forest Lawn (C)	Glendale	CA
Bob Nolan	(C) ashes scattered in desert		NV
Dave O'Brien	(C) ashes scattered in Pacific Ocean		
George O'Brien	(C) ashes scattered in Pacific Ocean		
Black Jack O'Shea	Paradise	Paradise	CA
Wheeler Oakman	Valhalla	Burbank	CA
Bud Osborne	Forest Lawn (C)	Hollywood Hills	CA
Dorothy Page	Allen Union	Northampton	PA
Tex Palmer	San Fernando Mission	San Fernando	CA
Cecilia Parker	Forest Lawn	Hollywood Hills	CA
Cliff Parkinson	Valhalla	N. Hollywood	CA
Hank Patterson	Forest Lawn	Hollywood Hills	CA
Sally Payne	(C)		
Barbara Pepper	Hollywood Forever	Hollywood	CA
Jack Perrin	Forest Lawn	Hollywood Hills	CA
Snub Pollard	Forest Lawn	Hollywood Hills	CA
Lee Powell	Nat. Cemetery of the Pacific	Oahu	HI
Hal Price	(C)		
Stanley Price	Rosedale (C)	Los Angeles	CA
Denver Pyle	Forreston	Forreston	TX
Jack Randall	Forest Lawn	Glendale	CA
Marshall Reed	Harbor Lawn (C)	Costa Mesa	CA
George Reeves	Mt. View	Altadena	CA
Duncan Renaldo	Calvary	Santa Barbara	CA
Warner Richmond	Chapel of the Pines (C)	Hollywood	CA
Tex Ritter	Oak Bluff	Port Neches	TX
Lynne Roberts	Forest Lawn	Hollywood Hills	CA
Jack Rockwell	Grand View (C)	Glendale	CA

NAME	CEMETERY	CITY	STATE
Estelita Rodrigues	San Fernando Mission	San Fernando	CA
Jimmy Rogers	(family plot)	Claremore	OK
Roy Rogers	Sunset Hills	Apple Valley	CA
Cesar Romero	Inglewood Park	Inglewood	CA
Betsy King Ross	Oakwood (C)	Chatsworth	CA
Gene Roth	Rosedale (C)	Los Angeles	CA
Fred Scott	(C) ashes scattered		
Randolph Scott	Elmwood	Charlotte	NC
Carl Sepulveda	Oak Hill	Red Bluff	CA
Jay Silverheels	(C) ashes sent to Canada		
Russell Simpson	Forest Lawn	Glendale	CA
Barbara Stanwyck	(C)		
Charles Starrett	(C) ashes scattered over Dartmouth College		
Bob Steele	Forest Lawn (C)	Hollywood Hills	CA
Charles Stevens	Valhalla	N. Hollywood	CA
Jimmy Stewart	Forest Lawn	Glendale	CA
Milburn Stone	El Camino	La Jolla	CA
Glenn Strange	Forest Lawn	Hollywood Hills	CA
Joe Strauch, Jr. (Tadpole)	Holy Cross	Culver City	CA
Sherry Tansey	Woodland	Yolo County	CA
Al Taylor	Los Angeles National	Los Angeles	CA
Dub Taylor	Forest Lawn	Hollywood Hills	CA
Duke Taylor	Forest Lawn	Hollywood Hills	CA
Forrest Taylor	Forest Lawn	Hollywood Hills	CA
Robert Taylor	Forest Lawn	Glendale	CA
Fred Thomson	Forest Lawn	Glendale	CA
Chief Thundercloud	Forest Lawn	Glendale	CA
Forrest Tucker	Forest Lawn	Hollywood Hills	CA
Tom Tyler	Mt. Olivet	Detroit	MI
Lee Van Cleef	Forest Lawn	Hollywood Hills	CA
Wally Vernon	Forest Lawn	Hollywood Hills	CA
Jimmy Wakely	Forest Lawn	Hollywood Hills	CA
Wally Wales	(C)		
Eddy Waller	Forest Lawn	Hollywood Hills	CA
John Wayne	Pacific View	Newport Beach	CA
Slim Whitaker	Valhalla	Glendale	CA
Blackie Whiteford	Vahalla	N. Hollywood	CA
Frank Wilcox	San Fernando Mission	Mission Hills	CA
Bob Wilke	(C) ashes scattered in Pacific Ocean		
Guy Wilkerson	Forest Lawn	Glendale	CA
Bill Williams	Forest Lawn	Hollywood Hills	CA
Guinn "Big Boy" Williams	Forest Lawn	Hollywood Hills	CA
Guy "Zorro" Williams	(C) ashes scattered in Pacific Ocean		
Tex Williams	Eternal Valley	Newhall	CA
Norman Willis	Chapel of the Pines (C)	Los Angeles	CA
Chill Wills	Grandview	Glendale	CA
Lois Wilson	Forest Lawn	Glendale	CA
Whip Wilson	Sunset Hills	Edwardsville	IL
Grant Withers	Forest Lawn	Glendale	CA
Harry Woods	Valhalla	N. Hollywood	CA
Hank Worden	Forest Lawn	Glendale	CA
Carleton Young	Hollywood Forever (C)	Los Angeles	CA
Polly Ann Young	Holy Cross	Culver City	CA

Gravesite of Gene Autry, Forest Lawn Cemetery, Glendale, California (photo by Norman Foster)

Gravesite of Noah Beery, Jr., Forest Lawn Cemetery, Hollywood Hills, California (photo by Scott Groll)

Crypt of Rex Bell and Clara Bow, Freedom Mausoleum, Sanctuary of Heritage, Forest Lawn Cemetery, Glendale, California (photo by Scott Groll)

Crypt of Monte Blue, Great Mausoleum, Forest Lawn, Glendale, California
(photo by Scott Groll)

Crypt of William Boyd, Great Mausoleum, Forest Lawn, Glendale, California
(photo by Scott Groll)

Johnny Mack Brown, Court of Freedom Mausoleum, Forest Lawn, Glendale, California (photo by Scott Groll)

Smiley Burnette's gravesite, Forest Lawn Cemetery, Glendale, California (photo by Norman Foster)

Pat Buttram's grave, Maxwell Chapel, Haleyville, Alabama (photo by Norman Foster)

Nathan Lemons, with grandfather Don Key, visited the gravesite of Sunset Carson in the Highland Memorial Park, Jackson, Tennessee. (photo by Rhonda Lemons)

Gravesite of Andy Clyde, Forest Lawn, Glendale, California (photo by Scott Groll)

Gravesite of Bill Cody, Jr., Forest Lawn Cemetery, Hollywood Hills, California (photo by Scott Groll)

Norman Foster visited Ray "Crash" Corrigan's unmarked grave, Inglewood Park, Inglewood, California. (Norman Foster collection)

Gravesite of Gail Davis, Forest Lawn Cemetery, Hollywood Hills. California
(photo by Scott Groll)

Gravesite of Jimmie Dodd, Forest Lawn Cemetery, Hollywood Hills,
California (photo by Scott Groll)

The gravesite of Cliff Edwards (Ukelele Ike), Valhalla Cemetery, North Hollywood, California (photo by Norman Foster)

Hoot Gibson's gravesite, Inglewood Park, Inglewood, California (photo by Scott Groll)

Gravesite of Russell Hayden, Oakwood Memorial Park, Chatsworth, California (photo by Scott Groll)

The gravesite of George "Gabby" Hayes, Forest Lawn, Hollywood Hills, California (photo by Norman Foster)

Norman Foster stands near Tim Holt's unmarked grave, Memory Lane, Harrah, Oklahoma. (Norman Foster collection)

Jack Hoxie is buried in the small town of Keyes, Oklahoma. (photo by Norman Foster)

Allan "Rocky" Lane's gravesite, Inglewood Park, Inglewood, California
(photo by Norman Foster)

Gravesite of Bob Livingston, Forest Lawn Cemetery, Glendale, California
(photo by Scott Groll)

Gravesite of Ken Maynard, Cypress Churchyard, Forest Lawn Cemetery, Cypress, California (photo by Scott Groll)

Gravesite of Kermit Maynard, Valhalla Memorial Park, Garden of Rest, North Hollywood, California (photo by Scott Groll)

Tim McCoy's tombstone, Mt. Olivet, Saginaw, Michigan (photo by Norman Foster)

Gravesite of Art Mix, Forest Lawn Cemetery, Glendale, California (photo by Norman Foster)

Gravesite of Tom Mix, Forest Lawn Cemetery, Glendale, California (photo by Norman Foster)

Audie Murphy's grave, Arlington National Cemetery, Arlington, Virginia (photo by Norman Foster)

Tombstone of Pete Morrison in Golden, Colorado (photo by Norman Foster)

Gravesite of Snub Pollard, Forest Lawn Cemetery, Hollywood Hills, California (photo by Scott Groll)

Gravesite of Lee Powell, National Cemetery of the Pacific, Oahu, Hawaii
(photo by Ed Phillips)

Gravesite of Jack Randall, Forest Lawn Cemetery, Glendale, California
(photo by Scott Groll)

Tex Ritter's grave, Oak Bluff Cemetery, Port Neches, Texas (photo by Norman Foster)

Gravesite of Lynne Roberts, Forest Lawn Cemetery, Hollywood Hills, California (photo by Scott Groll)

Roy Rogers' grave, Sunset Hills Cemetery, Apple Valley, Califonia (photo by Janey Miller)

Western star Buddy Roosevelt's grave, Meeker Colorado (photo by Norman Foster)

Reb Russell's grave, Coffeeville, Kansas (photo by Norman Foster)

Crypt of Bob Steele, Forest Lawn, Hollywood Hills, California (photo by Norman Foster)

Gravesite of Randolph Scott, Elmwood Cemetery, Charlotte, North Carolina
(photo by Norman Foster)

Gravesite of Glenn Strange, Forest Lawn Cemetery, Hollywood Hills, California (photo by Scott Groll)

Gravesite of Carl "Alfalfa" Switzer, Hollywood Memorial Park, Hollywood, California (photo by Don Key)

Gravesite of Jimmy Wakely, Forest Lawn Cemetery, Hollywood Hills, California (photo by Norman Foster)

John Wayne's gravesite, Pacific View Cemetery, Newport Beach, California (photo by Norman Foster)

Gravesite of Chill Wills, Grandview Cemetery, Glendale, California (photo by Scott Groll)

Gravesite of Whip Wilson, Sunset Hills Cemetery, Edwardsville, Illinois (photo by Norman Foster)

The following obituaries were added with the March 2002 reprint of B-WESTERN BOOT HILL.

REX ALLEN
Dies After Accident

PHOENIX – Singing cowboy star Rex Allen has died at a Tucson, Arizona, hospital after a female friend accidentally ran over him in his driveway, a hospital official said. Allen, 7, the last of Hollywood's singing cowboy stars, died at Tucson Medical Center at 5:20 p.m. Friday, said Cheri Schnepp, a nursing supervisor at Tucson medical Center.

Allen and the friend, whose name was not immediately released, were leaving for an appointment when she struck him s she backed up a Cadillac, police said. It was not clear if he fell before or after he was hit, police said. "He my have had a heart attack and collapsed," said Schnepp. "They're going to investigate that." Firefighters were called to the scene at about 10:50 a.m. MST when a man was reported trapped under a vehicle. It apparently took several minutes to extricate Allen, said Sgt. Judy Altieri, a Tucson police spokesman.

Allen, who was billed as "The Arizona Cowboy," made more than 20 films for Republic Studios, which had previously made stars of Gene Autry and Roy Rogers. He was supported in many of his pictures by stars Buddy Ebsen ad Slim Pickens.

He made his movie debut in 1949 in "The Arizona Cowboy," and other films included "Under Mexicali Stars" (1950), "The Old Overland Trail" (1952), "Down Laredo Way" and "The Phantom Stallion" (both 1953).

On television, he was the star of "Frontier Doctor" in 1958 and appeared on many variety shows. His voice became familiar to missions when he narrated a series of Walt Disney wildlife films in the 1960s.

Later Allen concentrated on television and radio voice-overs for commercials and also narrated the 1973 animated feature film "Charlotte's Web." *(Reuters – Associated Press December 18, 1999)*

TUCSON – Rex Allen Sr., whose Western singing and cowboy persona earned him fans around the world, died after being run over in the driveway of his Tucson home. Allen, 78, died at 5:20 p.m. at Tucson medical Center, said Tucson police Sgt. Judy Altieri.

Allen was struck by a gold Cadillac that was backing out of his driveway on North Hill Farm Drive near East Fort Lowell and North Swan roads about 10:40 a.m., according to Tucson Fire Department Capt. Joe Gulotta, whose agency was the first on the scene. Firefighters arrived at Allen's home at 10:49 a.m. and found the famed Western singer and movie star strapped under the Cadillac and being warmed by a blanket that the car's driver found in the trunk. It took firefighters four minutes to extricate Allen.

Tucson police, who are investigating the incident, would not release the name of the woman who was driving the car. Police would only say that Allen was a long time friend of the women. The pair were reportedly on the way to the doctor's appointment when the accident occurred. Altieri said Allen may have fallen down before the driver, who would have been able to see him, backed up. She added that the department does not intend to conduct a criminal investigation. "It was an accidental death on private property," Altieri said. "We found no evidence in our investigation leading us to believe that there was criminal intent involved." Altieri said an autopsy will be conducted.

Police and firefighters at the scene of the accident drew a crowd of neighbors outside Allen's home. None of the neighbors said they had seen or heard the accident

Allen's fame and popularity spawned the annual "Rex Allen Days" celebration in Willcox. In addition to crooning country tunes, Allen starred in more than 30 movies, many of them with his beloved horse, Koko. He also starred in his own television series, "Frontier Doctor."

DALE EVANS, 'Queen of the West,' dies at 88

By The Associated Press

LOS ANGELES – Dale Evans, the singer-actress who teamed with husband Roy Rogers in popular Westerns and wrote their theme song, "Happy Trails to You," died Wednesday at 88.

Evans died of congestive heart failure at her home in Apple Valley in the high desert east of Los Angeles, said Dave Koch, son-in-law of Evans' stepson Roy "Dusty" Rogers Jr. She had suffered a heart attack in 1992 and a stroke in 1996.

She was the "Queen of the West" to Rogers, the "King of the Cowboys."

The first movie she made with Rogers, already an established singing cowboy star, was "Cowboy and the Senorita" in 1944. They married in 1947, and together appeared in 35 movies, including such Saturday afternoon favorites as "My Pal Trigger," "Apache Rose" and "Don't Fence Me In."

When the B Western faded in the early 1950s, they began their television career. "The Roy Rogers Show" ran from 1951 to 1957; later incarnations included "The Roy Rogers and Dale Evans Show," 1962, and "Happy Trails Theatre," 1986-89, a show of repackaged Rogers and Evans movies on cable TV's Nashville Network.

In 1951, she wrote "Happy Trails," which became their theme song. She also wrote the 1955 gospel music standard "The Bible Tells Me So.' She and Rogers recorded more than 400 songs. Their most recent album was "Many Happy Trails," recorded in Nashville in 1985.

Rogers died in July 1998 at age 86.

Through her life, she was active in Christian evangelism, which she called "The most meaningful, the most enjoyable part of my life."

She wrote more than 20 books, including the best-selling "Angel Unaware," a poignant account of their daughter, Robin, the only child born to the couple. Robin, who had Down syndrome, died of complications from the mumps shortly before her second birthday in 1952.

It wasn't the couple's only taste of tragedy. Korean-born Debbie, one of the couple's adopted children, was killed with seven others in a 1964 church bus crash; the following year, their adopted son Jon choked to death while serving in the Army in Germany.

Besides Roy, Jr., she is survived by her son by her first marriage, Tom Fox; adopted daughter Dodie Sailors; foster daughter Marion Swift; stepdaughter Linda Lou Johnson; adopted stepdaughter Cheryl Barnett; 16 grandchildren; and more than 30 great-grandchildren.

Actor GEORGE MONTGOMERY Dies

One of the last of the true western screen stars, George Montgomery, 84, died of a heart failure in this Rancho Mirage, CA, home December 12, 2000, after a short illness. He had suffered from equilibrium problems over the past few years and was hospitalized recently after a fall at home. Although best known as a cowboy actor, the real George Montgomery was a sensitive, talented artist. He expressed himself in many ways as an actor, producer, sculptor, furniture maker, architect, builder, art collector, and philanthropist.

Born George Montgomery Letz in Brady, Montana, on August 28, 1916, the 15th child in a family of Russian immigrants, he studied architecture at the University of Montana, but moved to Hollywood to pursue acting. He obtained a job his second day in Hollywood, as a rider in Greta Garbo's "Conquest." Within a few months, Republic selected him as one of the five Texas Rangers for their "Lone Ranger" serial. In addition to his many large screen roles, he also starred in the television series, "Cimarron City."

'LONE RANGER' Dies At Age 85

LOS ANGELES – Clayton Moore, the masked man who played the Lone Ranger on television and raced horseback to the "William Tell Overture" and the cry of "Hi-Yo, Silver!" died Tuesday. He was 85.

Moore died of a heart attack in the emergency room at West Hills hospital, where he was taken early Tuesday, said Rick Miller, the hospital's vice president for business development. Moore's film career stretched back to the 1930s, but essentially he was known only as "The Lone Ranger" in the TV Western series of that name and a couple of movie spinoffs. He continued to appear in costume in personal appearances for decades after the show's heyday, and even fought and eventually won a court battle over the rights to the image. "Once I got the Lone Ranger role, I didn't want any other," Moore said in a 1985 *Los Angeles Times* interview. "I like playing the good guy." He said that as a childe, 'I wanted to e either a cowboy or a policeman. As the Lone Ranger, I got to be both.

"The Lone Ranger" was originally a radio program and the basis of a few low-budget films in the 1930s. It its TV form, it was one of the first shows filmed especially for the medium, debuting in 1949 and running for eight years, not counting endless reruns. Moore appeared in all but a couple of the seasons in the early '50s when he sat out a contract dispute with the producers and actor John Hart replaced him,

The Ranger, with his Indian companion Tonto, rode through the West bringing law and order in every half-hour episode. Moore liked to say that the character embodied a creed that "everyone has within himself the power to make this a better world." The masked Ranger disguised himself because he was the lone survivor of a group of Texas Rangers who were ambushed by a gang of bad guys;

Tonto had nursed him back to health.

The show was ABC's biggest hit for a time in the early '50s, when the fledgling network was far overshadowed by CBS and NBC. Fans loved the show's trademarks: the opening theme, from "The William Tell Overture"; the Ranger's horse, Silver, described by the show's announcer as "a fiery horse with the speed of light"; Tonto's name for the Ranger, "kemosabe"; the silver bullets; the Ranger's habits of never shooting to kill and never removing his mask, unless the plot had him donning some other disguise.

It was finally the courts that forced Moore to remove the mask, when producers planning a new, big-screen version of "The Lone Ranger" got a court order against Moore's use of the character in 1979. The move brought Moore, who was reduced to doing personal appearances in a pair of wraparound sunglasses, an avalanche of sympathetic publicity and fan support. The film "The Legend of the Long Ranger," starring Klinton Spilsbury as the Ranger, came out in 1981 and promptly flopped. In 1984, a court lifted the restraining order.

Moore was born September 14, 1914 – some sources give an earlier year—in Chicago, son of a real estate developer. He worked in a circus trapeze act and as a model before heading to Hollywood, first appearing in movie serials such as "Dick Tracy Returns," 1938.

He was largely retired in recent years, living at his home in

Calabasas. He and his late wife, former actress Sally Allen, had one daughter, Gwen. "I'll wear the white hat the rest of my life," Moore said in 1985. "The Lone Ranger is a great character, a great American. Playing him made me a better person."

WALTER REED: 1916-2001

SANTA CRUZ – Walter Reed, a Hollywood character actor who appeared in more than 150 films and 400 TV shows, dies Monday of heart failure. He was 85.

Born in 1916, Reed grew up in Los Angeles and had made Santa Cruz his home since 1962.

He got his start in motion pictures at age 13, cast as an Indian boy in "Redskins" (1929). He honed his craft on the stage in New York. He was "discovered" there by Hollywood talent scouts who sent him back to Los Angeles, where he landed a contract at RKO.

Reed was cast as a leading man in such films as "Seven Days' Leave" (1942) with Lucille Ball and "Bombardier" (1943) with Robert Ryan, Eddie Albert and Randolph Scott. After serving in the Army in World War II, her returned to Hollywood to make his living as a character actor.

His decision led to 20 years of steady employment. Reed appeared in such classics as "Young Man with a Horn," "The Carpetbaggers," "I was a Teenage Werewolf," "The Horse Soldiers," "How the West Was Won," and "Tora, Tora, Tora." He also acted in episodes of "Dragnet," "Dennis the Menace," "The Twilight Zone," and "77 Sunset Strip."

Tall, barrel-chested and able to handle a horse, Reed appeared in many Westerns and was a regular in films by legendary directors John Ford ad Bud Boetticher.

After suffering a massive heart attack in 1962, Reed moved to Santa Cruz with his wife and three children. Reed became active in the real estate business while his wife earned a doctorate in theology.

Las year in Hollywood, Reed was presented with the prestigious Golden Boot – the Western movies' equivalent of the Academy Award.

July 14 of this year as declared "Walter Reed Day" in Santa Cruz County. Arriving at The Nickelodeon Theatre in a horse-drawn carriage, Reed imprinted his hand- and footprints in a cement square in front of the film art house to commemorate the occasion.

Reed is survived by a brother, Jack Smith; three children, Kim Tice, Kirk Reed, and Peggy Reed; and numerous grandchildren and great-grandchildren.

His wife, Elizabeth Reed, died in 1998. In the final years of his life, Reed donated his Western movie memorabilia to the collection in the university of Wyoming archives.

He had a business card he loved to hand out, with his name, address, phone number, and occupation: "Moderately important Actor."

ABOUT THE AUTHOR

Reared in Oak Ridge, Tennessee, Bobby Copeland began going to the Saturday matinee B-Western movies at nearby theaters. He was immediately impressed by the moral code of these films, and has tried to pattern his life after the example set by the cowboy heroes. After graduating from high school and attending Carson-Newman College and the University of Tennessee, he set out to raise a family and start a career at the Oak Ridge National Laboratory. His love for the old Western films was put on the shelf and lay dormant for some 35 years. One Saturday, in the mid-eighties, he happened to turn on his television and the station was showing a Lash LaRue picture. This rekindled his interest. He contacted the TV program's host ("Marshal" Andy Smalls), and was invited to appear on the program. Since that time, Bobby has had some 100 articles published, contributed to twelve books, made several speeches, appeared on television over 20 times, and has been interviewed by several newspapers and four independent radio stations as well as the Public Radio Broadcasting System to provide commentary and promote interest in B-Western films. In 1985 he was a co-founder of the Knoxville, Tennessee-based "Riders of the Silver Screen Club," serving five times as president. He initiated and continues to edit the club's newsletter. In 1996, his book *Trail Talk* was published by Empire Publishing, Inc. (one of the world's largest publishers of books on Western films and performers), and in 1998, he published *The Bob Baker Story*, and *The Whip Wilson Story*. He has attended some 45 Western film festivals, and met many of the Western movie performers. He continues to contribute articles to the various Western magazines, and he is a regular columnist for *Western Clippings*. In 1988, Bobby received the "Buck Jones Rangers Trophy," presented annually to individuals demonstrating consistent dedication to keeping the spirit of the B-Western alive. In 1994, Don Key (Empire Publishing) and Boyd Magers (Video West, Inc. & *Western Clippings*) awarded Bobby the "Buck Rainey Shoot-em-Ups Pioneer Award," which yearly honors a fan who has made significant contributions towards the preservation of interest in the B-Westerns.

Bobby is a deacon, Sunday School teacher and an usher at Oak Ridge's Central Baptist Church. He retired in 1996 after 40 years at the same workplace. Bobby plans to continue his church work, write more B-Western articles, and enjoy his retirement with his faithful sidekick, Joan.

Bobby Copeland

More Western Books Available from Empire Publishing, Inc.

ABC'S OF MOVIE COWBOYS by Edgar M. Wyatt. This book is an alphabetical countdown to western film actors and producers. Photos throughout. **Only $5.00.**

AUDIE MURPHY: NOW SHOWING by Sue Gossett. Contains 200+ pages and more than 500 photo illustrations of advertising materials used to promote the 44 films given to Audie's credit. Hardcover. **$30.00.**

BACK IN THE SADDLE: ESSAYS ON WESTERN FILM AND TELEVISION ACTORS edited by Gary A. Yoggy. This collection of essays offers expert analyses of the performances of some of the most famous of Hollywood's leading Western sars, including G. M. "Bronco Billy" Anderson, Tom Mix, Buck Jones, Tex Ritter, Roy Rogers, James Stewart, Barbara Stanwyck, Steve McQueen, and James Arness. Softcover. 216 pages. **$24.95.**

BILL ELLIOTT, THE PEACEABLE MAN by Bobby Copeland. Includes biography, filmography, many, many photos. **$15.00.**

BITS AND SPURS: B-WESTERN TRIVIA by Bob Nareau. Contains hundreds of facts—both known and unknown—about players who appeared in B-Western movies. Includes complete name index for easy reference. 134 pages. Softcover. **$20.00.**

BUSTER CRABBE: A SELF-PORTRAIT as told to Karl Whitezel. This autobiography displays the heart of a true champion molded by the hands of a loving family and forged by the disciplines needed to win. **$24.95.**

B WESTERN ACTORS ENCYCLOPEDIA: FACTS, PHOTOS AND FILMOGRAPHIES FOR MORE THAN 250 FAMILIAR FACES by Ted Holland. 512 pages. Softcover. **$30.00.**

B-WESTERN BOOT HILL: A Final Tribute to the Cowboys and Cowgirls Who Rode the Saturday Matinee Movie Range by Bobby Copeland. 1000+ entries—the most complete list ever assembled of birth dates, death dates, and real names of those beloved B-Western performers. **$15.00.**

THE COWBOY AND THE KID by J. Brim Crow III and Jack H. Smith. This book explores memories of the Saturday matinee with over 230 photographs. Published at $12.95; **SPECIAL: NOW ONLY $5.90.**

DUKE: THE LIFE AND IMAGE OF JOHN WAYNE by Ronald L. Davis. "I have read every book written about John Wayne. This is the best!" — Burt Kennedy. Softcover, 400 pages, 27 photographs. **$14.95.**

FEATURE PLAYERS: THE STORIES BEHIND THE FACES, Vol. 2 by Jim & Tom Goldrup. This book includes the story of forty performers. Intermingled amidst their experiences is a history of the acting profession as seen and lived by the players. **$20.00.**

FEATURE PLAYERS: THE STORIES BEHIND THE FACES, Vol. 3 by Jim and Tom Goldrup. Explores the lives and careers of John Agar, Michael Ansara, Pierce Lyden, James Best, John Hart and 35 others. 352 pages. **$29.95.**

THE FILMS AND CAREER OF AUDIE MURPHY by Sue Gossett. The story of "America's Real Hero." More than 100 photos, 200 pages, softcover. **$18.00.**

THE GENE AUTRY Reference - Trivia - Scrapbook BOOK by David Rothel. This book contains all you ever wanted to know about America's Favorite Cowboy. Over 200 photos. Softcover— **$25.00.**

THE GOLDEN CORRAL: A Roundup of Magnificent Western Films by Ed Andreychuk. 192 pages, softcover. **$29.95.**

THE HAVE GUN—WILL TRAVEL COMPANION by Martin Grams, Jr. and Les Rayburn. The complete story of how this series originated. A behind-the-scenes look at the formation of the Paladin character, the success sories, awards received, ad Richard Boone's control over the hoice of scripts and casting. Includes complete episode guide. **$29.95.**

THE HOLLYWOOD POSSE: THE STORY OF A GALLANT BAND OF HORSEMEN WHO MADE MOVIE HISTORY by Diana Serra Cary. 276 pages. **$16.95.**

THE HOXIE BOYS: The Lives and Films of Jack and Al Hoxie by Edgar M. Wyatt. This is the story of the Hoxie boys with their struggles and triumphs in real life and their experiences in motion pictures, circuses, and wild west shows. **$15.95.**

IN A DOOR, INTO A FIGHT, OUT A DOOR, INTO A CHASE: Movie making Remembered by the Guy at the Door by William Witney. 246 pages, hardcover. **$32.50.**

IN THE NICK OF TIME: MOTION PICTURE SOUND SERIALS by William C. Cline. 293 pages. Softcover. **$25.00.**

I WAS THAT MASKED MAN by Clayton Moore. Moore shares his real-life adventure of becoming an American icon. Softcover. **$17.95.**

JAMES ARNESS: AN AUTOBIOGRAPHY by James Arness with James E. Wise, Jr. Foreword by Burt Reynolds. This is the long-anticipated, never-before-told account of one of the icons of twentieth century television. As the principal performer of *Gunsmoke* for twenty years, the actor and the character took on mythic proportions—a born leader, honest, and strong. Many personal revelations. Previously unpublished photographs. Hardcover. **$35.00.**

JOHN FORD: HOLLYWOOD'S OLD MASTER by Ronald L. Davis. According to Richard Widmark: "A well-researched study of a great filmmaker and a complex, fascinating man." **$14.95.**

JOHN WAYNE: Actor, Artist, Hero by Richard D. McGhee. Softcover, 339 pages, 51 photos, filmography, index. **$25.00.**

JOHN WAYNE: An American Legend by Roger M. Crowley. A tribute to John Wayne on the 20th Anniversary of his death. 160 pages; over 200 photos; beautiful full-color hardcover **$29.95.**

LADIES OF THE WESTERN: Interviews with Fifty-One More Actresses from the Silent Era to the Television Westerns of the 1950s and 1960s by Michael G. Fitzgerald and Boyd Magers. Forewords by Kathryn Adams, Mala Powers, and Marion Shilling. This work features interviews with 51 leading ladies who starred in B-Westerns, A-Westerns, and television Westerns. 288 pages. 150 photos. Hardcover **$36.50.**

LASH LaRUE, KING OF THE BULLWHIP by Chuck Thornton and David Rothel. 2003 reprint. All you ever wanted to know about this cowboy enigma. Hardcover. 160 glossy stock pages. **$25.00.**

LAST OF THE COWBOY HEROES: The Westerns of Randolph Scott, Joel McCrea, and Audie Murphy, by Robert Nott; foreword by Budd Boetticher. This chronological account of the three stars' careers begins in 1946 and concludes with Audie Murphy's last Western in 1967. Includes 70 photographs and a filmography for each of the three. Hardcover. 196 pages. **$32.50.**

MORE COWBOY MOVIE POSTERS by Bruce Hershenson. Features over 350 full-color images from western films—from the earliest silents to the present day. **$20.00.**

MORE COWBOY SHOOTING STARS by John A. Rutherford and Richard B. Smith, III. The handiest A- and B-Western book ever devised! Includes a listing of each star's films chronologically in release order with running time and studios listed for each film. Photos throughout. Hardcover. **$18.00.**

MORE THAN A COWBOY: The Life and Films of FRED THOMSON and Silver King by Edgar M. Wyatt. This book is the first complete biography of Fred Thomson, the almost forgotten cowboy star of the silent era. It contains over 300 illustrations, including rare shots never before published. Hardcover. **$29.95.**

MOVIE ADS FROM THE PAST: A Classic Collection of Movie Advertising from the '40s and '50s. This book is a nice collector's item. It has 80 pages and 450 total illustrations, including 150 ads from Western films. **$10.00.**

THE OFFICIAL TV WESTERN ROUND-UP BOOK by Neil Summers and Roger M. Crowley. Includes interviews of: Will Hutchins, Kelo Henderso, Whitey Hughes, Gail Davis, John Hart, Rand Brooks, Dick Jones, and many more. 8-1/2 x 11" hardcover, glossy stock, 6 pages of color photos inside, 208 pages, over 200 photos. **$34.95.**

RANDOLPH SCOTT / A FILM BIOGRAPHY by Jefferson Brim Crow, III. (Originally titled RANDOLPH SCOTT, THE GENTLEMAN FROM VIRGINIA) The only complete film biography of this legendary star. Over 250 photographs. 302 pages, Softcover. **$25.00.**

Please add $3.00 shipping for first book + $1.00 for each additional book. Send order to: Empire Publishing, Inc. • PO Box 717 • Madison, NC 27025. Phone 336-427-5850 • Fax 336-427-7372 • email: movietv@vnet.net.

More Western Books Available from Empire Publishing, Inc.

THE REPUBLIC CHAPTERPLAYS: A Complete Filmography of the Serials Released by Republic Pictures Corporation, 1934-1955 by R. M. Hayes. Just released in softcover. **$25.00.**

REPUBLIC CONFIDENTIAL: VOLUME 1 — THE STUDIO by Jack Mathis. The long-awaited sequel is finally available. 512 oversized pages, more than 2000 photos and illustrations (400+ in full color). This is the MUST-HAVE book for all Republic Pictures fans. **$175.00 postpaid in USA.**

REPUBLIC CONFIDENTIAL: VOLUME 2 - THE PLAYERS by Jack Mathis. Section 1—Contractees details Republic's players in five contract categories plus the popular Western stars; many familiar faces have multiple photos. Section 2—Super-index lists every player ever credited on screen in all Republic films, over 4500 players in all; also series listings and more player photos. **$60.00** (+ $5.00 for UPS shipping).

RICHARD BOONE: A KNIGHT WITHOUT ARMOR IN A SAVAGE LAND by David Rothel. Here is almost everything you ever wanted to know about one of America's favorite actors. Includes free Johnny Western CD featuring "The Ballad of Palladin" and "The Guns of Rio Muerto." Beautiful hardcover book, loaded with photographs. Softcover—**$30.00** postpaid.

RIDING THE (SILVER SCREEN) RANGE: The Ultimate Western Movie Trivia Book by Ann Snuggs. More that 1000 great questions and answers (spanning the 1930s thru the 1990s) in this fun-filled collection for the Western fan. **$15.00.**

RIDING THE VIDEO RANGE: The Rise and Fall of the Western on Television by Gary A. Yoggy. 710 pages, hardcover. **$75.00.**

THE RKO FEATURES: A Complete Filmography of the Feature Films Released or Produced by RKO Radio Pictures, 1929-1960 by James L. Neibaur. Hardcover. **$52.50.**

THE ROUND-UP, compiled and edited by Donald R. Key. This book is a pictorial history of Western movie and television stars through the years. Has full page photos of more than 300 stars, sidekicks, heroines, villains, and assorted players. Hardcover. **$27.00.**

ROY BARCROFT: King of the Badmen by Bobby Copeland. Finally. . . a long-awaited book about this great character actor. Includes a detailed biography, filmography, and much more! **$15.00.**

ROY ROGERS: A Biography, Radio History, Television Career Chronicle, Discography, Filmography, Comicography, Merchandising and Advertising History, Collectibles Description, Bibliograpy, and Index by Robert W. Phillips. 446 pages, hardcover. **$75.00.**

THE ROY ROGERS Reference - Trivia - Scrapbook BOOK by David Rothel. Contains all you ever wanted to know about the King of the Cowboys! Almost 200 vivid photos. Softcover —**$25.00.**

SADDLE GALS by Edgar M. Wyatt and Steve Turner. This book is a filmography of female players in B-Westerns of the sound era. Softcover. **$10.00.**

SERIALS-LY SPEAKING: Essays on Cliffhangers by William C. Cline. 271 pages, softcover. **$25.00.**

SILENT HOOFBEATS: A Salute to the Horses and Riders of the Bygone B-Western Era by Bobby Copeland. This book salutes the great and beautiful horses of the Saturday matinee Westerns. Loaded with wonderful photos and extensive commentary by the cowboy heroes. **$20.00.**

SINGING IN THE SADDLE: The History of the Singing Cowboy by Douglas B. Green. Better known as "Ranger Doug" from the Grammy-award-winning group, Riders in the Sky, the author is uniquely suited to write the history of the singing cowboy. Hardcover. Many rare photos. Approx. 400 pages. **$34.95.**

SIXTY GREAT COWBOY MOVIE POSTERS by Bruce Hershenson. Includes 60 full-page color images suitable for framing or matting. **$14.99.**

SIXTY GREAT HORROR MOVIE POSTERS by Bruce Hershenson. Includes 60 full-page color images suitable for framing or matting. **$14.99.**

SIXTY GREAT SCI-FI MOVIE POSTERS by Bruce Hershenson. Includes 60 full-page color images suitable for framing or matting. **$14.99.**

STROKE OF FORTUNE: Adventures of a Motion Picture Showman by William C. Cline, author of *In the Nick of Time* and *Serials-ly Speaking*. Published at $15.00; Now only **$5.00.**

THE SONS OF THE PIONEERS by Bill O'Neal and Fred Goodwin. The story of the most famous singing group in the history of Western music. A *must* for any fan of Western movies and music. 250 pages. Softcover. **$26.95.**

SO YOU WANNA SEE COWBOY STUFF? The Western Movie/TV Tour Guide by Boyd Magers. Here is the only complete tour guide ever assembled leading you to all the western movie and TV memorabilia as well as filming locations in the entire USA. Hardcover. 264 pages. **$35.00.**

STUNT MAN: THE AUTOBIOGRAPHY OF YAKIMA CANUTT with Oliver Drake. Foreword by Charlton Heston, afterword by John Wayne. Includes 42 illustrations. **$15.95.**

TELEVISION WESTERNS EPISODE GUIDE: All United States series, 1949-1996, by Harris M. Lentz, III. 568 pages. **$95.00.**

TELEVISION WESTERNS: MAJOR AND MINOR SERIES, 1946-1978 by Richard West. 168 pages softcover **$20.00.**

TEX RITTER: AMERICA'S MOST BELOVED COWBOY by Bill O'Neal. More than 200 photos from the family files illustrate the remarkable story of country music and movie cowboy legend Tex Ritter. Includes film list and discography. Softcover. 168 pages. **$21.95.**

THOSE GREAT COWBOY SIDEKICKS by David Rothel. Revised and updated edition. Features in-depth profiles of those fondly-remembered character actors including Smiley Burnette, Gabby Hayes, Fuzzy St. John, Pat Buttram, and many, many, more. Loaded with photos. 300 pages. Softcover— **$25.00.**

TO BE CONTINUED, 2nd Edition by Ken Weiss. This is an update and is almost three times the size of the original book, published in 1972. Includes a complete chronologidcal listing, arranged by year, of every sound serial made. For each serial made, there is an in depth cast listing, studio, director, producer(s), screenplay, editing, photog-raphy, music, chapter titles, and extensive synopsis. Supply is limited! **$195.00.**

TRAIL TALK by Bobby J. Copeland. Contains quotes and comments (compiled by the author while attending almost 40 Western film conventions through the years) from those lovable and memorable participants of Western movies. 25 photos, 168 pages, softcover. **$12.50.**

VALLEY OF THE CLIFFHANGERS SUPPLEMENT by Jack Mathis. Includes chapter by chapter synopses of the 849 episodes of Republic's 66 serials. Many, many photos throughout. Hardcover. **$55.00** (+ $5.00 for UPS shipping).

WESTERN AND FRONTIER FILM AND TELEVSION CREDITS, 1903-1995, by Harris M. Lentz, III.. Hardcover, 1796 pages in 2 volumes. **$210.00.**

WESTERN FILMS OF SUNSET CARSON by Bob Carman and Dan Scapperotti. Lots of photographs. *Limited Supply.* **$20.00.**

WESTERN MOVIE QUOTATIONS compiled by Jim Kane. Includes 159 photos in 559 pages. Hardcover **$75.00.**

WESTERN MOVIES: A TV and Video Guide to 4200 Genre Films. Compled by Michael R. Pitts. 635 pages, softcover. **$25.00.**

WESTERNS AND THE TRAIL OF TRADITION: A Year-by-Year History, 1929-1962 by Barry Hanfling. The author discussed the cultural and industry trends, the directors, producers, studios, and especially the stars, and how their personalities affected the way westerns were shot. 270 pages. Hardcover. **$36.50.**

WESTERNS WOMEN: Interviews with 50 leading Ladies of Movie and Television Westerns from the 1930s to the 1960s by Boy Magers and Michael G. Fitzgerald. Hardcover, 312 pages, 150 photos. **$36.50.**

WHATEVER HAPPENED TO RANDOLPH SCOTT? by C. H. Scott. With this book, you can go behind the walls of this actor's Beverly Hills home and learn about his personal life. Written by Randolph Scott's only son. **$12.95.**

Please add $3.00 shipping for first book + $1.00 for each additional book. Send order to: Empire Publishing, Inc. • PO Box 717 • Madison, NC 27025. Phone 336-427-5850 • Fax 336-427-7372 • email: movietv@vnet.net.